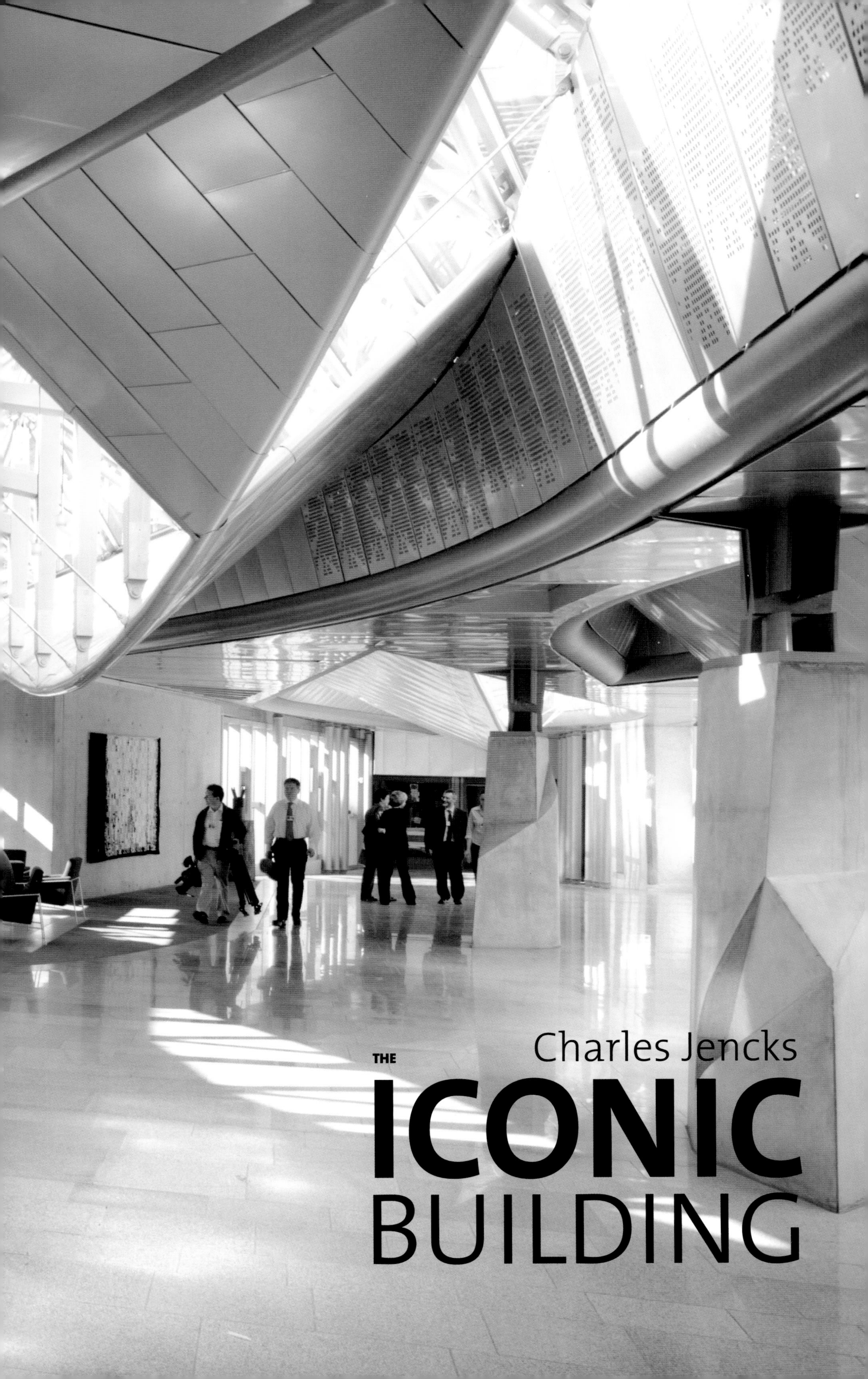

Charles Jencks

THE
ICONIC
BUILDING

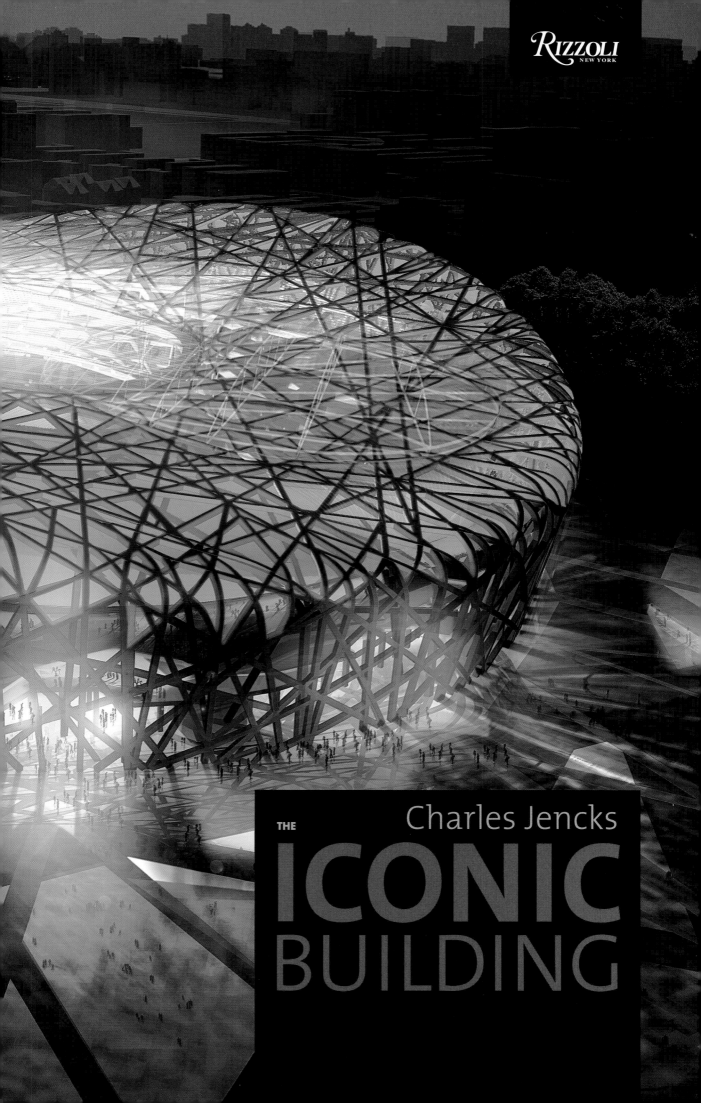

RIZZOLI
NEW YORK

Charles Jencks

THE
ICONIC
BUILDING

contents

Introduction The Bilbao Effect

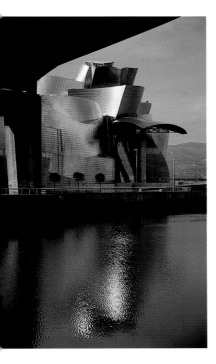

Frank Gehry, New
Guggenheim Museum,
Bilbao, 1993–7.

The War of the Hot Labels

A specter is haunting the global village—the specter of the iconic building. In the last ten years a new type of architecture has emerged. Driven by social forces, the demand for instant fame and economic growth, the expressive landmark has challenged the previous tradition of the architectural monument. In the past, important public buildings, such as the cathedral and the city hall, expressed shared meaning and conveyed it through well-known conventions. They stood out from the background—the houses, shops and factories—as poetry rose above prose, the statesman above the citizen. Some old towns retain these relationships of power and meaning today: the tallest building may still be the central church or clock tower, the less prominent types might be the school and public library, and the minor civic buildings—the railroad and the police station—adopt a modest demeanor. There was a hierarchy of public worth, not perfectly agreed and finely graded to be sure, but akin to that of everyday dress and civil address. Decency and appropriateness were its watchwords; deference and conformity were its curse. But in a world marketplace competing for attention, decency and deference carry little weight and even attacks on iconic buildings fail to register. In fact the insults often add a welcome *frisson*, the desired element of controversy and column inches—publicity.

It sounds bad, and many bemoan celebrity architecture. They want to turn the clock back; they tend to damn any deviance from minimalist modernism as kitsch; and they get very angry, not observing that their reaction may amplify the sins they slate, for paranoia, as we shall see, is an essential part of our media situation. Furthermore, when a global culture has no unifying faith, the iconic building will continue to prosper, perhaps even increase in volume. We might then step back from reaction and learn to understand the new genre. We might distinguish the few superlative creations from the more numerous failures, for the best work, like all good architecture, shows the basic temper of the times and, as Ruskin said, judges its character. The iconic building, when successful, puts architecture on a par with the best contemporary art to explore freely the possibilities of open-ended creativity.

We might also freely condemn the mistakes when they happen, the pretentious nonsense and waste of money. The new global landmark can be a jumped-up museum that proclaims itself, according to the cliché, as the new cathedral of the age. This pretence is, of course, supported by the belief that paintings selling for hundreds of dollars in the 1950s will go on to gather millions. Consider the evidence from the art market. It bears on what is considered the iconic work of an iconic artist, and shows just how far the notion of an icon has traveled, starting life in the Christian past as an object of religious veneration to now become an object of shopping.

While dotcoms collapse and Enrons run away, an abstract painting by Willem De Kooning, a few gestural lines and swaths of color, will only increase in value. One, called appropriately *Spike's Folly 1*—a hard-to-fathom work—was put on the block at Sotheby's New York in November 2003. The bidding war was won ultimately by a Mr. Rales at $11.2 million, "just above the low estimate of $10,000,000." The low estimate was two-thirds of the high one, $15 million. This figure is normal, averagely low for a De Kooning; just as Rothko's *No. 8 (White Stripe)*, a 1958 abstract with a red background and central white stripe foreground, also went that night for a customarily low $8.8 million. Customarily low. "Just," as *The New York Times* reported, "above the $8 million low estimate". "Of course," "naturally," "to be expected," these "low" figures. Since the 1950s they have multiplied, from $200, about fifty thousand times.

Art as religion, the museum as cathedral, the buyer as priest? "For these shoppers at Sotheby's that night," *The New York Times* went on, "the hot labels are Warhol and Rothko rather than Gucci and Prada." And it quoted Tobias Meyer, the director of contemporary art at Sotheby's worldwide and that evening's auctioneer: "They're jumping into the market, and they want to buy iconic postwar works." Exactly: the "I-word" works wonders.

When asked for an explanation a Miami collector offered: "It's the kids who studied art at a younger age. They're the ones who are supporting the bottom part of the market."[1]

The bottom, which was nearly reached by *Spike's Folly 1*, was the low estimate of $11 million. Just a little above one-tenth the cost of Frank Gehry's New Guggenheim Museum in Bilbao, at $100 million. Ten averagely low De Koonings is the price of one big Gehry. Normal, to be expected.

TOP: Portrait of Frank Gehry.

ABOVE: Frank Gehry, New Guggenheim Museum, Bilbao, 1993–7.

Frank Gehry Opens the Door

Frank Gehry, a Los Angeles designer in his mid-seventies, changed the course of architecture with his museum at Bilbao, though, as he has told me, he didn't quite mean to do so. I have had many conversations with him over the years and, as I did with other architects interviewed for this book, I asked him to clarify his attitude toward the new building type.

CJ: Frank, there has been a shift toward the icon, even within High Modernism, and there is no going back.

FG: In a way I did open that door because, since Bilbao, I get called to do "Frank Gehry buildings." They actually say that to me. We want a "Frank Gehry." I run into trouble when I put a design on the table and they say, "Well, that isn't a Gehry building." It doesn't have enough of whatever these buildings are supposed to have—yet.

CJ: That is the problem with having a public persona. Yet, just because you *helped* open a door does not mean it wasn't going to happen, anyway. Look at the Pacific Design Center in LA, known as the "blue whale." That was way back in 1975—a whale-like building, not appropriate to its context though it *was* an effective commercial icon that brought in business for the interior decorators.

FG: The door was opening; maybe I pushed it over the edge a bit.

What a revealing comment: "pushing the door over the edge!" The mixed metaphor is also absolutely typical of the iconic building, and either makes the architect look like a genius or a fool. One can see this by examining such buildings or, if one wants external evidence, summarizing the response of critics, who invariably follow the architect in going over the top of the edge. I have analyzed such critical reaction to the Bilbao Guggenheim and to subsequent iconic buildings, and these drawings, by Madelon Vriesendorp—seeing the building as fish, artichoke, or mermaid—tell their own story, an instructive one, even if it is not a full or adequate response to the buildings. With Bilbao (as the building is now known among architects), Gehry opened Pandora's Box or, according to taste, destroyed the box, the taboos, the constraints of decorum, square architecture, the right-angled world, what was damned as the Dumb Box. So interesting and convincing was his wiggling museum, his exploding flashes of titanium, that critics dropped their usual skepticism, warring architects came to praise, King

LEFT: Metaphorical analysis of some of the terms critics used to describe Gehry's building: a fish, a sequined mermaid, a narcissistic swan, a duck, a window box, a Constructivist artichoke, etc. Drawings by Madelon Vriesendorp.

ABOVE: *Bravo Spain*. Frank Gehry's New Guggenheim, Bilbao, becomes the icon for travel to Spain as this ad appears in upscale magazines (www.tourspain.es).

Carlos came to crown the opening, and the world's travel companies, especially the Spanish, came for the ads. At its unveiling in October 1997, it became, instantaneously, the most famous building of the 20th century. The twenty-six Millennium Landmarks of Britain, the £8 billion worth of architectural competition put on the block, led by Richard Rogers' Dome, didn't stand a chance.

I asked Frank when the tradition of recent iconic buildings started, and he gave me a surprising answer.

FG: Philip Johnson's AT&T Building—that was the first one that got that kind of attention, in the press.

CJ: 1978—Philip woke up the world—the AT&T was front page of *The New York Times*.

FG: Front cover of *Time* magazine. That was a big first, it hadn't happened for many years.

CJ: It made the front pages of *The Times* in London, in Hong Kong, in Buenos Aires, and the rest of the world—but it is an *American* experience you are describing.

FG: Right.

CJ: And you think the iconic building started in the 1970s?

FG: That was the turning point in bringing public attention to that kind of architecture, to a new kind of expressive architecture.

CJ: But what about the Sydney Opera House, before it; or even Saarinen's TWA Building in New York, way before it?

FG: Yes, but the Sydney Opera House got immersed in all kinds of economic and political problems, so it cast a pall on the concept. The AT&T was out there and glorious and everybody liked it.

CJ: The AT&T was supposed to blow smoke rings at the top, like the Lucky Strike Man in Times Square.

FG: I don't remember that.

CJ: Paul Goldberger christened it a "Chippendale High Boy," the 18th-century piece of furniture, not the stripper. What I am getting at is the Sydney Opera House was an *Australian* icon.

FG: Danish architect?

CJ: It was meant to sell tickets for Qantas Airways, to fly you to Sydney, and it did.

FG: I thought Eero Saarinen had picked that scheme in the competition.

CJ: Yes, but it was built to be an icon for all of Australia. Obviously, opera is not what every Australian thinks of every day, but it captures the harbor site.

FG: It worked, didn't it?

CJ: It worked, so much so that, after they fired the architect in the 1970s, by 2000 the Australians had to *apologize* to him.

FG: Now he is re-building the inside.

CJ: The country had to apologize to an architect. That's iconic.

It is significant that each nation sees an iconic building through its own press and that therefore for Americans such as Gehry the AT&T would mark the significant shift; but just as important is what Frank then said about the global importance of the Sydney Opera House.

FG: When I was called for Bilbao, they asked me for an equivalent to the Sydney Opera House—that was part of the brief.

CJ: Fascinating. Tell me about that.

FG: It was a small competition with Arata Isozaki, Coop Himmelblau and me and they—Thomas Krens and the Basques—said that they needed a "hit" there, like the Sydney Opera House. They needed the building to do for Bilbao what the Sydney Opera House did for Australia.

CJ: Why did you win the competition?

FG: When I went there and met with them they were very conservative, like everybody else, and they wanted me to look at Basque classical architecture and things like that. But, they picked me as the winner because they thought they had a chance of getting the Sydney Opera House out of it. Because Isozaki's design was a big oval, and they couldn't see how Coop Himmelblau's could be built— it looked uneconomic. So by picking the weird-looking scheme of mine, in their terms they were picking the economically conservative choice. After it was built people started going to Bilbao and that changed the economics of the city. It was wildly successful. The building worked and did not have the sort of problems that the Sydney Opera House had.

CJ: Exactly, it shows that if you can take a rustbelt city like Bilbao and transform it, then the iconic building works wonders for the city. The economics drive the icon in architecture today.

Gehry didn't mean to blow them away. But the door was kicked wider open and, after Bilbao, the trickle of icons became a flood, the mixed metaphors poured through it—the I-word set the market price for landmarks.

Now every new corporate headquarters seeks to be an icon, has to have a nickname that sums it up, a one-liner, a bullet point that journalists love to hate, love to spice up their workaday prose—"erotic gherkin," or "shard," or "crystal beacon." Tall buildings are no longer content to be concealed phallic symbols, they have to come out of the closet, declare their sex, strut their stuff. Office workers are no longer corporate drones; they are Gordon Gekkoes, scoring millions in their high-flying missiles. Norman Foster's Swiss Re headquarters challenges the dome of St. Paul's, and every previous symbol in the City of London: the other skyscrapers around, especially the taller ones. It is simply better, more interesting, cooler, more convincingly built, more ecological, more inventive, more optical . . . and more iconic. As its skycourts spiral on the diagonal heavenward this rocket

Norman Foster, Swiss Re headquarters, London, 1996–2003. The office dome challenges St. Paul's dome and releases a flurry of metaphors, the most unlikely of which sticks —"erotic gherkin."

inspires a kind of cosmic awe that makes Christianity look a bit like yesterday's faith, one reason that the church fathers near by came out against it. Who wants to be an earthbound Dean of St. Paul's, a John Donne writing poetry for the few, when you can be an upward-busting trader heading for the mile-high club. And these self-proclaimed landmarks are in some ways more democratic, especially if no one can prescribe or proscribe their looks.

Yet this proposition is disquieting. How does one distinguish different building types, navigate the city fabric, tell if a building is grammatical or even appropriate, if there are no conventional rules? How does a client recognize a mistake and know when to sue? In a Gehry building corners join in transgressive ways; sheets of metal buckle and dimple because they are meant to. Above all, the libertarian aspect of this movement engenders paranoia because any building type can now have its moment in the sun, even the lowest of the low, even a corner shop. Furthermore, this paranoia is an essential part of the message, its *frisson* of overturning, of lese-majesty.

The recent corner shop in Birmingham, located on the edge of its famous Bullring, for Selfridges, shows the power of upstaging the hierarchy. It is placed right next to a large church and shares a pedestrianized square with this superannuated building. Moreover, the department store, with its concessions given to brand names such as Paul Smith and Prada, became, on its opening in September 2003, *the* icon, not only for Selfridges but for the city as a whole. Birmingham, like other 19th-century cities, tried to reinvent itself in the 1960s without much success, conceiving the Modernist Bullring, a neutral,

BELOW AND RIGHT: Amanda Levete and Jan Kaplicky (Future Systems), Selfridges, Birmingham, 2001–3. The unfathomable shop becomes the icon of the company. The view from the parking garage with the old church far left. The overt escalator, detail of the aluminum discs as silver hubcaps, and view up to main hall.

abstract public space. But when that non-gesture failed, the developers came to Selfridges and gave them a green light to try something spectacular, to add a corner shop with a difference. The architects, Amanda Levete and Jan Kaplicky, were inspired, naturally, by a woman undulating in a metallic, Paco Rabanne dress. Of course, most of the high-end shops inside have women undulating in and out of clothes, so why can't the whole building do so? As Amanda Levete pointed out, there is no need for a Selfridges sign or any identification—"the building *is* the sign," is the logo.

"Your shop will be on postcards in every shop in the city," adds her partner and, as the reporter totes up the reproduction of images, before its opening it had already appeared on Barclays Bank ads, on the sides of vans and on cool CD covers. The sensuality is irresistible for architect and newspaper alike. Photographs, and suggestive metaphors, overcome the resistance. "Each floor," the architectural critic Tom Dyckhoff stresses, "is marked by fat white polished lips of balustrades, stepped back like terraces, to the skylight, and sliced by chunky fat matt escalator tubes like ribs."[2] We will probe the sexuality of the building in more detail later, but the point here is that spectacular images banish all doubts before them, and inflame the writer's imagination to find potential copulation in anything that moves. "A second, smaller atrium," he notes "is a plump-lipped ovoid penetrated by thick rounded shafts of escalators: 'The sensuality is very overt sometimes, isn't it?' laughs Levete, sheepishly." And, she adds bringing out the somewhat subversive message, "More people will pass through here than Tate Modern. This building questions the nature of a public building."

Indeed it does. Not only does it upstage the church next door, other civic monuments near by, and possibly London's famous new Tate museum, but it takes most critical opinion before it. Virtually the whole mainstream press, from the tabloids to the Sundays to the weekly *Economist*, buy into its hard sell. This over-endowed shopping center, bursting through its sequins like some Rubensesque vamp, had become that self-fulfilling prophecy—the icon.

The editor of the *Architectural Review*, Peter Davey, tried to resist. Writing the monthly "Outrage" column in this, the leading British architectural journal, he faulted the building's scale and its assault on the context:

> The result is sadly like a blue blancmange with chicken-pox. As a contribution to the cityscape, it is scaleless, uninviting and completely out of sympathy with its surroundings (although admittedly they are difficult to sympathize with). Some 16,000 aluminium discs have been attached to the exterior blue rendered insulation of the carapace by a process not unakin to sticking in drawing pins. They are entirely decorative, and from certain angles, give the impression of reptilian skin. Doubtless they work extremely well, though their use is most daring in terms of construction, cleaning and maintenance. But what are they for? They scarcely modulate the scale of the bulging monster they cover, and in many ways serve to emphasize its grossness.[3]

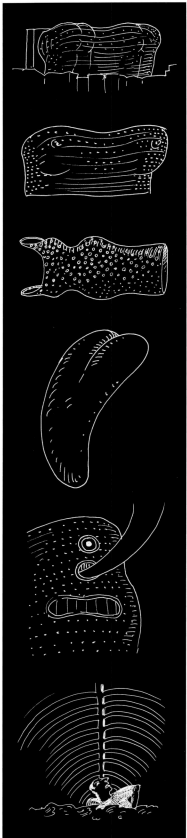

But that, as Davey almost grants, is the point of a democratic icon. It is meant to upset the context, overturn convention, challenge the hierarchy, get away with the crime—use paranoia, as Nietzsche advised his supermen to do, in order to overcome the existing order. The building was designed to get into the "Outrage" column.

Even factories, houses, and warehouses are getting into the act. No building task is too low to make a grab for instant repute, added column inches in *Wallpaper** and *Time* magazines. And why not? Any celebrity, no matter how lacking in talent, can today outshine a politician; any artist willing to deface a few Goyas can take a shot at the Turner Prize. Any warrior president can up his ratings by night-

LEFT: Metaphorical analysis of intended and accidental overtones. Drawings by Madelon Vriesendorp.

BELOW: Las Vegas (left) and Shanghai (right), 2003. As iconic buildings fill up the world's fastest-growing cities they come to resemble a World Fair.

time bombing, especially set up so that CNN and the BBC can film the recurrent fireworks safely, and from the best angles, for evening TV consumption. Why can't architecture follow this trend? After all, as many prophets wrote in the 19th century, this building art reflects its time, and the Modern Age is, well, commercial.

There is, of course, an objection. As we will see, the iconic building has its discontents, a chorus to support Davey's Outrage. Buildings hang around taking up precious space and forming the urban stage and background scenery, while most celebrities are cast on to the fashion heap as last year's dead stock. And who wants to live in a continuous World Fair, where each overstatement shouts down the last? Urban decorum, common decency, shared streets, and collective transport are necessary for the city to work. That's why there are building codes. Yet the new iconic building, with its will to artistic power, challenges the very notion of appropriateness and commonalty. It says any shed can be a temple, any abode can be a landmark. This radical form of democracy and egalitarianism seems to strike at the heart of collective notions of the same faith. Is democracy turning against itself? Is rampant individualism killing the public realm?

Two apparently opposite cities illustrate this phenomenon: Las Vegas, the fastest-growing city in America during the 1990s, and Shanghai, the fastest-growing city in China for even longer. Both translate the inflated construction of the icon from the building into the city as a whole; both have relaxed the usual constraints of urban

propriety, even good taste; both have embraced a form of centralized accumulation that ought to be called Late Cowboy Capitalism (to distinguish it from the early examples in Los Angeles and Houston). Large, extra large, chunks of city space are molded and stacked in any shape that doesn't defy the laws of engineering. The result is a permanent exhibition of landmarks, indeed, an exhibitionism of trademarks, each city intent on gathering up the gawks, on pulling in the Newly Indebted Rich. Put me on the map, give my industrial city a second chance, make me the centerfold of the Sunday supplements, the cover of in-flight magazines, the backdrop for fashion shoots, give me an iconic landmark, give me—architectural—Shock and Awe!

It works, at least according to the market researchers who have studied Frank Gehry's icon that transformed Bilbao. His New Guggenheim, as mentioned, cost ten low-rated De Kooning's—$100 million—a lot of money for a museum but not for a rustbelt city setting out to reinvent itself. Through the new museum-as-cathedral, this city transformed its failing shipbuilding industry into the emerging culture industry. This outstanding building brought in an extra 1.3 million visitors the first year, 1998, and 1.1 million the second, and, by 2000, the total had reached 3 million. Shock and tourism.

These figures were supplied at a Gehry exhibition at the old Guggenheim museum in New York—the uptown one designed by Frank Lloyd Wright—as it launched another new improved one for Lower Manhattan to be designed by Frank Gehry. By 2001, and this show, he was being hailed as a celebrity architect, America's greatest since Wright, and crowned, because he was a worthy successor, "Frank II." The gallery section, featuring his new designs for the billion-dollar downtown Guggenheim, was called "Measures of Success," an important idea because Thomas Krens, the director of this emergent art empire, had to raise the money and, following September 11th that year, money was very tight. "Measures of Success" is an unusual label to come across as the heading to a gallery room, a strange art concept that seems to have wandered up Fifth Avenue from Wall Street. It's not the usual abstract or conceptual art that you're used to finding in this museum dedicated to abstraction, not the kind of "spiritual art" of Wassily Kandinsky, on which the Guggenheim was founded.

But for the large multinational expanding museum-corp it made perfect sense, just as it did for factory cities on the skid, for Bilbao or

Norman Foster, Sage Music Centre, Gateshead, 1997–2004, another enigmatic icon meant to revive the fortunes of an industrial city. Three concert halls are wrapped in an undulating bubble of rectilineal scales that glisten in various shades like the skin of a reptile.

Manchester or Pittsburgh or that tired old Modernist steel production center, Magnitogorsk. After Gehry's structure was completed in 1997, the Bilbao museum attracted many more visitors from outside the Basque region. Eighty-seven percent were foreign to the area, and they directly increased the tourist spending by over $400 million in two years. "Measure of Success" indeed: that figure would cover the cost of four New Guggenheims. Or it would build two Tate Moderns, the understated icon that London did produce in order to catch up with the rest of the art world. (Is "understated icon," an English paradox? We'll see the importance of oxymoron and the double bind later.)

The additional tax revenue for the city of Bilbao amounted to more than $70 million and the museum attracted 137 corporate members, with all that implies for the fortune of the region, an area often trying to secede from the rest of Spain. The Basques were initially skeptical and resentful of what they took to be an imperial American gesture, and some terrorists planted bombs for the opening by King Carlos. However, the local citizenry did in the end come around to love the building, partly because it revived the city's fortunes and partly because it is lovable. Frank II had taken the time to create more than a sensation, and he found some architectural moves that had never been made.

But it was the implications of the "Bilbao Effect" that were obvious to the media, and to every aspiring metropolis. If a city can get the right architect at the right creative moment in his or her career, and take the economic and cultural risk, it can make double the initial investment in about three years. It can also change the fortunes of a declining industrial region. To put it crudely, the tertiary economy of the culture industry is a way out of Modernist decline: Postmodernize or sink! Shanghai and Beijing are like Florence and Siena before them, competing for supremacy through architectural mania, the former aiming at the 2010 EXPO the latter at the 2008 Olympics. As one reporter, Robert Booth, summarized the contest: "Cities are competing against each other for icons and are using international architects to drum up the "something different."[4] Something different—the iconic building?

Judging the Icon

How did things get this way? How did global culture evolve so that one trend-setting building could reverse the economic trends of a flagging conurbation? That question would take us far from architecture into the greater orbits of political power, the world art market, the celebrity system and branding. While these well-aired realms already receive the lion's share of attention, I prefer to look at the story from within architecture's point of view: how it has changed and is changing in response to these same pressures. If architecture is not any more immune to the media and commerce than art, and if the iconic building is creating an epochal shift, then the real question becomes how to judge these unlikely concoctions, how to differentiate between an interesting departure and a dull stab at sensation. In spite of the eccentricity and madcap surrealism—the overkill and under-thought—that characterize the genre, there are ways of distinguishing the suggestive creation from the hyperactive one-liner.

A valid objection might be raised at this point: who really cares how good they are? An iconic building is created to make a splash, to make money, and the normal criteria of valuation do not apply. Moreover, to object in "Outrage" to their failures, as Peter Davey has done, risks not only being drowned out by the swell of hype, but taking these spectacles more seriously than they do themselves. This may be true in some cases; however, partially obscured by the media froth, are some important issues and real qualities. These deserve appreciation and a means for judgement.

One method, which I will elucidate in the brief survey that follows, is to show how enigmatic meanings do or do not relate to each other and the possible significance of the building. In effect, I will look at how uncanny connotations work as a small, internal world. My argument is that "enigmatic signifiers" can be used in an effective way to support the deeper meaning of the building.

A second litmus test is to see how the architect negotiates the very difficult terrain between the explicit sign and implicit symbol: a false step on this thin ice and he or she falls into one of the twin dangers that come with the territory, either vacuity or bombast.

A third approach follows the traditional pattern of judging: by understanding the history of the new genre, by getting a feel for its possibilities and limits, by looking and speculating on emergent qualities. The example is wine tasting and comparison: first educate the senses to understand the historically new. Experience comes before a detailed judgement can be made, so we will look very briefly at an overall picture of the iconic landmark, where it came from and how it recently rose to global prominence.

Definitions: The Religious and Secular Tensions

The iconic building shares certain aspects both with an iconic object, such as a Byzantine painting of Jesus, and the philosophical definition of an icon, that is, a sign with some factor in common with the thing it represents. An icon (*eikon*) is literally a "likeness, image, or similitude," such as that of a saint painted on a wooden devotional panel. The word always carries this old religious meaning as does its negative, iconoclasm—God's prohibition of image worship in *Exodus* 20:4 or the actual destruction of such objects or images. We will see some of the latter architectural and symbolic implications in the destruction of the World Trade Center, seen as an icon of Western capitalism by Al Qaeda.

But the word also carries a harmless denotation, equally important, referring to such things as a footprint in the sand. This has a direct likeness to the foot that caused it, a similarity in some respect. An iconic building, as we will see, has many and often divergent likenesses to the most bizarre and contradictory things. This is a primary reason they are often so powerful and amazing (as with Bilbao, above, "the building as fish, mermaid, and artichoke").

Like the sacred icon in front of the Russian altar, the iconic building often occupies a prominent place in the city or carries out a function regarded as important although, as mentioned, today that can mean almost anything. Moreover, when successful, the iconic landmark does inspire the kind of awe and veneration fixed on an object of religious or artistic devotion. Picasso's *Guernica* has occupied a position comparable to a sacred relic, and the modern museum tries to convey this kind of aura to prized works in its collection.

A more recent definition of "icon" is also relevant. In computing, the small symbolic pictures on a monitor look like the options they represent. For instance, the folder icon and recycle bin icon have a similarity to their function. The iconic building usually, but not always, has this same compressibility. It can be shrunk to the size of a TV screen, or smaller, to a letterhead or stamp. This property, which

ABOVE: Religious and technical meanings of the icon remain potent. The pyramids, the first architectural icons, were places of veneration and, like the computer icon, are reduced to a minimal image. A footprint in the sand shares the shape and shadow of a foot; similitude is the technical meaning of an icon.

allows it to become a brand image, also threatens to make it a cliché or one-liner.

To summarize these meanings is to understand the tensions at work within the new genre of architecture. On the one hand, to become iconic a building must provide a new and condensed image, be high in figural shape or gestalt, and stand out from the city. On the other hand, to become powerful it must be reminiscent in some ways of unlikely but important metaphors and be a symbol fit to be worshipped, a hard task in a secular society. The way it sometimes succeeds in reconciling these meanings will slowly become apparent and explicitly faced in the final chapters.

With these various meanings, it is apparent that the architectural icon has grown out of its predecessors in other fields and, while it may seem strange to venerate a mere building with the devotion applied to a saint, this also has precedents within architectural history.

Ancient Icons

While the *amount* of iconic building that goes on today is unique, the practice is old. Architects and engineers have always had one eye fixed on the outrageous gesture and the big spender. Think of the Seven Wonders of the World: the Pyramids or the Colossus of Rhodes, which was erected toward the end of the 3rd century BC. This amplified statue, a naked equivalent of Arnold Schwarzenegger eight stories high, held a lighthouse beacon in one hand while standing at the mouth of a harbor. His very male legs stretched to either side of the port entrance. Ships, according to some paintings, would sail in below the fig leaf and sail out below the backside, a strong reminder that iconic buildings were around long before the Statue of Liberty cleaned up and dressed the gesture two thousand years later. A building in the bizarre shape of the human body goes back thousands of years.

Ancient accounts of the motives involved can be traced to the 1st century BC. The Roman authority Vitruvius gives a wonderfully ridiculous description of how Dinocrates got to be the architect for Alexander the Great. This frustrated designer happened to have a good physique and a "pleasing countenance," so naturally he took advantage of these qualities. One day, when the King was administering justice in front of a tribunal, Dinocrates undressed, anointed his body with oil, threw a lion's skin over his left shoulder and, half naked, stalked up to the ruler. Not surprisingly, Dinocrates

BELOW: The Colossus of Rhodes: the building as body, a double icon given the similitude between architecture and human shape (from Fischer von Erlach, *Entwürf einer historischen architecktur*, 1721).

stood out from the crowd, and was invited to explain himself to Alexander.

"Dinocrates," quoth he, "a Macedonian architect, who brings thee ideas and designs worthy of renown. I have made a design for the shaping of Mount Athos into the statue of a man, in whose left hand I have represented a very spacious fortified city, and in his right a bowl to receive the water of all the streams which are in the mountain, so that it may pour from the bowl into the sea."[1] A convincing icon? City as man; reservoir as bowl? Alexander the Great, not a complete fool, answers that while the "design is commendable,"—that is, a whole city shaped like himself is a good idea—it wouldn't work on the site Dinocrates had in mind. The context was wrong because there wasn't enough "corn" to feed the city (in the usual sense of corn). Nevertheless, flattery and outrage succeeded, as they usually do when directed by a good designer at a willing target. And so Dinocrates got the job of designing the most famous ancient city of Alexandria, in Egypt. Stupendous icons may not work the first time round, but clients don't forget.

The First Modern Icons

Jump a few thousand years to the situation of modern architecture after the Second World War. Nothing much was happening except reconstruction and austerity—the rationing of petrol, food, and building materials. The pioneers of modern architecture were, for the most part, a spent force, exhausted by war and exile. Young architects wishing to make a mark had few opportunities and little patronage, so all remained relatively quiet on the architectural front. There was one important exception, to which we shall return, the first post-war icon, the little church at Ronchamp by Le Corbusier, the building that was to set the standard for all subsequent work in the genre, the sculptural explosion that opened the door to what becomes the hero of the tale, the "enigmatic signifier." But I want to skirt around this masterpiece designed in 1950, and look first at the froth created in its wake, to see the turbulent waves for what they became because to judge any part of a new genre it helps to see the whole. So, a quick *tour d'horizon*.

One building type that emerged center stage after the war shows the radical egalitarianism that comes with the contemporary icon, the inversion of the customary hierarchy: public housing. Partly because there was an aggravated shortage of cheap places to live and partly for ideological reasons, modernists put mass housing near the top of the

Le Corbusier, Unité d'Habitation, Marseilles, 1947–52: mass housing as a collective icon.

conceptual pyramid. It could be summarized by Le Corbusier's polemic of 1928, *Une Maison un palais*, as if the two were equivalent. A house should be a palace, a château for the masses with every citizen having a single, detached villa in the sky. Le Corbusier was committed enough to this goal for thirty years to design utopian schemes for most European cities. They became paper icons, all were frustrated until a few Unités d'Habitation were commissioned for Marseilles, and one was actually constructed, after five long, bitter years of fighting by the architect.

This unity of "living functions," with shops and a hotel on the seventh floor, and many functions on the roof, became an instant icon for, and of, the modern movement. In 1953, just after its opening, the Congress of International Modern Architecture (CIAM) was held here, the building was praised and condemned in the world press (again, paranoia is always helpful for iconic status) because it proposed many radical departures for collective living. Visually (or retinally, as Duchamp would say), the massive cube was equally challenging. It was as heavy as Brutalist concrete could make it yet, because of the strong color painted on the reveals, it seemed to dance lightly in the Mediterranean sun. Its bold sculptural stacks on the roofscape and thigh-like supports called up obvious associations with the human body. Shades of the Colossus of Rhodes. The eminent American critic Peter Blake praised it as "as graceful as Joe Louis on tiptoe." "Joe Louis?" "Tiptoe?" Get serious. Well, that's how critics respond when they are both conceptually and retinally challenged: they respond with metaphors gone mad (yet with some truth, some visual metaphors of value). The citizens of Marseilles took to their city icon, christened it on highway signs "Le Corbusier" and, after fifty years, members of the third generation have started happily to inhabit it, including, as one would expect, a family of architects.

The conceit of "housing = palace" goes back to 19th-century France and the utopian socialism of Fourier, and lasted until 20th-century Romania and the dystopian socialism of Ceausescu. There is something comical, logical, and fearful about the equation. The Nietzschean transvaluation of all values makes a certain sense in a mass democracy where the consumer is king for a day. Since people are now multiplying, with the runaway growth found in populations of locusts before they go extinct, then why not build vast hive-palaces for them, and transform peasants into aristocrats? This promise of state communism found architectural expression throughout the 1950s, from Warsaw to the Moscow Underground (the metro, that is, not the subversives). The conceit is obviously a totalitarian version of "let them eat cake," or "bread and circuses," but before one condescends too quickly to Imperial France or Rome, it is worth recalling the fantasies of Las Vegas and late capitalism.

People multiplied together generate towers and skyscrapers, and a variety of different iconic types. Ricardo Bofill, trading on *Une Maison un palais*, designed in 1972 a twenty-story version in Barcelona, called Walden 7. Named after B.F. Skinner's would-be utopia of conditioned automata, *Walden II*, this palace of mass housing is ingenious in two respects: its intricate geometry of interlocking apartments and its shady internal courtyards—opening as twelve-story holes! They provide excellent, natural air-conditioning. Red tiles and curved balconies syncopate marvelously in the strong sunlight, and the glistening blue tiles on the inner courtyards, with their burbling fountains, convey "coolth." The iconic image is not so much a palace as a fort, with hundreds of turrets. All this slightly surreal and spooky connotation takes the sting out of mass housing. I remember being taken around the twentieth-floor bridge-walkways by Peter Hodgkinson, one of the English architects working with Bofill. Acknowledging the mad logic of the whole thing, he described with a bit of pride the first reactions as the inhabitants moved in. The height gave some of them vertigo. They were sick on their front doors. Agoraphobia on the outside combined with claustrophobia on the inside intensified the architectural experience. After they got used to

Ricardo Bofill, Walden 7, Barcelona, 1972–5: housing as fortress.

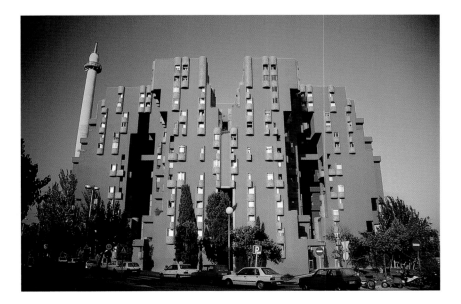

these feelings, as with Le Corbusier's Unité, the locals began to love the paranoia of their icon. Fear and attraction overlap somewhere in the brain.

Piranesi, the architectural visionary of the 18th century, exploited this truth in his grandiose sketches of prisons, which have a complex space that is dark, horrible, impossible to build because it is contradictory, and sublime. These megalomaniacal drawings lie behind so much inflationary architecture today that the phrase "Piranesian space" has become a cliché. The Piranesis have just multiplied and amplified further in scale. Ricardo Bofill is, once more, a prime beneficiary and culprit. Just outside Paris, and again for mass housing, he takes Le Corbusier's metaphor a stage further in his Theater, Arch and Palace of Abraxas. The Theater is a ten-story amphitheater surrounded by dark fluted columns of glass. These house the living rooms of the impoverished aristocrats, while above them is a triple crescendo of balconies and planters and, to cap it all off, obelisk-like cypress trees. The château topiary-work is straight out of *Last Year at Marienbad*. It is Vaux-le-Vicomte for the masses, an idea that becomes even more absurd yet compelling in the two monuments that confront the theater. The first, lower one is a ten-story, live-in Arc de Triomphe in beautifully finished, dark concrete; the one behind is a fifteen-story *palazzo* in light concrete. It sports prefab Tuscan pilasters. Pretentious and collaged from clichés, this is the kind of post-modern surrealism that modernists love to hate.

Again, the anger provoked by such an outrageous gesture is an important part of the iconic experience, and calculated by Bofill as carefully as his self-comparison to Michelangelo. For a short time after it was finished, in 1982, it became a global focus for architectural obsession and envy. This was due not only to its amplified historicism but also the fact that it turned modernist mass housing on its head and, if that wasn't bad enough, it was better constructed than Le Corbusier's Brutalist concrete. "Eat your heart out" is a metaphor never far away from the icon, playing its magic of jealous rage to fester away in the heart, amplifying the building to even bigger proportions.

The psychology of constructing the biggest building in the world feeds these feelings, and they recall a statement made in the Renaissance by the Medici princes as they commissioned a palace, the biggest in Florence. Brunelleschi, the leading architect, who had constructed the icon of the time, the city's cathedral dome, presented a design for a powerful fortress of a palazzo. The Medici looked at

Ricardo Bofill, Theater, Arch and Palace of Abraxas, Marne-la-Vallée, 1978–82: three monumental types turned into an icon of low-cost housing.

what they had commissioned, thought about their enemies, the Strozzi and Pitti families, and then came to their decision. "Envy is a plant one should never water," they pronounced, as they axed the structure. An aggressive icon in a small Renaissance city, brimming with competitive genius, may cause the wrong brand of Outrage. The desired outcome is the fury of one's competitors. Yes, by all means use paranoia as an empowering boomerang, sweet victory. But it should be directed toward an impersonal public good. In short, housing or palaces are dangerous; one needs an unchallengeable necessity, or a recognized monumental task such as a museum or airport.

The Iconic Icon

When most people think about the recent history of iconic buildings they call to mind such structures as the Sydney Opera House. This is obviously because of its prominence in the harbor, its white beauty and its unusual shapes that recall other things—the white sails or white breakers that can be seen so strikingly near by. In effect, this type of building is doubly iconic. Firstly it is a bizarre reduced image—like a logo. Secondly, like an iconic sign, there is similitude between visual images. One uncanny shape calls up surprising metaphors. There is no question that Frank Lloyd Wright's Guggenheim Museum, designed in 1943 but only finished after his death in 1959, is the first example of the iconic icon.

On the outside, it flings extremely simplified, bulging curves at Fifth Avenue. Four massive, flat, white discs flare out above each other and their absolute black shadows—ultimate gun-slits, unarguable voids. This kind of icon can be, and has been, reduced to the size of a postage stamp and still hold up. It was incessantly painted by the one of the fathers of Pop Art, Richard Hamilton, because it is a final word in gestalt, in figural closure, in visual completion. Moreover, the inside balconies and ramps mirror this iconicity, reflect the primary definition of the word: the likeness of an image with another artifact or image. Bursting out on Fifth Avenue, amid the yellow cabs and flat-chested buildings (as Wright called boxes), the Guggenheim had, by the 1970s, become an icon of the contemporary museum. This occurred in spite of the fact that the first director and later curators were driven to distraction by the continually low exhibition spaces that, more maddeningly, were always tilted as ramps. It didn't really matter. The excitement of the

ABOVE: Frank Lloyd Wright, Guggenheim Museum, New York, 1954–9. The interior is an icon of the outside and an effective reduced background for displaying art and people.

ABOVE RIGHT: As an iconic icon this reduced image resembles discs, stacked plates, and vehicular ramps, among other things.

space, the drama of the art opening as a parade of black tuxedoes and colorful peacocks seen across a dramatic space—like the paintings and sculptures themselves—more than compensated for the tilts. An important lesson was learned: a faulty design can succeed if the excess is convincing enough. You can't be a half-hearted icon, as the arrogant Wright never doubted. His flowing cape, TV interviews, and studied poses as the romantic, misunderstood (but accepted) genius set the new level of publicity. The architectural celebrity had arrived, to be crowned in the pages of *Life* and *Time*.

By the 1950s, as the architectural star system began to gather strength, Eero Saarinen emerged as a protean force to challenge Wright. Each one of his differently styled buildings was a striking departure, often one more reduced image of structure and space. If the Dulles Airport in Washington DC is a good example of this approach, his TWA Terminal in New York's Kennedy Airport is even better. Again it is an unusual, curving building, again it recalls other images—a bird's beak, wings, and flight path. Again it is made from reinforced concrete. Again the critics were outraged at its supposed functional shortcomings, for instance, the way TWA agents had to lift their skirts to surmount a sculptural flourish of concrete, or duck under flying beams. Nikolaus Pevsner, speaking for the modernists on the BBC, slated the "Anti-Pioneers," as he called them, for deviance from the true creed. Saarinen's terminal was a prime sinner:

> Why should an airline departure and arrival building rise to such heights of expression? Surely the spiritual function, if you call it that, of an airline terminal is neither elating or edifying. Does anybody

want to receive information on Flight 230 from a trim girl busy inside a coral reef?[2]

"Yes," might be the answer in the age of the icon, "why not?" The critics may act as if they disapprove but, as with Pevsner's recurrent outrage, censoring every departure from the straight and narrow, one suspects he is taking a bit too much pleasure in describing the sin. Critical hypocrisy, we will find, is flushed out by the icon. One mustn't blame the writers for this. As I never tire of pointing out, we need their paranoia to amplify the message and describe some very real provocations (as well as to deflate architectural egos). Do I object to Pevsnerian Puritanism, or the critic who can't stop enumerating deviances, peeking between his fingers at naughty behavior? It certainly sells newspapers, a consideration not be underrated when sin is exposed.

Saarinen was one of the judges who picked Jörn Utzon's Sydney Opera House as the winner in a competition. After it had been overlooked once he went back to the rejection pile and resurrected this, the second most notorious icon of the 20th century. Saarinen was right to do so. The opera house may have been an outrageous example of costs being fudged so that the building could get started. Like the new Scottish Parliament, recently completed in Edinburgh, it jumped ten times in price, from an initial $7 million to $70 million. Ever paid ten times the estimate on a building? It means all those whose costs are fixed by percentage, including the architect, are paid ten times as much; and they don't have to do much more on the job, except defend themselves from an angry client.

Underestimation is a well-known tactic, perfected by Robert Moses in New York, who was the first in the age of architectural inflation to show that "once the concrete is poured and the starting bars are in there's no going back." The Sydney Opera House may have obscured its huge fly tower and real functions behind a set of soaring wings, but Santiago Calatrava does the same with his opera house recently completed in Tenerife (see pages 138–9). It may have necessitated several national lotteries, changes on the interior, the resignation of the architect and a host of lesser problems, but Sydney undoubtedly got the harbor icon of the age. It put the city on the tourist map and, in 2000, the nation even went so far as to publicly apologize to the architect for treating him shabbily. How many times a millennium does that happen?

ABOVE: Eero Saarinen, TWA Terminal, Kennedy Airport, New York, 1956–62. An icon of flight: a bird's beak, wings, and legs.

MIDDLE AND BELOW: TWA interior with sculptural information desk and the circulation system as an icon of blood vessels.

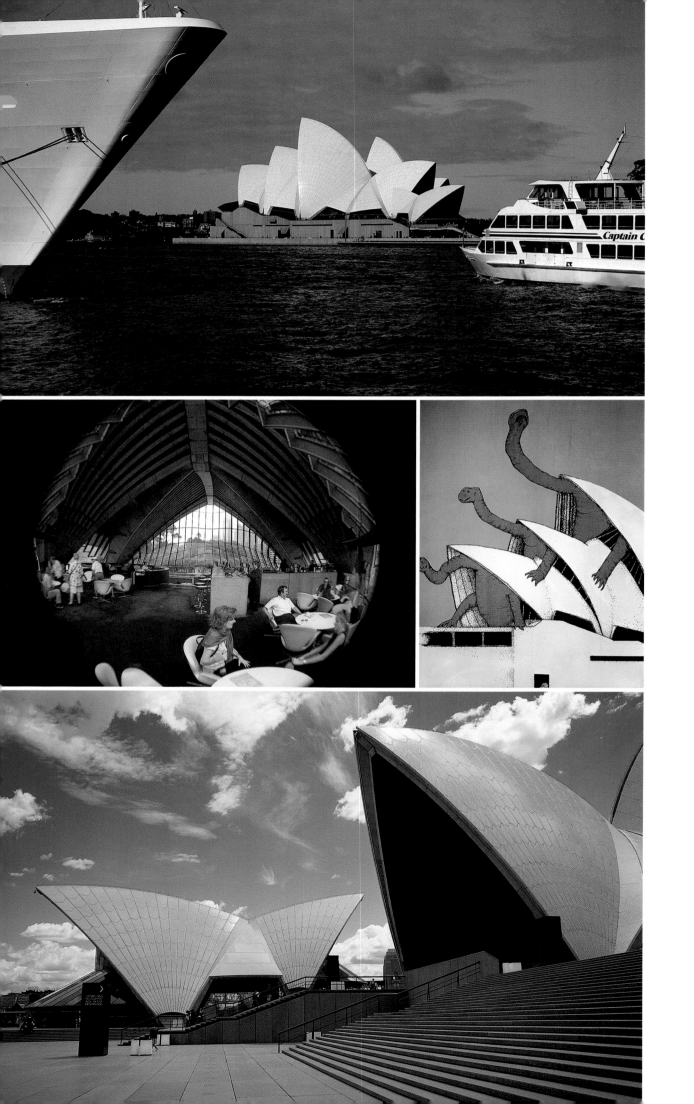

ABOVE: Jörn Utzon, Sydney Opera House, 1956–73, seen between white boats with similar shapes. Sails, shells, fish, waves, and other maritime metaphors are also embedded in this enigmatic signifier.

MIDDLE LEFT: The structural shells are uneconomic and have to be supported by very heavy, dark ribs.

MIDDLE RIGHT: A Sydney student's interpretation, 1973.

BELOW: Although structurally expensive, the shell forms became the icon for Sydney, for its harbor and for travel to Australia—the Bilbao Effect before the fact.

In terms of metaphors, the building not only picked up the sails and waves of the harbor, but more clearly the glistening white vessels that constantly pass in front. From one angle, where the white cowl-like curves confront each other, it looks like "a scrum of nuns." From another "a car accident with no survivors." The students of Sydney celebrated it as "turtles making love," while many visitors pick up the marine metaphors of "superimposed seashells," or "fish eating each other." (The "scales" of the building support this reading.) Inevitably, the architect had a different metaphor in mind: he generated the design by cutting segments of a sphere, and concertinaed them together like "orange peels."

Does all of this metaphorical froth tell us anything important? At the very least it reveals that writers, critics, and the general public react spontaneously to an unusual set of provocative forms with concepts, phrases, and similes they already know. We map the unknown on to the already said and a successful iconic building will always elicit a flurry of bizarre comparisons, a veritable blizzard of idiotic similes, an absolute snowstorm of ridiculous conceits. The icon won't calm down. Hence the Sydney student's cartoon, hence the drawings and analyses on the following pages. They suggest an historical opening to a new type of sign, a shift from the conventional monument to the unconventional landmark. This is the age of the enigmatic signifier.

Returning to building reality for a moment we should pause and note, as did the foremost engineer in concrete, Pier Luigi Nervi, that the Sydney shells are horribly uneconomic. They have to be supported by heavy ribs, so closely packed that they look dense, dark, threatening. When we realize that concrete vaults, logically employed by an engineer such as Felix Candela, can span such a space and be only one inch thick—and a tenth of the cost—it takes some of the shine off the building. Frank Gehry, as we will see, has some thoughts on the question of this inflationary city symbol.

Influenced by Saarinen and Utzon, and the previous Expressionist movement of the 1910s including the work of Antonio Gaudi, a host of expressive icons were constructed in the 1960s. A church outside of Florence, located right next to the highway, was designed especially to appeal to the passing motorist, to be seen at 120 kph. Naturally, at this speed, it had to be an icon of movement, a swoop to be taken in at a glance—and so La Chiesa dell'Autostrada del Sole has a pleasant ski-jump of a shape and, both inside and out, a series of angled

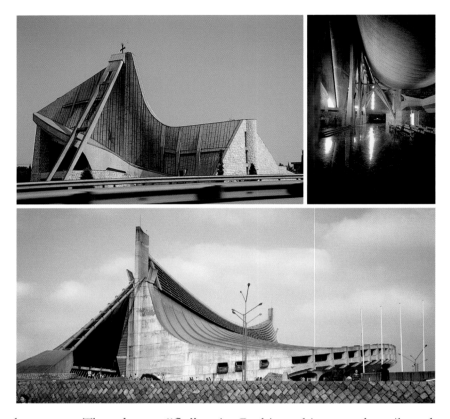

ABOVE, LEFT AND RIGHT: Giovanni Michelucci, Church of San Giovanni Battista, near Florence, 1960–63, known as La Chiesa dell'Autostrada del Sole because it has been designed to be seen from the car at high speed.

MIDDLE: Kenzo Tange, National Gymnasium for the Olympics, Tokyo, 1963–4. This graceful structural expression of catenary curves became the icon of the Tokyo Olympics and Japan's new presence on the world stage.

BELOW: Norman Foster, Willis Faber Head Office, Ipswich, 1972–6. The "big black piano," as it was called, emerged from architectural determinants reduced to their simplest integration.

buttresses. They do not "fly," as in Gothic architecture, but tilt and slam around like angry props thrown at the structure by a kid in a hurry. This, of course, was the time of Rauschenberg's assemblages and the junk sculpture of Chamberlain, who took real car collisions and improved on them. Again, if artists open the door why can't architects go through it? The more common case, however, is shown by the Olympic structures of Kenzo Tange and Frei Otto, where swooping and expressive shapes are exploited for a harmonious integration.

The question of intention is raised by these iconic icons. Did Norman Foster realize he was designing a "big black piano" when he simply followed the outline of a curved site plan and clothed his structure in black reflective glass? The intention was, among other things, to create a startling, reduced image that would look good as a logo, but as Foster mentions in conversation, below, a successful icon always has more than one determinant. The Pacific Design Center, Cesar Pelli's "blue whale" in Los Angeles, created at the same time as Foster's "black piano," had a fortuitous but important connotation in common with the products and functions going on inside. It displayed and sold architectural moldings, and looks like a gigantic one. But it is absurd to imagine that the architect started his design from the fish-

eating place near by, which has a big blue whale mouth for an entrance. That restaurant gave journalists, and locals, the sobriquet, the cue for the nickname, but the building became iconic in the area for all the classic reasons: it was big, compressed as a form, and highly unusual.

By contrast, some iconic buildings are so aggressive in their reference and intent that one has to defuse their charge, tone it down to make it bearable. The trick here is carefully to avoid mentioning the obvious, to look at other things. This response was perfected as a defense against the sexual explicitness of Pop Art, its brazen, in-your-face pelvic thrust. *Chiquita the Banana*, a lubricious Mel Ramos nude of the 1960s, struts her stuff at eye height, so you can't look at the painting without confronting her aggressively-aimed unmentionable. The criticism of the time thus went into panic escape mode and

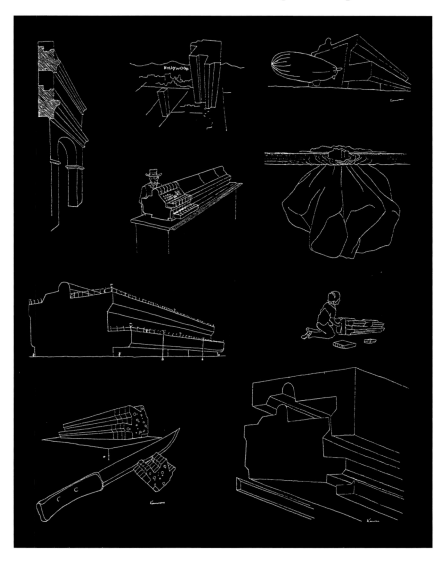

analyzed the formal flatness of the graphic image, just about anything to avoid commenting on the soft porn.

I.M. Pei's three pyramids, placed in front of the Louvre in Paris, were built with Egyptian proportions and literally recalled those of Cheops, Chephren, and Mycerinus. The conceit was so stunningly banal and obvious that critics tended to overlook it. They concentrated on the way the building blocked all axial views of Lefuel's 19th-century façades. Modernists defended this *grand projet* as another High-Tech insertion (after the Pompidou Center) in the city's historic core. I criticized the scheme as a typical example of *blasphemesis*, an architectural disease that spreads quickly when a lot of pomp and money are involved. Note the way good architects are inventive. Pei was asked by President Mitterand to add a simple entrance to the Louvre, a *porte cochère*, the equivalent to the front door of a palace. He "expanded the brief," as the phrase has it, and came up with these three pyramids and an underground museum at $1 billion. That is creative architectural thinking. A Parisian newspaper lampooned the presidential pretension of Mitterameses I, and depicted him as a sphinx in the bloodline of Rameses II. Shades of the Colossus of Rhodes or Alexander the Great? But the public accepted it, came in droves, and didn't bother with niceties of meaning, historical theft or architectural inflation. The Egyptians joked they would reply with a glass version of the Louvre to surround their sacred forms. After the controversy died down, the money was forgotten, the tourists came, and the photographers celebrated the aesthetic, the icon had its way and became, simply, a city icon. Unimpugnable, a fact of life, a self-fulfilling prophecy. It underlined the fact that, if a proposition is put with enough aesthetic surety, and exaggerated reduction, it doesn't matter what it is. Iconic design is not for the faint-hearted.

On the other hand, rhetorical strength doesn't always succeed. There are some good architects who try so hard to be iconic that certain images take over and they fail. A case in point is Imre Makovecz's Hungarian Pavilion at EXPO 92 in Seville. In many public buildings in his home country he succeeds in making a grand statement but, perhaps because it was a world exhibition or because he became too self-consciously historicist, here the attempts at national symbolism are embarrassing. The icons that resemble wooden steeples are neither historically accurate nor new and powerful enough to be convincing.

ABOVE: Mitterameses I as seen by the Paris press.

RIGHT: I.M. Pei, Louvre Entrance, Paris, 1984–8. Pei argued that his thin, see-through glass would not block all three main views of the old Louvre, an absurd hope. More defensible was the notion that these pavilions were undistinguished and not worth much of a look. In any case, the icon worked its magic in attracting the crowds and the arguments were forgotten.

Daniel Libeskind, for the Imperial War Museum North, just outside Manchester, is being equally obvious when he uses the iconic icon of shards of the globe. These, like Utzon's orange peels, are recognizably fragments of a sphere, but it is only when one makes the connection with war in the world that the connotation of shards in strife hits home. The viewer has to do some work, complete the simile, think about the great power settlement, world wars, the fact that at any one time there are about forty-five major conflicts under way around the globe and that these are cutting up territories into slices of earth. Moreover, war tends to be fought in three theaters—land, sea, and air—hence the major three shards in juxtaposition. These metaphors are made explicit several times, in sculpture and drawing, so the amplified symbolism can be understood. The fragmented peels even appear on the stationary and directional signs to the museum, becoming at once explanation and icon. Then they are translated into architectural experience, in the slightly curved floor of the main hall that is a "disoriented earth plane," the tilted walls and slashes of light. What is more, when the sun is right the overall building explodes in violent light as a piece of communicative land art.

I have not mentioned, in this summary, those iconic icons that are used as roadside advertisement—the hot dog stand in the shape of a hot dog—or those which are huge amplifications of living beings—whales, elephants, and any animal big enough to use, such as a dinosaur (see next page). Explicitness, cliché, and lack of multiple determinants render these conspicuous icons one-liners, certainly worth a look at sixty miles per hour but not much slower unless one wants to hallucinate. They contribute to city life, and used to make driving in Los Angeles an amusing game of spot the building in the shape of a bowler hat, a camera, a fruit bowl—Pop icons that often portrayed what they sold within—until they were killed off by the more unfunny chains of Jack-in-the Box, Little Chef, KFC, and McDonalds (which, incidentally, borrowed its icon from Eero Saarinen's St. Louis parabolic arch). But enough has been said to establish several points concerning the iconic icon. It works best when it is both obvious and veiled, a compressed striking shape that is similar to something and open to completion in the viewer's mind. It is most potent, as in Libeskind's war museum, when translated into architectural experience that underlines the point of the building, its symbolic programme or meaning.

ABOVE: Imre Makovecz, Hungarian Pavilion, EXPO 92, Seville: spatially challenging but iconographically regressive.

RIGHT, ABOVE: Daniel Libeskind, Imperial War Museum North, Manchester, 1998–2002. The three shards symbolize the three theaters of war—land, sea, and air—as well as the globe in fragments.

RIGHT, MIDDLE: War as the globe in fragments—an iconic model.

RIGHT, BELOW: The interior floor slopes, sign of earth and a slightly destabilizing experience; walls, with cuts of light, hold objects of war and provide a background for a light and sound show.

Anything can be an Icon

We live in a permissive, radically egalitarian era when any building type can be an icon. I have so far mentioned mass housing, an airport, and a dinosaur, among other things, but the strongest contenders for the most upwardly mobile buildings of our time—the structures with the least respect for their proper place in society—are offices, Millennium projects, and shops.

Frank Gehry, asked to name the first recent iconic building replied, "Philip Johnson's AT&T." This seemed a strange answer because, after its first explosion on the front pages, it seemed to disappear, an example of Warhol's fifteen minutes of fame. An icon for North America, maybe, but not for the rest of the world. And yet, on reflection, in a very real media sense it was the symbol of change for the global village. Much to my disappointment (because it is not an exemplar of the genre) on its birth date of 1978, it came to signify the shift to post-modernism. That is, Johnson jumped on a bandwagon, and helped drive it into the ditch but, as he did so, at least he made a world splash. He appeared in articles announcing post-modernism, on the front page not only of *Time* magazine, but *The New York Times*, and *The Times* in Britain. This had never happened with a building before, especially just the rendering of one, or a mere model. In-flight magazines and the *Observer*, and every weekly from Hong Kong to Buenos Aires carried major articles on the "Tower of Power" (as *New York Magazine* called it). To put it with American understatement, it was the biggest media event in architecture in the history of the world. Gehry was right, in terms of publicity this was the first recent global icon.

Both the building and its architect illustrated several realities of the High-Rise Icon Style, as it was termed (Ada Louise Huxtable called it "flashcard architecture").[3] Stereotyped, produced on the run, quickly built, guaranteed high style, compressed as an image, and, of course,

FAR LEFT: The LA tradition of Pop Roadside Icons.

LEFT: Philip Johnson, AT&T Building, New York, 1978–82. This media event of post-modernism was more a traditional New York skyscraper, but nonetheless an icon of change from the flat-topped office.

LEFT, BELOW: Philip Johnson, *Genius of Electicity* on the black altar.

inflated in size and self-importance. Johnson had $2.5 billion worth of work in 1984, when it was completed, and major projects—all would-be icons in different styles—in San Francisco, Boston, Denver, New York, Los Angeles, Houston, Dallas, Pittsburgh, and Washington DC. He announced at the time, indeed several times, that he was "a whore," a truth that cost him a Boston skyscraper when the story was printed in *The New York Times*. One has to applaud Johnson's candor, and self-insight. Most successful corporate architects—indeed all of them, Johnson would claim—have to be prostitutes to get the job and keep it, to keep their firms rolling over. It goes without saying they are golden-hearted whores, because they keep their eye firmly on the aesthetics, not on the pocket book. And I am forced to admit his insight may be true of the big boys, the big firms such as SOM (which currently has thirty major commissions now under way in China).[4]

Nothing illustrates architectural inflation in the age of the icon better than the reality of mega-fast-build. It colors every aspect of practice, as we will see in the battle of Libeskind versus SOM. It bends the avant-garde architect, like Rem Koolhaas, to its will. It smothers dissent and, to put it in Ruskinian terms, makes slaves of its workmen. Big boys cannot escape its inexorable logic.

What concerns me here is the way the corporate icon has usurped the throne, captured the urban hierarchy. Put another way, the two million shareholders of AT&T (in 1980 the largest public company in the world) effectively built the city cathedral. To ram home the Nietzschean truth, Johnson put in its entrance lobby a kitsch, gilded statue on a black high altar he designed especially for it: the *Genius of Electicity*. What genius, what honesty, what madness! What has happened to public symbolism? Was Philip Johnson's real intention to reveal the pretentious shallowness of corporate culture with this fey gesture? Is he making some kind of pre-emptive attack on the Enronization of America? Is he really being subversive from within? Did he give a thought to the content?

In the age of the runaway icon, there isn't much reflection about symbolism, except that of power and glamor. Perhaps this is too pessimistic, although I think not. In Europe, in the 1970s and 1980s, High-Tech architects such as Richard Rogers, Norman Foster, and Jean Nouvel designed iconic buildings that were more nuanced and distributed in their symbolism than their American counterparts. Rogers and Piano's Pompidou Center, with its bright colors and exposed pipes and structure, with its emphasis on a public square and urban spectacle, signified the liberation of technology and the idea of an egalitarian shopping for culture. Equally iconic were Rogers' Lloyd's of London and Millennium Dome, two landmarks that also symbolized the optimistic potential of expressive structure. The former gave the high-tech services such a high stainless steel polish that they became almost transcendental; the latter, although conceived as the icon of the year 2000 and called a dome, was neither. It was fundamentally a hybrid structure held in tension by twelve yellow struts and became a symbol, unfortunately, of the Blair government's inability to take culture seriously, and especially the content of the Millennium. On the inside of the Dome, a series of trivial exhibitions, with no vision in common except banality, became the biggest let-down of the thousand-year celebrations.

This is not a minor failing, in economic, iconic, or, of course, cultural terms. Spending close to £8 billion of Lottery money on twenty-six landmark projects and other cultural interventions, and garnering thereby a matching amount of £8 million from the public, the pump was well primed for an effort as great as was required for the cathedrals in AD 1000.[5] But, for the most part farmed out to focus groups or those in a hurry, the results did not live up to expectations. Perhaps the most iconic buildings were Michael Hopkins' Dynamic Earth in Edinburgh and Nicholas Grimshaw's Eden Project in southwest England. Both are marvelously airy spaces inventively enclosed by light-giving membranes. The first housed an inspiring narrative of the earth. However, it was recounted in the most childlike way and with simulations, while the real spectacular rocks, just outside, were hidden from view. Since the science of geology started here, the missed opportunity was a stroke of malign genius, rather like locating a Museum of Skyscrapers in the heart of New York in a subterranean bunker with no exterior views! The Eden Project also told an inspirational story: that of the earth's varied plant life, which, thankfully, it planted and grew on the inside (rather than reproducing them in plastic, as Dynamic Earth did). In these two cases, one has the beginnings of a challenging content sufficient to our time.

Yet there are problems with these eminent structures, however beautiful they might be. Firstly, they do not reflect the interior content; conceptually they are, as Hopkins admitted, "black boxes" (albeit white and full of light). Secondly, the expression of content on the inside has not reached a level of artistry remotely comparable to its equivalent in, say, the Renaissance or even with the Victorians. The

LEFT, TOP TO BOTTOM:

Richard Rogers and Renzo Piano, Pompidou Center, Paris, 1971–7. The building that sought and achieved mass popularity became a symbol for the public realm as a place of spectacle and cultural shopping.

Richard Rogers and Partners, Millennium Dome, London, 2000. Unfortunately, the architects took the blame for the failure of the content and thus this, the most prominent of many millennial *grand projets*, became an icon of politicians' failure to address the cultural issues of the year 2000.

Michael Hopkins, Dynamic Earth, Edinburgh, 2000: a strong white image against the dark Salisbury Crags, one of the origins of geological study. This icon only draws attention to the retrograde policy of the interior display—geological wonders shown in plastic and simulation.

Nicholas Grimshaw, The Eden Project, St. Austell, Cornwall, 1998–2001. Placed in a former china clay quarry, the millennial project houses distinct habitats, demonstrates sustainability and a novel use of inflated pillows of ETFE, yet fails to make an architectural virtue of its globular form.

Jean Nouvel, Institut du Monde Arabe, Paris, 1984–7. The window lenses open and close, giving a contemporary twist to Muslim screens and ornament—a convincing High-Tech icon of the Arab world in Paris?

architectural shells, which were mere containers, were mainstream essays on existing well-known structures and, in that sense, not iconic. They failed to excite the imagination and, as symbols, were self-referential. That is, Hopkins' white tent referred not to the earth story but to other tensile structures, while Grimshaw's geodesic domes referred to these structures rather than, say, the way they were stacked like globular clusters.

Ponder the missed opportunity of the Eden Project. Think of the relation of its domes to mineral globular clusters, those bubbles of malachite or turquoise or any number of beautiful structures that Mother Earth creates as a giveaway, at no cost. A globular cluster is one of the eight "forms" that nature uses, one of its underlying archetypes, its rules for construction. Bear in mind the Eden Project's goal of recreating the world's ecology, even rainforests, in southwest England. Imagine the opportunity to design the biggest, lightest set of geodesic pillows—a marvelous technological innovation. Finally, imagine placing them higgledy-piggledy on top of each other and missing the symbolic connection to the workings of Mother Nature. As far as the iconic building is concerned, this neutrality toward content itself signifies the problem of the High-Tech approach. Beyond a polite agnosticism and occasional populism, it studiously avoids social, political or symbolic commitment. In comparison, Jean Nouvel's High-Tech is more focussed on the affect, the emotional rhetoric of the means he is using. His Institut du Monde Arabe in Paris intentionally symbolizes Muslim geometries with its fifty-six giant window lenses that modulate the exterior light. This High-Tech virtuosity produced a contemporary equivalent of the ubiquitous Muslim screen and an instant icon of an Arab world meeting the Western challenge. It may not be the most profound interpretation of ethnic identity, but the structure does address content and culture specifically. Equally amazing as an image, though questionable in other ways, is Nouvel's interior of the French department store in Berlin. His Galleries Lafayette has a central void in the shape of an egg, where one can survey all the products glistening on different levels. Look up and you find shopping turned into a cosmic egg, a mystery, a celebration of the central solar disc and the thousands of surrounding planets (they are light bulbs). Look down and you discover the same enchantments vortexing toward a black hole (is it consumer debt?). Ironic thoughts do not disappear when shopping becomes as sublime as this.

Museum = Shop = Icon

Nouvel's transcendental buying experience was constructed in the mid-1990s and five years later, by the time of the Millennium celebrations, it was clear that the almighty dollar, rather than the Almighty, was the greater cause for global joy. The market was at a record high, after an unprecedented climb of eighteen years. A Dow of 36,000 was predicted and, in spite of several attempts to deflate this "irrational exuberance," money continued to pour into America, $50 billion per month, to balance the deficit spending. Enron, WorldCom, and Parmalat were not even a gleam in Gordon Gekko's eye.

All this liquidity had to go somewhere and a possible safe haven was the art market. Reflect on my opening remarks and the insight of the Sotheby's experts. The kids supporting the bottom end of the art market—$10 million for a de Kooning and $8 million for a Rothko— not only supported these brands but Gucci and Prada as well. The result? The museum became more like the department store and architects were given the job of branding them both. A spate of exhibitions sought to unravel the mysteries of the icon, fashion, and shopping, as if they needed museum analysis (or was it that museums needed the cash?).

London's Victoria & Albert Museum celebrated the Millennium with an exhibition cleverly branded as Brand.New, a display of 4,000 brand images and a few of their wares. Later, two different shows appeared in Frankfurt, one called simply Shopping (that went on to Tate Liverpool) and the other I Think Therefore I Shop. These shows made explicit the equation "museum = shop" and underscored Andy Warhol's gnomic comment about the future: "All department stores will become museums, and all museums will become department stores." In architecture, Rem Koolhaas got into the act with a more intellectual string of gnomic utterances, a fat book of statistics and analysis, *The Harvard Design School Guide to Shopping* (2001), and a few Prada stores (and yet another fat book on Prada). After excoriating the "junk space" and junk mentality behind consumerism, terming shopping "the terminal state of mankind," Koolhaas began to play both sides of the junk with a vengeance, and an almost heroic disgust. "Shopping is doubtless the last form of public activity," he asserted in a doubtlessly false one-liner, as a moment's thought about sport, the Olympics, and going to museums might have told him. Nonetheless, he stresses both sides of the equation: shopping is killing the city even as it gives it the kiss of life.

TOP AND ABOVE: Jean Nouvel, Galleries Lafayette, Berlin, 1992–5: the shopper's gaze at the world's products laid out floor by floor becomes the pretext for some amazing cosmic symbolism.

Koolhaas became Koolworld as he purveyed his thoughts, alongside Miuccia Prada's and Martha Stewart's, through a guest-edited issue of *Wired*. He reached this acme of fashion after designing two brand spaces for the Guggenheim and Hermitage museums. These were located in that notoriously fastest growing city, Las Vegas, in its Venetian Resort-Hotel-Casino. The Guggenheim quickly failed, and closed. Koolhaas' statistics had predicted this. They showed the inflationary growth of shops was accompanied by their inflationary demise. He designed, for Miuccia Prada herself, the flagship store in New York—for something approaching $50 million. This was the cost of the bottom two floors of an interior. He denounced the very idea of the "flagship syndrome" as megalomaniac repetition and then re-launched her policy as one of reinvention through different "epicenters"—"Street" for New York, "Solid" for San Francisco, "Plastic" for Los Angeles, and "Void" for Tokyo. Oh those differentiated epicenters, veritable hubs of unique identity for all those 166 spokes, the smaller Pradas and little "Miu Mius" (Prada's younger line) that revolved around them. Miu Mius, little kitten Miuccias, carried out her new philosophy, as amplified by Koolhaas' little fat book. Miuccia was restructuring her conceptual space to outgun the other rag-brands in sight: the new-look Armani, the reinvented Comme des Garçons, and Gucci, and LVMH. Everyone was hiring architects to distinguish their brand.

Tadao Ando did up Armani's image; John Pawson minimalized Jigsaw's face; Future Systems face-lifted Comme des Garçons; David Chipperfield essentialized Gucci; and Christian de Portzamparc relaunched the New York flagship of LVMH. Oh poor multinational flagship with its integrated collection of repetitive imagery—Louis Vuitton luggage, Moët & Chandon champagne, Guerlain perfume and Christian Dior, among other icons! Hadn't they heard about "flagship syndrome," the wrong way to brand? Hadn't they read Rem's fat little red book, or listened to Miuccia's new philosophy—reinvention through architectural space? She essentialized the Koolhaas message in Koolhaas' guest-edited issue of *Wired*: "Every piece of clothing shapes your body but also the space around you, the emptiness around you." And then, capturing the deeper idea of emptiness, the Japanese "Void," she explained its existential contrast with your body: "This raincoat, from our 2002 winter collection, plays off that divide. It's transparent, but when it gets wet—from rain or perspiration—it becomes opaque. So you have the space of the

ABOVE: Rem Koolhaas, Guggenheim Museum, Venetian Hotel, Las Vegas, 2001. The motorcycle show, installed by Frank Gehry, typified the new global Guggenheim policy of less Kandinsky and more Armani.

body and then also this outer space outside the clothes: it changes the relationship between what's inside and outside."[6] Here is real reinvention, the reprise of modernist space seventy-five years old, the connection between inside and outside, that great old futurism of plate glass. Think about it: you're walking down Fifth Avenue singing in the rain with little on except this opaque wet Miu Miu plastic and then suddenly the sun comes out, and presto!—it's you, you in the altogether, changing the relationship between inside and outside space. Very profound.

Koolhaas and other Prada architects in differentiated global epicenters designed changing rooms on the same interactive idea. At the touch of a button, a kind of electro-chromatic glass changes "the emptiness around you" and transparency becomes opaque, so you are more in control of nudity than when the sun comes out. This and other major contributions to putting on and taking off clothes, were pioneered in further epicenters, the most ambitious being Herzog & de Meuron's Prada located in the Aoyama district of Tokyo, the ground zero of fashion. At a cost of $87 million, this was the "largest single investment made by an Italian company since the Second World War."[7] More than a mere interior, it was notable because it gave the city a generous open space from which to be seen in 360-degree splendor, and enclosed the bottom of this public face in moss-covered walls. It gave the company an iconic image of diagonal ribs punctuated by bizarre lens-like windows and horizontal tubes of VIP changing rooms (now completely opaque). Thus two defining aspects of the successful icon were realized, reduction and strangeness. And it gave shoppers some techno-innovations to distinguish itself from competitors: uncanny snorkels that coiled down from the ceiling allowing the knowing consumer to compare a choice with the entire Prada collection.

Herzog & de Meuron, like Koolhaas, received architecture's so-called Nobel for architecture, the Pritztker Prize, and, like so many of the other architects re-branding a fashion house, they are minimalists. Their reductionism, however, expands way above the others' by incorporating extraordinary juxtapositions of idiosyncratic materials—here green moss versus wet-look bubble glass, or latex snorkels versus raw oak floors. This is important. The subject of fashion is materialism squared, luxury contrasts taken to the nth-degree, and in this sense shopping has found its perfect foil in this Tokyo epicenter. Its cost was 87 percent that of Gehry's Bilbao

ABOVE: Christian de Portzamparc, LVMH Tower, New York, 1996–2000. Corporate empires started commissioning architects for flagship icons as well as their museum collections: art and architecture became momentary sites of competitive struggle.

RIGHT: Herzog & de Meuron, Prada, Aoyama, Tokyo, 2001–3. A lattice of diagonal ribs contrasts with the horizontal tubes of changing rooms; "snorkels" disgorging information are juxtaposed with mesh ceilings and raw oak floors—all very Prada-Dada.

museum, thus supporting Warhol's equation of the department store = the museum. Grazing for clothes becomes like grazing for art; on average each work gets a ten-second, dreamy walk-by. Tokyo Prada does for spending cash inattentively what the American missile program did for the Cold War: throw money at a symbolic problem until the opponent (the Soviet Union, the consumer) gives up.

This triumph of shopping and the Millennial failures of content bring us face to face with two related issues: the commercialization of culture and the disappearance of belief. It sounds depressing but there is a bonus. The loss of faith is still accompanied by the desire to build inflationary symbols to something or other and if you put the two forces together—the loss of content with the influx of egoistic money—they point toward the only solution possible: the enigmatic signifier. This unlikely answer to an impossible conundrum generates the iconic building, just as Christianity generated the cathedrals. But before we look at how architects stumbled on the solution, we must conclude this overview with a glance at the acceptable face of the icon: the civic building.

A Suitable Case for Icons?

The seat of government and the museum are two building tasks that, in an agnostic age, still command some respect. Democracies teach the arts of doubt, but citizens still pay taxes for public works such as a parliament and a national museum, two building types that have enjoyed a minor resurgence. When India achieved independence, in 1947, Pandit Nehru oversaw the building of what he called "a temple of a new India," that is, the new city of Chandigarh and, more particularly, its temples of government designed by Le Corbusier. These included many icons of the new faith: a monumental High Court, a Secretariat, and a General Assembly. The General Assembly established a precedent for civic architecture and, in some ways, remains the most convincing public building constructed since the Second World War. Built between 1953 and 1961, it houses a council chamber, general assembly, and collective space, both on the rooftop and inside, protected from the sun. It is this murderous sun and the terrifying monsoon rain that become the justification for a cosmic symbolism that Le Corbusier was developing at the time.

Among the various things that make an iconic building successful, one that I haven't stressed is its relationship to local realities. Here, the new, powerful forms of the Assembly are for collecting rainwater and shielding people from both the seasonal torrents and the 100-degree heat. An exaggerated entrance canopy, which channels water to a reflective pool below, is in the shape of a giant upturned cistern. From the side this has a U-shape similar to the horns of the cows and bulls that roam the site. Thus what might, with another architect, be an empty formal gesture, with Le Corbusier connects to two immediate realities. Gargantuan sunshades on the side and a rooftop explosion of solar symbolism are also sculptural gestures that are more than one-liners. They relate to an annual solar festival that Le Corbusier imagines for the public realm, "reminding man once every year that he is the son of the sun."[8] This idea is carried beyond the external forms, the pyramid council chamber and cooling tower assembly, both of which are traditional and modern signs of energy. The tower cap was meant to open at the solar festival and a shaft of light hit the speaker's rostrum, a secular altar celebrating the truth that political power emanates ultimately from the sun. The pyramidal council chamber also incorporates cosmic symbols into the political process. A huge tapestry covering one wall, dampening the echo and providing vivid colors, portrays the abstract dance of the twenty-four hour sun, a carriage wheel borrowed from the national arms of India, the open hand and footprints (also Indian icons), a mango tree, clouds, and a series of signs more esoteric or personal to Le Corbusier.

The whole building radiates with these markers, some cast in concrete, others made permanent and shiny on large enamel doors. Here we confront the only architect capable, daring, and arrogant enough to supply an emergent culture with a ready-made set of

ABOVE: Le Corbusier, General Assembly, Chandigarh, 1953–61. The powerful forms partly related to local and cosmic meanings: indigenous animals, the monsoon, and extreme heat.

MIDDLE: The rooftop sun symbolism extends into the assembly room, as once a year a solar festival focuses light on the rostrum. The sun and its path generate the side *brise soleil* as well as the top curves and the conventional solar symbol, the pyramid.

BELOW: The pyramidal council chamber, Chandigarh. Cosmic and local symbolism pervades the architecture and forms a backdrop for debate.

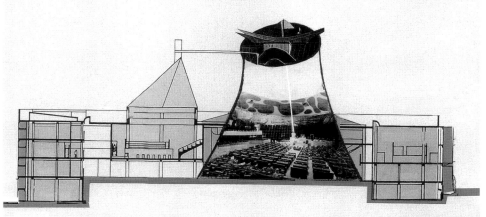

symbols. The risk seems to have paid off. The temple complex at Chandigarh remains the only seat of government to have reached this resolution of iconic building. By comparison, the new capital of Brazil, Brasilia, is a series of abstract one-liners open to misinterpretation. Its focus is a large phallic secretariat set between two domes, one upside-down. Brazilians read this composition, according to customary signs, as salad bowls. The government sits down to dinner and then, when finished eating, turns over the bowl (that is, consumes the people's cash). By contrast, Le Corbusier's local and esoteric icons root his governmental buildings in place and usage. Again, think of how different this is from other architects' practice. This is because Le Corbusier, unlike them, draws, paints, sculpts, and has an interest in iconography. He cares about the totality of signs and their meaning. Two examples bring out the point, both which derive from his work. Boston City Hall, designed in the 1960s, and Norman Foster's London City Hall, finished after the Millennium, are both expressive iconic buildings and are intended as contemporary symbols of democracy. Neither has an iconographic programme, nor art that carries through its intentions in a systematic way. As provocative signs the former is misread as a fortress, the latter as a testicle, inadvertent meanings that were hardly intended.

A whole class of malapropistic metaphors flourishes today, exuberant signs that on the road to some unspecified Damascus have lost their way. This is the revenge of the enigmatic signifier, the expressive form with the wrong kind of content. When it misfires it shoots the architect in the backside.

Norman Foster, on another outing in Berlin, produces a rather beautiful icon of democracy. The Reichstag, a heavy brooding hulk of Germanic classicism, reminds the nation not only how Hitler burned it, and his way to power, but of the dark side of imperial bombast. Potent symbols of national identity carry that paranoiac charge that is essential to the successful icon, so the grim visage of the burnt and blasted Reichstag—that suffered Russian occupation and humiliation for thirty years—was not without its affect. Germans knew they had to keep these signs of their horrific past and guilt and, at the same time, transform them. So choosing the Englishman Foster, the perfect icon of lightness, technological supremacy, openness, and British fair play, was a brilliant foil. In the initial competition he produced a High-Tech cover to the old building; but then on winning it he was encouraged, step by step, to invent an amazing icon—the non-dome

ABOVE: Norman Foster, London City Hall, 1999–2002. The icon of a thousand nicknames.

ABOVE RIGHT: Norman Foster, Reichstag Renovation, Berlin, competition 1992, construction 1995–9. The beacon of democracy shines out as the citizens walk above their representatives and survey the city, an intentional icon of a new Germany.

dome. At night, like some Expressionist beacon of a new faith, this radiates out beams of light, a reminder that many Berlin architects adopted crystal metaphors of spirituality in the early 1920s. What a brilliant opposition to Hitlerian classicism: a great, democratic light-bulb sits in triumph over the past. People walk all over their representatives debating below in the main chamber. They look out in wonderful vistas over their city, stroll to the top and see the heavens framed by a circular void—an icon adopted from the Pantheon. And, lest anyone is in doubt as to where the power is meant to lie, a missile-shaped light reflector sends its sharp dagger-point at the heart of the assembled politicians. Here is an echo of Le Corbusier's shaft of light on the rostrum, even if unintentional. The only critique of this otherwise cogent expression of democracy is that there is little iconographic support. The double-headed eagle of the Germanic imperium carries no weight; the signs of Russian occupation are welcome expressions of pluralism, but they find no echo in paintings, sculpture, or the multiple media that Le Corbusier employed at Chandigarh.

Sadly, we live in an age where iconography has become something of an embarrassment. Politicians are unsure of what public meanings to symbolize; they have to make U-turns on the spot and deny a change of direction. The history of monumental buildings in post-revolutionary France is not a happy one. These had a habit of changing names, and meanings, with each republic, and between them. Better to be ambiguous and hide behind generalities that transcend time and party than declare something specific. The slide into platitude is particularly evident when designers are given an impossibly divided program such as that for the World Trade Center site. This demanded both a particular recognition of individuals and

ABOVE: The light reflector brings enlightenment to the politicians below, and also its dagger of truth.

BELOW: The dome of the sky, an idea adapted from the Pantheon, culminates the walk to the top, another example of cosmic symbolism used in a civic building.

RIGHT: Romaldo Giurgola, Parliament House, Canberra, Australia, 1984–8. Won in competition in 1980, this huge governmental center is sunk into the landscape and surmounted by the national flag, sign that all nature and culture is subject to law.

groups, such as the firefighters and police who lost their lives and the different nations who lost citizens and the country as a whole and the globe—after all it was the *World* Trade Center. This conundrum of pluralism will be examined in the following chapter, but it is already apparent in such attempts at iconic building as Australia's new parliament building in Canberra. Designed by Romaldo Giurgola in 1979, it was an early example of symbolizing people power by having them walk all over their representatives—here below grass rather than Foster's glass. The national flag, on large upturned supports, becomes the ultimate icon, rather than the buildings, which are sunk out of sight. Because of their heavenward swoop, the stainless steel supports signify an almost sacred version of democratic nationalism: the flag is above all the people, no one is above the law of the land.

That is the idea; icons do not have to be true, but they are best if they appeal to faith, ideals, our better self, what we want to see in the mirror. With Parliament House, the Australians wanted to see identity politics, pluralism, cultural diversity, and a benign attitude toward Greeks, Italians, and other non-Anglo-Saxon minorities, above all their aboriginal population. So they suppressed the British colonial identity, so evident elsewhere, and repressed the buildings under a grassy knoll, instead instituting an art program giving sixty major commissions to artists for site-specific, identity works. Michael Nelson Tjakamarra, a leading aboriginal artist, designed the forecourt's granite mosaic pavement. This was a first step in what became, twenty years later, a millennial shower of post-modern icons to pluralism.

The Melbourne Museum, designed by DCM in 1999, is typical of the new mood of realism. Upfront about the continuous murder of its inhabitants and the destruction of ethnic art, it presents different groupings of Australian culture with a studied egalitarian honesty, and within a colorful *mélange* of abstract forms. Another architectural group, LAB, pushes the formal pluralism further with their fractal monument to urban diversity, Federation Square. Celebrating the centennial federation of eight different states, it goes beyond American essays in architectural diversity by fragmenting the existing city materials and colors—sandstone, steel, and glass—into self-similar shapes that are readable at various scales. The layout is a superb transformation of the alleyways one finds in medieval cities. It mediates between the two opposite realities of the site, the grid of the modern city to one side and the fractal forms of the river and trees to the other.

Turning diversity itself into a symbol is the most difficult of all iconic themes. Yet recently it has caught the imagination of the Australians as of no other nation. ARM, another architectural group, takes pluralism to the limit at the National Museum of Australia. This stupendous exercise in the carnivalesque is set right across the lake from the understated Parliament House, that exercise in identity politics which hides its face under a hill. The National Museum, by contrast, welcomes the visitor to a crash course in Aussie realism with an echo of the Parliament's abstract flag, that is, a giant loop-the-loop icon at the entrance, which then runs throughout the building. This is a coiling snake-like ribbon of exploding color, with obvious aboriginal overtones. Where Giurgola provides a harmonious sweep of unity in icy metal, ARM hits you with the image of "tangled destinies," a powerful metaphor of Australian realities. Here is the architectural equivalent of Robert Hughes' *The Fatal Shore*. No equivocation here, no pieties about unity in diversity, just bloody tangled destinies with their hot-spots marked out on a blown-up map of the country that forms the central courtyard, and various signs of competitive diversity threaded through each other. The curators have welcomed the theme and given the various architectural symbols a particular grounding in events and cultural artifact.

Those who do not want a building to narrate cultural reality should stay away. It does not produce high architecture (impossible given the budget and time constraints), but rather low burlesque with high intentions. Given its vigor and honesty you come away from the museum with an insight into iconic buildings that should not be forgotten. They intensify experience and make it more vivid so that it gnaws at the memory. The truth is worth underlining since it foregrounds the paradox that a great icon need not be a great work of architecture, but it must be a captivating one. It has to move your viscera, whether you like it or not, and stay around as a memory image that attracts other thoughts into its orbit. Pain and pleasure, love and

TOP: LAB, Federation Square, Melbourne, 1997–2002: a symbol of diverse urban tissue readable at many scales.

ABOVE: ARM, National Museum of Australia, Canberra, 1998–2001. The icon of "tangled destinies," a ribbon that greets the visitor, connects up the narratives of Australian life as it circles the map of struggle and crime.

RIGHT: Daniel Libeskind, Jewish Museum, Berlin, 1989–2001. History as the zigzag drunken walk bisected by the void.

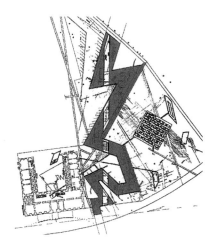

fear create lasting impressions, which may be why many people cannot forget the Coliseum in Rome, or a visit to a Holocaust museum.

Emotion-laden experience is a necessary aspect of the successful iconic building and it is one of the reasons why Daniel Libeskind's Jewish Museum attached to the old Berlin German Museum became one of the foremost icons of the 1990s. Even before it was filled with Jewish memorabilia, the building was visited as a striking memorial to the fraught but deep relations between the Germans and Jews. For various reasons, Libeskind called it "between the lines." Lines of windows and plan elements connected up particular Jews and Germans who were related through acquaintance or profession; the zigzag line of the twentieth century, searching and getting lost, is incorporated in one aspect of the plan. And the straight line that passes through this angular chaotic line signifies what he called "the voided void," the concrete cavern that runs down the museum, a path that one traverses but on which one cannot walk. It is a vivid metaphor of the unspeakable and unforgettable way the Berlin Jews were systematically catalogued and sent to their death. These are striking architectural metaphors for emotional states. To look into the gray voided void is to see the door shut, escape cut off, and finality imposed. The shafts of light are meant to remind one either of the hope glimpsed through cuts in a railroad car, or something more general, such as an inchoate glow, an unfathomable source of energy. The architecture, in spite of these strong images of loss, remains surprisingly optimistic. This is due to the contrasts in material, the gray caverns versus the white galleries, the slashes of view and the light through the windows, and the juxtaposition of a white grid of high planters and the zinc background on the exterior. Libeskind has deepened the experience of such abstract metaphors with more particular signs of Jewish identity, some quite obvious such as the Star of David, and others more esoteric, such as the references to Schoenberg and E.T.A. Hoffmann.

No doubt a Holocaust museum, to which this is comparable, and a national museum in Australia are suitable cases for iconography. The preconditions for a good icon, of course, are that people believe in something, have a developed idea of how to represent their faith, and that architects and artists are trained to carry through these signs and symbols—and want to do so. None of this is self-evident anymore. Parliaments and churches, two other potent building types, also continued a fitful existence into the new millennium and they too received some

symbolic treatment. But I end this quick overview of recent iconic buildings on the architect with whom I started, Le Corbusier, because his remains the most fully developed and seminal of all such work. It influenced the whole new genre, and is worth a closer look.

The Spiritual Icon

The iconic building is unthinkable today without reference to the little pilgrimage church Le Corbusier designed in 1950 in western France, called after its tiny hamlet, Ronchamp. An old church on the site had been destroyed by the Nazis in the early 1940s and Le Corbusier, during this time, had been going through a tortuous process of re-examination. First he tried to collaborate with the Petain government. Meeting no success in this pragmatic folly, he went into self-imposed exile, far from any town, indeed all other people except his wife. Here, in an old farmhouse, he rethought his painting, architecture, iconography, and, one imagines, his attempt at compromise. Out of this personal crisis came a bizarre set of new forms, most notably some "ear" shapes. These Le Corbusier called after the crazy character Père Ubu, for him a symbol of the madness of war, and these uncanny shapes multiplied throughout his paintings. They then inspired the new architecture at Ronchamp. Four ear-forms are here assembled, four signs of the mad surrealist king or, as he called him, "the ludicrous person created by Alfred Jarry." The architect also termed the ears "acoustic curves," and they can be found in the church's plan, section, and elevation, and in the basic way it addresses the four horizons.

ABOVE LEFT: Daniel Libeskind, Jewish Museum, Berlin, 1989–2001. "Between the lines" of a zigzagging history are further lines and, in front, the titled Garden of Exile with nature growing out of incarceration.

ABOVE: Libeskind's "voided void" of empty, concrete space runs down the middle of the zigzags but one cannot understand it or walk in it.

When it was finished, in 1955, the building became an international icon. It featured on a French stamp, on French tourist advertisements, in countless newspaper articles, and on the cover of many architectural magazines. The little chapel at Ronchamp became such a *succès de scandale* that it disoriented otherwise intelligent critics. The architect James Stirling saw in it "the crisis of rationalism," because it was not built with contemporary techniques (as if concrete were not of our time). For the historian Nikolaus Pevsner, who disliked curved buildings but also granted Ronchamp's power it was, in 1966, "the most famous building of the last twenty years."[9] In his *Outline of European Architecture* he labels it "the most discussed monument of the new irrationalism" and goes back into Puritan mode: "Woe to him who succumbs to the temptation of reproducing the same effect in another building, a building less isolated, less remote." Woe, woe: paranoia and misreading once again accompany the iconic building, especially when it heralds a shift in architecture, when it is good enough to make intelligent people feel challenged. Since Ronchamp is today familiar, and has so many offspring, including Gehry's work in Bilbao, it is worth recalling this initial disorientation and excitement.

It is, of course, absurd to think curved buildings are "irrational," or "rational" for that matter: it depends on the context, cost, appropriateness, etc. But it was true that for modern architects, in the late 1950s, straight lines, right angles, and boxes were assumed to be normal, understated, and more easily mass-produced, and in those senses "rational." Now that computer production and taste have rendered these previous conventions obsolete we can see them for the preconceptions they were, but the extreme reactions to Ronchamp—positive and negative—have other important lessons. They show that people respond to unusual shapes emotionally and with metaphorical comparisons. They tend to love (and hate) strikingly new forms, and map them on to

RIGHT: Le Corbusier, Ronchamp Church, 1950–5, from the south-west with "ear" forms both left and behind the pulpit to the right.

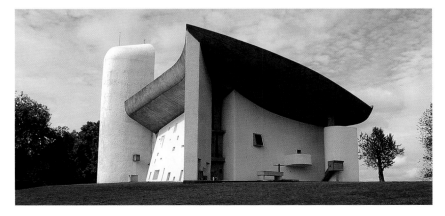

familiar images. This reaction to the iconic building is normal and what turns it into an enigmatic signifier: either an appropriate or errant stimulus. No building brings this out more than Ronchamp.

All sorts of images are suggested that relate to its function — a "nun's cowl," a "monk's hood," "mother and children," "praying hands," and that ancient metaphor of the church, a "ship at sea." The monks and local inhabitants offer such comparisons. Other popular signs that can be mapped directly on to the provocative shapes — such as a duck—are not clearly religious though indeed they may have spiritual overtones. Beyond these images are the various meanings historians and architects have found, more esoteric overtones, such as the relationship to a Roman building at Hadrian's Villa, to vernacular buildings of the Mediterranean, and to a storehouse of alchemical symbols. Like a great work of art, like *Hamlet*, it provokes new interpretation, and these multiple meanings were quite intentional. Ronchamp was constructed at the time Le Corbusier was developing an iconostasis, a set of personal and alchemical symbols, and the building can be interpreted through these icons.[10] Rather than repeating this analysis here, it is more relevant to mention the emotional response to Ronchamp.

When you first see it from afar it perches like a little white sculpture, a dove, on top of the wild, rolling hills of the Haute-Saone part of France. The approach has to be one of pilgrimage because it is a struggle to mount the hill and, in this ascent, the radiant form comes in and out of view like an elusive goal. Up close, and when circled, it explodes with sculptural vitality. There is no question that every element is part of a visual drama, a violent battle of light versus the dark roof and the green background. You penetrate between two of the ear forms (in Le Corbusier's paintings these curves do suggest other human parts) to find a mysterious inversion of religious space—the roof hangs down—and from the sides the "ears" push up, to grab the light. Mixing the metaphors can heighten experience, and it certainly does here since one of these light periscopes is painted red. The result is a suffused, Day-Glo bath of blood-light. When someone chants in it, or elsewhere in this reverberant space, the chapel suddenly changes again in feeling and becomes a sound box, an amplifier, or an echo chamber. Such violent and affective forms are then played in a different key as one approaches the south wall to find that the small holes of the outside have become flared, truncated pyramids of space that explode straight at you. The excitement of this new idea is overwhelming. The musical instrument has suddenly become a light

RIGHT: Metaphorical analysis of some popular signs. Le Corbusier admitted acoustic metaphors and the roof generated by a crab shell. He also intimated a veritable cornucopia of esoteric symbols, hints that have sparked decoding on an industrial scale. Drawings by Hillel Schocken.

FOLLOWING PAGES:
LEFT ABOVE: Ronchamp back entrance: penetration between two "ears," or periscope-chapels.

LEFT BELOW: Interior south wall: truncated pyramids of light, with tiny cosmic signs in color, expand toward the viewer.

RIGHT The acoustic metaphor is deepened by the reflective properties of the overhanging roof and canted surfaces and these forms aid outdoor services—a temple in and of nature.

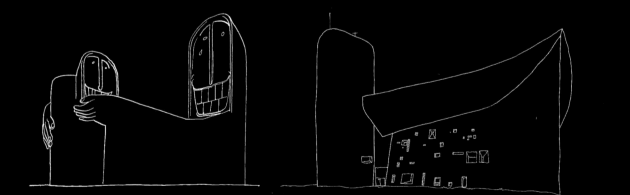

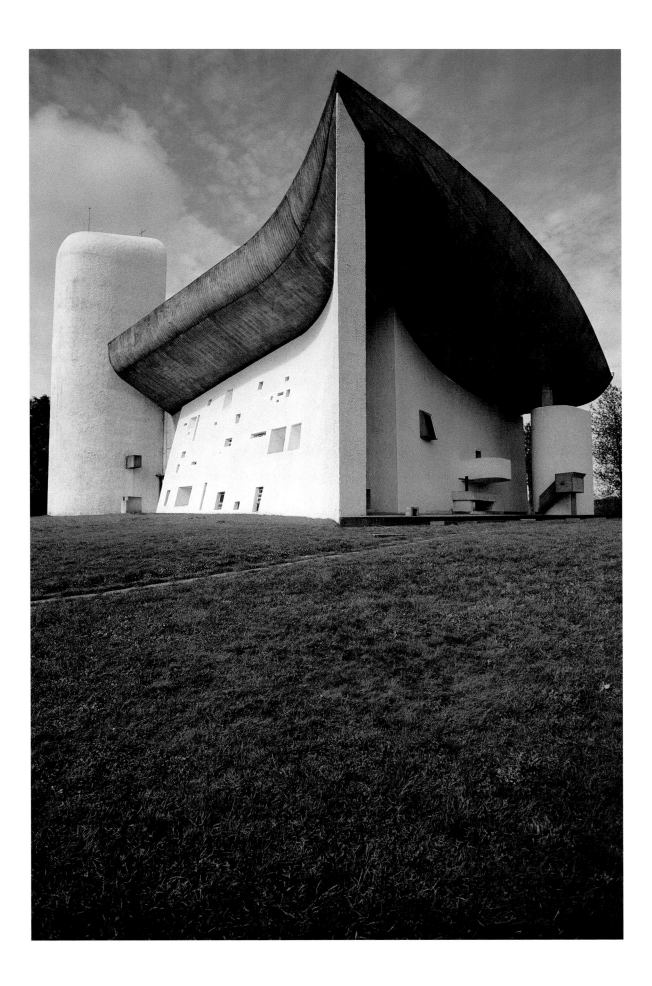

box, and one spies at the end of each perspectival slot of space a view of the outside and, often, a painting of nature, or a spiritual theme. It is all extremely moving, and my description concerns only a small part of the bigger experience. But it is enough to see why many people, even those who are not religious, respond to the building so forcefully.

The forms convince one that there has to be some deeper significance. It is as if some mystical interpretation existed for every shape and sign while the language, which would unlock their secrets, had been lost. Because the forms are sculpturally determined and powerful, they appear to be have been fixed by years of religious ritual. Yet Le Corbusier, who could be considered a pantheist, specifically rejected all conventional religious motifs and approached the problem psychologically.[11] As he expressed it emphatically:

> [Journalists at Ronchamp] virtually machine-gunned me with their flash cameras. I told the workmen near me: "If these people don't get out of here immediately take them by the shoulders and . . ." One of these fellows who had pursued me in front of the altar of pilgrimage outside, called to me, "Mister Le Corbusier, in the name of the manager of *The Chicago Tribune*, answer this question: was it necessary to be a Catholic to build this chapel?" I replied, "Foutez-moi le camp!"[12]

In polite parlance, "get the hell out of here." But the reporter's question is, in a psychological sense, perfectly valid, even pertinent, and it goes to the heart of the whole iconic enterprise. What is the referent to all this architectural rhetoric? What is the point of designing amazing buildings, or spending $100 million on Gehry's Bilbao, or $1,000 million on Pei's Pyramid (and underground), or $10,000 million on millennial projects? Why bother? Prestige, glamor, archiphilia, selling more clothes, amusement? For Le Corbusier, at least, Ronchamp referred back to a moment when he was a young man, in his teens, following the ideas and projects of a teacher, who was leader of a small flock of devotees. They were called, in the local Swiss school, the New Section of Art and they were devoted to creating a new spiritual equivalent to the religious art of the past, but one based on Nature rather than on God. He writes, in a book of 1925 appropriately called *Confession*, of a situation similar to creating Ronchamp, that is, building on the top of a small mountain, in the Swiss wilderness: "We were preparing the future. 'Here', [at the top

Red light spills down one of the chapels. The acoustic metaphor is deepened when a monk chants here, filling the church with a reverberent sound lasting three seconds. Painted signs (below) also underscore the iconography.

of the highest hill, with uninterrupted horizons] said the master, 'we will build a monument dedicated to nature and we will make it our lives' purpose'."

That temple was never constructed, but it is not fanciful to see Ronchamp, with its many colorful symbols and sculptural forms, its icons without a religious iconography, as a cosmic celebration. Then, reflecting back on the iconic buildings we have surveyed, particularly Le Corbusier's work at Chandigarh and Daniel Libeskind's in Berlin, we might see them as further offspring in the same bloodline. There is a tradition unfolding here, a common thread even if it has no label. But if a name is sought, one might call it "the open work," after Umberto Eco's book of that title, the work that demands to be decoded, but not according to any script. The open work, the enigmatic signifier, has many suggestive meanings that point in a direction and ask that one travels along an unknown route with the search as part of the goal. When used by Le Corbusier at Ronchamp they imply a temple to the universe and a spiritual exploration without a religion. Perhaps, in the end, that is a motive of all successful enigmatic signifiers? In any case, Ronchamp, because it was built by an artist adept at fashioning new symbols, is a standard against which to measure the iconic buildings of our time, and a hard one to equal.

Iconic Media Wars

The I-Word Goes Public

In late February 2003 Daniel Libeskind beat six other architects competing to build the successor to the World Trade Center at Ground Zero. He won with an iconic building, the Freedom Tower. It was 1776 feet tall and contained several other, more architecturally underlined, symbols of democracy. But the Battle of the Icons wasn't over. Winning competitions isn't really about coming first any more, especially when the most important commission on the most important site is at stake. It is worth taking a detailed look at what amounts to a war of symbols lasting three years and one that shows no signs of ending. The struggle casts a strong light on the way iconic building has moved center stage and taken on a life of its own.

The strife was due partly to the politicization of Ground Zero, a site of world dispute, and partly to the ambiguities of power and who had it. The owners of the area, the New York Port Authority, and the developer, Larry Silverstein, had their favorite schemes and architects. Indeed, Silverstein had even hired the New York skyscraper firm SOM to redesign the World Trade Center *before* September 11th, and he never changed his mind. There were further complications of power, and claims on the site. The families of the victims had their agenda, the Republican Mayor and the Governor of New York had a strong influence on the decision and, besides, Libeskind only won the competition for an outline scheme, the concept, and had never built a tall tower. To compound the confusion, the master-planner of a site is not the architect of all the buildings, a fact never sufficiently understood by the public or the press.

Hence the drama played out on the world stage, amplified by the media. In the end, Silverstein's favorite, David Childs, leader of SOM, was given the task of designing the Freedom Tower *somewhat* to Libeskind's guidelines: that is, with a surmounting spire 1776 feet high, and an abstract echo of the Statue of Liberty, whose raised torch is within view of the site.

Making Childs conform to Libeskind's building codes was never going to be easy, rather like making a man in a pin-stripe suit dress in designer clothes. SOM—Skidmore, Owings and Merrill—is *the* corporate American firm, one that Frank Lloyd Wright mocked as a business conglomerate. Skiddings, Ownmore and Sterile, he called it.

TOP : Daniel Libeskind, proposal for the Freedom Tower for Ground Zero.

ABOVE : David Childs' design, Decemeber 2003.

For five months the two designers struggled with each other. Finally, only a few days before the end of the year, Governor Pataki informed them they must have a joint result, before Christmas, of which they both could be proud, which they could both sign off without rancor. The Libeskind team had been accused of trying to pre-empt the Childs design, and had even been charged with a Watergate-style break-in, when on a visit the worst crime they committed was to take a few photos of some ideas (surely acceptable for a supposed collaborator). Governor Pataki banged the designers' heads together and, on December 19th, with a smiling developer and two apparently happy architects, they jointly presented the hybrid scheme to a press conference.

Libeskind, wearing his signature thick, black-rimmed glasses, hugged the developer, sporting his thin-rimmed spectacles; the property magnate, moved by this sudden burst of emotion, returned the gesture, with amazed laughter, and tears flooded his bifocals for all the assembled to see. "Working with David Childs wasn't just easy," Libeskind confessed, "It wasn't just a couple of meetings. It was a struggle to create something great." "It's been fractious and difficult," his wife and business partner Nina admitted to a reporter, "but we expected that," and it wasn't over. "It's a work in progress."[1]

As the reporter for the *Financial Times* put the story of conflict, "the two men did not always see eye-to-eye when collaborating on the design for Freedom Tower, the 1776-foot building. . . . They both wanted an iconic building. But they agreed on little else."[2]

That sounds right: different philosophy, different values. They liked different kinds of architecture, different suits. Is the need for an icon the only area of agreement left in our agnostic age?

Mr. Childs, with the kind of self-effacement that only the head of an architectural empire can muster, admitted he wanted a building without someone's "name on it." "Nobody knows the name of the architect who built the Washington Monument, same with the Chrysler Building." Childs was invoking that old humble architect, Anon., who crops up everywhere. The Architect with a Thousand Faces, the hero of SOM, the firm that brought America background architecture, the business vernacular. Our self-effacing architect designed a couple of turns to the Freedom Tower, giving it that contextual relationship to the twisting Statue of Liberty across the water, which Libeskind had mandated, and he added at the top some cables and a wind farm of turbines, that had a kind of anonymous relationship to the Brooklyn Bridge, up the river. In keeping and

The Collaboration—a collage frames the media-framing of the event.

The Architect, The Governor, The Developer, The Architect

THE COLLABORATION OF OPPOSITES

Jewish Museum, left, and David M. Childs's Time Warner Center: meshing styles, personalities and bosses to design a tower for ground ze

Scenes From a Forced Marriage

modest, that was it, he admitted *sotte voce* to the English reporter, and gave away his real motive: "A cable latticework in the sky with windmills—it's very simple, very fast [to build] and though it's been used before in bridges, it has never been used before in a building." He added with pride, "We think it's quite iconic." Of course, those anonymous wind propellers buzzing away around the 90th floor are *quite* iconic.

Framing the Event—the double explosion and the surviving fragments became the two media icons, repeated for many months.

On December 19th, 2003, the I-word had gone public to become *the* area of agreement in an otherwise fractious dispute. Whereas in the past an icon enjoyed a venerated status because of its reference to a specific saint or valued meaning, now it claimed legitimacy because it validated itself. This circularity, or self-referential nature of the sign, is typical of the mediated world where celebrities are famous for being famous and then, when that fades, famous for recharging their notoriety by appearing as reality TV has-beens in *I'm a Celebrity. Get Me Out of Here!*

The word and concept of the iconic building has had, as we have seen, a long and continuous history and in that sense there was nothing new in its emergence that December day, except, perhaps, the empty circularity of its meaning, its appearance as pure sign with only media significance. Even deep ecologists would have trouble worshipping wind farms as the crown of a skyscraper. And yet, at another level of meaning, in a competition commanding world attention, there was a deep logic to its emergence as pure sign. Never had there been such a public focus on picking an architect and project; the designs for the World Trade Center site became a kind of world exercise in self-psychoanalysis and it is revealing to look at this process for the light it casts on the iconic building.

Global Ritual

Since so much of the globe watched the Twin Towers on TV being hit and falling, and re-watched it again and again, the event itself became etched in the collective memory in an unforgettable way, as a trauma. Monument, memorial, and icon are all connected by their prime place in our memory and nothing is so memorable, neurologists and psychologists argue, as a horrible, painful experience. It fuses neuronal clusters into repeated firing patterns. The slightest association with the original trauma can ignite the entire cascade of these feelings and thoughts. Moreover, newspapers and magazines dramatized what were already the most recorded dramatic images, and a veritable

Framing the Event

ON THE FIRST DAY – The Iconic Shots

ON THE SECOND DAY – Ruins as Memorial Icon

industry grew around purveying them. They appeared on the cover of countless artefacts and this repetition itself added to their iconic nature. In the most ill-considered remark of what this might mean the composer Karlheinz Stockhausen proclaimed the attack "the greatest work of art ever."[3]

The unparalleled nature of the event, the mediated experience, and its vivid shock memory led to the question of how to memorialize these terrorist acts. There were a thousand answers. The immediate notices of missing relatives, placed on boards near the site, had the most poignant impact, the photograph as a specific memorial and a question mark. The small shrines to the police and firefighters who died trying to save other lives also had this factual charge, a reality that later memorials had difficulty recapturing. The badges, memorabilia, photos, and accompanying text—"These 37 brothers and sisters of the P.A.P.D. became victims of a despicable terrorist act"—kept the moment vivid and particular, where later monuments became abstract and generic. As time passed, and politics entered, the complexity of signs and mourning was reduced: the police and firefighters became, simply, "Heroes of September 11th," as if they had chosen their fate beforehand and knew what they were in for.

For a few days, the curtain wall fragment of one twin tower remained above the smouldering ruins and many people, including Philippe De Montebello, the head of the Metropolitan Museum in New York, called for the skeletal fragment to be preserved. As he pointed out, it was "already so frequently photographed and televised that is has become nearly as familiar to us as the buildings that once stood there." In fact, several books used these images to memorialize the event, and De Montebello makes clear why the jagged fragment was such a natural monument. "Though tilted slightly, it somehow survived, emerging from the fire and smoke of September 11th— inexplicably durable, still pointing to the heavens, and now a fitting, realistic and moving monument to those who died there. Already an icon, it should stand forever."[4] Permanence, connection to the event, and expressiveness are three powerful qualities of the successful icon.

In addition, the subsequent ritualization of the whole tragedy by the media, including the wars in Afghanistan and Iraq, turned the events of September 11th into a classical icon itself. It took on the aspect of a sacred or holy occurrence, a kind of negative miracle, and a "defining moment" as so many said, as if it had changed the world forever. Just as the crucifixion became a numinous instant for

BELOW: Immediate memorials to the police and firefighters.

BELOW RIGHT: *On the Fourth Day*—the British Press picks up the framing for war.

Christians, just as the French Revolution defines a part of French identity, "9/11" became a symbol to be put on the level of Pearl Harbor and the Civil War. The continuous, everyday transmission of a similar message through the media lasted for several months, creating the peculiar modern ritual of the secular society. Has any other recent event become so reified and repeated as a formula? In global society the modern form of ritual is created by media, not religious, repetition, hence the way it is re-presented here as the layered accumulation of text, headline, and image. This meta-media is part analysis, part the art of amplification.

The mediation reveals an important truth, perhaps so obvious as to escape comment. A building becomes iconic not just for the reasons I have enumerated but also when it is part of an unfolding media event that takes time. In other words, the building plus its reception over many months creates the necessary ritual. In a secular society, only the newspapers, magazines, and TV can engender the proper aura, establish legitimacy, create taboos, and define what can be said and felt and what is unacceptable. In the case of September 11th, this lengthy

process is still under way. The world ritual continues as each stage in the unfolding drama is reached, as each part of the puzzle is fit into the narrative. The terrorists are named, the heroes and villains are defined, Bush and Blair declare you are either for us or against us, the wars are started, the body count is made, the victim's relatives form pressure groups, public meetings of all sizes take place, Governor Pataki and Mayor Bloomberg define the political discourse, the Port Authority, the owner, maps out the functional and economic parameters, the developer Larry Silverstein lays down architectural guidelines, the insurers of the Twin Towers dispute how much they should pay, the press and architectural critics define who and what might be acceptable for the building, and the rest of the world is invited to express opinion. The fallible opinion poll, backed up by the even more fallible measuring on the Internet, is brought in on the act. The result is pure global ritual, and architecture, for the first time, is at its center.

Significantly, soon after September 11th, the profession reacted with proposals. Within a few months the New York Gallery owner Max Protech had put together an exhibition of sixty world architects who he considered worthy to speculate, in artistic ways, on what might be done on the site. The quick sketches were interesting as provocations that opened a space for imagination. Typical of these is Daniel Libeskind's entry called "Stone and Spirit," an upward explosion of four rectangular shards. Resembling a mannerist version of Constructivist work of the 1920s, or his own prophetic designs of the late 1980s, Aleph Wing, or, in more pop terms, a clutch of stacked pencils, the design was clearly rhetorical, not a realistic proposal. But the heavenward spire of his later scheme, and De Montebello's ruined skeleton "inexplicably durable, still pointing to the heavens" is here, the expression of disaster versus hope. After Libeskind's work on the Jewish Museum, such oppositions became his staple, his way of portraying tragedy. It is worth hearing his language because it was to become standard, even for others, over the years.

> Following the attacks that destroyed the World Trade Center, one has to evaluate architecture in completely new terms. It is a delicate task to ask what should be built in place of such an icon, especially given the power of its destruction.

While he terms the World Trade Center an icon, few in the architectural community thought the original towers were worth much

Daniel Libeskind, "Stone and Spirit," entry for the Max Protech exhibition, "A New World Trade Center," featuring design proposals from leading architects worldwide, 2002.

until they were destroyed. However, Libeskind is sensitive to the media icon of destruction as the defining memory image and realizes its challenge. He goes on to question commercial use on the site, notes that "the real question is about memory," and reiterates the newness, uniqueness, and irreversibility of what has occurred. For him, as for so many others, September 11th has not only changed the site but the world. Thus the response must take "into consideration the relationships between the uniqueness of a site and its global significance; fragility and stability; stone and spirit. Whatever is built will have to acknowledge the permanent loss. This emptiness will remain and cannot be obliterated by any building."[5] His images, though, express both sides of a duality, not only loss and explosion but also emergence and hope. It was this combination of opposite signs that was to drive his project forward.

Choosing an architect and design over the next year was partly a benevolent process of public participation, partly a series of accidents, and partly a mixture of power politics, power money, and shameless infighting. With so many actors and no single client or brief, except as the architect Richard Meier put it—"to produce the most meaningful architectural project in the city's history"—the process was bound to be melodramatic. Indeed, this narrative of commercial democracy in action, the stupidest system except most of the others, became itself the media ritual that drew the world's attention.

A Drama in Five Acts

Act One. Worthy civil architects, Beyer Blinder Belle and Steven Peterson and Barbara Littenberg are commissioned to produce six analyses that show how the Ground Zero site could be transformed. They are paid something over $3 million for these first complex studies. This amount so dwarfed the subsequent figures that were paid to some of the world's top designers for actual designs, that architectural fees themselves became politicized. However, the initial concepts were meant to be anodyne sketches, not fully worked out propositions, concerned with transportation, engineering, and the best use of the site. They were not meant to be architectural solutions and they did influence the final designs in positive ways. Noteworthy were such ideas as turning a wide traffic artery, West Street, into a boulevard and reconnecting the sixteen acres of Ground Zero with the fabric of the downtown. Peterson and Littenberg's urban concept of a "loop penetrated by a spine" even finds an echo in Libeskind's ring of skyscrapers bisected by Greenwich Street.

But, whatever the intentions, the ideas were perceived as architectural solutions, and this had unfortunate results. In the last scene of Act One—July 2002—five thousand people assemble in the Javits Convention Center to debate the concepts. To facilitate the interactive process of such a large number, each seat is provided with a computer terminal so everybody could answer questions, react, and make comments. Their overwhelming response is, as Alex Garvin, coordinator of these plans puts it, "No, this is not good enough."[6] The public outside, the relatives of the victims, and the architectural critics give the same verdict. But some positive lessons do emerge. The public do not want the original 11 million square feet of office space put back on the site because, with the new memorial area that they also demanded, there would be much less room. The idea of preserving the two footprints of the old towers is also solidified. Over-exploitation became an issue; an acceptable ratio of mammon to memorial. Finally, responding to directed questions, the five thousand assembled at their computer terminals ask for some great architecture. Hence there is a public mandate for iconic building.

At the beginning of Act Two, the city's press enters the fray, above all *The New York Times*. Its architectural critic Herbert Muschamp and a series of local architects work on imaginative urban ideas with some of the world's top designers. They are paid very little for their thoughts. At the end of Act Two, on the anniversary of the event in September 2002, these are presented in a *New York Times* Sunday supplement and at the Venice Biennale. The basic urban notion is a wide boulevard like the Champs Elysées, a new version of West Street leading south to the harbor, to Battery Park. This is fronted with some grand icons by Peter Eisenman (twisted skyscrapers) and Rem Koolhaas (an upside-down skyscraper) and the bright ideas of other superstars. Two twisted towers are placed around Ground Zero, an early premonition of the final twist by SOM. While these buildings were open to criticism as gestural architecture, their importance was to inject fresh thinking and major talent into the discussion.

Act Three is one of the longest and most fraught. After the unveiling at the Biennale the debate heats up. The political machine running the show set up by New York State Governor, George Pataki, is the Lower Manhattan Development Corporation (LMDC), with a boring name as long as it is powerful. It initiates the final push. World designers, now known to be more than willing participants in this

Consortium of architects, September 2002, led by Herbert Muschamp and Frederic Schwartz. The West Street Boulevard has been opened and, in order to be visible, the architects' models are here moved into the Hudson River.

drama, are canvassed for their willingness, and all but Frank Gehry comply. Stupidly, he lets it be known to an interviewer that he finds the $40,000 fee on offer an insult to architecture, pure exploitation, derisory, etc., which, from him, is a throwaway understatement, quoted out of context. Given the millions previously paid for the concept plans, the fee is a joke, a brilliant piece of inspiration from an acronymn looking for a cheap solution. So four hundred world architects apply and they are reduced to seven teams, most of whom have at least one luminary in attendance. With their $40,000, they are given just eight weeks to produce the most important symbolic design in the world. Having no time makes up for being paid next to nothing.

Paul Goldberger, the *New Yorker* architectural critic, worked out the design labor involved: the money on offer would pay for "little more than two hours' work on the competition."[7] But truth is not the virtue required when the "most meaningful architectural project in the city's history" is on the table. What is needed is selfless passion and total commitment to architecture, etc. Peter Eisenman, well known for these virtues, naturally slated the small-mindedness in a public forum to which the seven new competitors were invited. "It doesn't matter a damn, Frank Gehry," he said at a New York meeting, addressing the architect 3,000 miles away in Los Angeles, "that we were paid only $40,000."

The Port Authority and LMDC smiled approvingly at such outspoken altruism. Here was the kind of architect you could really do business with. Cesar Pelli, the skyscraper architect, estimated that the competition cost the architects a combined figure of $4 million, thus saving the Corporation a handsome three and a half. The exploitation did, as Pelli added, give something back to the architects in terms of publicity.[8]

Such ridiculous fees provided the spark for a fight. The posturing and bitchiness of a good old professional ding-dong was in the offing, and few of the architects wished to disappoint their, by now, worldwide audience. Act Three was a show-stopper, by the local standards of the theaters along Times Square. The proposal by Eisenman, Meier, Gwathmy, and Holl, with its upright rectangular slabs connected by horizontals—in the manner of a war cemetery of white crosses—was dubbed by the media a "tic-tac-toe board." Bernard Tschumi, the Dean of Architecture at Columbia University, found the result "too monumental and iconic to be effective." "Too iconic!" This sly comment seems to confirm that enigmatic icons are often more effective, in an agnostic age, than explicit ones. Tschumi then went on to advise that the best parts of each scheme might be combined, an impossibility in a competition although something hinted at by the initial brief.[9] Another contributor, Ms. Littenberg, surprised and angry that every architect at the meeting turned out to be nice to each other, attacked them for their inhuman scale: "A lot of these designs engage in gigantism. That kind of arrogant thinking led to the construction of the first towers." And, by implication, their destruction. This convivial meeting occurred in New York on January 9th, after the first presentation of the seven schemes, on December 18th, and well before the final day of judgment, February 27th, 2003.

It typified the insecurity of the situation. The client and the brief were somewhat vague; the bottom had fallen out of the skyscraper market; public opinion was leading events; formal meetings of all types were trying to determine the indeterminant and architects were now proclaiming the whole spectacle "the greatest architecture show ever." At their presentations on December 18th, the seven competitors were televised live for more than three hours. Suddenly it was no longer architecture, or even September 11th, or memorialization that was the subject, but the unfolding media event itself—the modern ritual.

The workings of this ritual, over the two and a half months, had a life of their own. Norman Foster, or Lord Foster of Thames Bank as he is officially known, had produced the most suavely perfected scheme, two faceted towers. These, designed like other entries to be the largest building in the world, zigzagged in and out and touched at several point, "kissed," as he explained, to create both gardens in the air and safety features, the ability to escape from one tower to the other. As reborn versions of the old World Trade Center, they looked at once more elegant and fragile, and thereby became an appropriate memorial, less aggressive than the original. Within minutes of his live TV presentation, Foster launched the most sophisticated website devoted to the scheme, and quickly emerged as the public favorite. Early American opinion polls, and CNN, made him the man to beat. Such was the intensity of the designer-race that careful measurements were made of "unscientific indicators—the volume of applause from New York businesspeople passing alongside the invitation-only presentation." These clapometers also put him ahead. As a colleague said, "I've never seen Norman so fired-up" or as the reporter flagged the piece, "He wants the job so badly it hurts."[10] Foster called the

The New York Times

the News
Fit to Print"

.... No. 52,337   Copyright © 2002 The New York Times   THURSDAY, DECEMBER 19, 2002

7 Design Teams Offer New Ideas For Attack Site

Towers and Plazas Seen in Manhattan Plans

By EDWARD WYATT

Seven teams of architects from around the world unveiled new designs for the World Trade Center site yesterday, giving a remarkable tutorial on architecture contemporary urban design ing the hole left by the S...

...scaffolding...canopies of ...what would be ...ing in the world, and ...e an area for a memorial victims of 9/11.

"The architects have responded with great depth to the question, 'What does Sept. 11 represent?'" said John C. Whitehead, the chairman of the Lower Manhattan Development Corporation, the joint city-state agency that is overseeing the rebuilding project. "Their response vary, just as our own reaction... trauma, the aftermath...

...io Romero/The New York Times
...appointment last summer.

The battle for ground zero

ZERO: Back From the Drawi...

...al ...space in ...efeller Center. ...reflecting pools are ...d footprints of the twin ...ers; beneath them, the shafts below the footprints become sites for memorial rooms. Cultural facilities include Memorial Museum and Freedom Library, a concert hall, an opera house and performing arts theaters framing the edges of the site. The transit station is reminisce... of the "glass shed" architect...

...spaces, ...loors what the ...16 acres of sky ...d 16 acres of cultural ...e as well as a million square ...eet of retail space around the transit station. The architects described this as "the vertical city." While there was no estimate given of the total amount of office space, the presentation showed that "over time buildings emerge from the site" to give "more than adequate retail and commercial space." A reflecting pool with bridges passing over the footprints of the former towers brings light to the station, which is situated below street level, between Greenwich and Church Streets.

7 WORLD - CLASS ARCHITECTS

GIVEN JUST $40,000 & 8 WEEKS

Seven architects vie to redraw New York's skyline

Vision of Manhattan: how a replacement for the Twin Towers might look, left, from Lord Foster of Thames Bank and two of the other seven finalists (themes from 400 entries from 34 countries. The winning design will be decided in February

FOSTER & PARTNERS

PETERSON/LITTENBERG

The Seven Architects present to the world media, and Foster sprints ahead.

footprints of the missing towers "sacred voids" and, like Richard Meier, who turned them into reflecting pools, he adopted the language of memorialization that had become so prevalent since Libeskind's Jewish Museum and Maya Lin's Vietnam Memorial, the symbolism of pregnant absence, of potent emptiness.

Of course, it was Libeskind who could articulate this vision with the most persuasive force because of his previous work and first-hand experience. "To acknowledge the terrible deaths which occurred on this site, while looking to the future with hope, seemed like two moments which could not be joined," he said at his presentation. "I sought to find a solution which would bring these seemingly contradictory viewpoints into an unexpected unity." Libeskind's rhetorical strength throughout these two and a half months was not only in the direct way he combined the opposites of death and hope, but also in the personal way he talked about visiting the site and the feelings and thoughts he had when he did so. The other architects were more bound up in design language and less willing to talk about the emotional and symbolic urgency of their design. As a result Libeskind emerged as one of the media favorites to win and was supported by *The New York Times'* critic, Herbert Muschamp. "If you are looking for the marvelous, here's where you will find it. Daniel Libeskind's project attains a perfect balance between aggression and desire. . . . The project's power is partly rooted in Mr. Libeskind's immigrant experience: this guy actually arrived by boat . . . [He] has fashioned a new set of crystals, brilliantly faceted skyscrapers, forms that recreate the aspiration many architects felt when plate glass was new."[11] Muschamp's comments about another entry, in the shape of two helical lattices, that of the team called THINK, led by Rafael Viñoly and Frederic Schwartz, were tepid by comparison.

A dramatic development in Act Three was Muschamp's switch of allegiance from Libeskind to the THINK team, a reversal that had all sorts of repercussions because of Muschamp's position on *The New York Times* and the Libeskind counterattack. Behind this turnabout were several cross-currents. President Bush was becoming ever more strident in his lead up to Gulf War II and the World Trade Center competition was becoming embroiled, by implication, in this imperial adventure. New York architects, especially the influential avant-garde, were angered by the Libeskinds' explicit use of national symbolism, such as the Freedom Tower and its 1776-foot height. The mutual jealousy of the competitors was amplifying any sign into a political declaration. Daniel Libeskind donned cowboy boots on occasion, and put a tiny badge with an American flag in his lapel, and these acts were read as some kind of pledge of allegiance to the right wing, or support for pro-Israeli American foreign policy. And he and his wife Nina were not about to succumb to tough New York street-fighting conducted with *faux politesse* but, on the contrary, even more ready to do what they had done to get the Jewish Museum in Berlin completed: fight for the job.

So, as the drama developed, in a series of articles Muschamp produced a new interpretation of what he had previously called these "crystals, brilliantly faceted skyscrapers." No longer were they "a perfect balance between aggression and desire." Now they were suddenly "a startlingly aggressive *tour de force*, a war memorial to a conflict that has scarcely begun." President Bush's war rhetoric had shifted the background against which all of this could be seen, so now suddenly, and by association, Libeskind was guilty of "an emotionally manipulative exercise in visual codes," which was "demagogic," even "kitsch." "Unintentionally," Muschamp contends, "the plan embodies the Orwellian condition America's detractors accuse us of embracing: perpetual war for perpetual peace."[12] Strange that a mere site plan could embody all this, even if unintentionally, but such is the potency of an enigmatic signifier that, when the atmosphere becomes electric, any conceivable overtone suddenly becomes supercharged with particular meaning. The uncertain enigma coalesces into precision. This focussing was enhanced by every step Bush took toward war, and every step the anti-war movement took against him.

The potency of the enigmatic signifier was also amplified by the party politics of the site. The Republican Mayor Rudolph Guliani, one of the visible "heroes" of September 11th because of the way he took charge that day, and the Republican Governor George Pataki did not want their hated Democratic opponent Mark Green to take charge of rebuilding the World Trade Center, and they managed to help the election of Republican Michael Bloomberg as the new Mayor of the city. With Republicans in the seats of power, and Pataki in control of the LMDC, it looked to conspiracy theorists as if the winner had to be a Republican, and a likely supporter of the Iraq invasion. So politically electric had architectural symbolism become that, when the ground-breaking ceremony for the icon building was determined as September 2004, Pataki had to deny, on several occasions, that it had anything to do with the Republican convention in the City at that date.

His protestations may have been too much but, because the anniversary of September 11th was an obvious choice for laying the first stone, they contained good political spin, that "high degree of deniability."

Libeskind also had to parry such suppositions, and they naturally stemmed from the explicitness of certain signs—the Park of Heroes, the Freedom Tower, 1776, and so on. He argued on several occasions that the right wing did not have a monopoly on democratic symbols and shouldn't be allowed to steal the American flag, or even a pair of cowboy boots. His wife Nina has always been on the center-left of the spectrum, and comes from a political family that includes Naomi (*No Logo*) Klein as a niece. On the London scene, responding to queries, Libeskind said that he was determined to protect his design, and the "experience of the US [embodied in it] from being appropriated by the US 'far right'." Obviously he was referring to the immigrant's experience of the Statue of Liberty and various other symbols of freedom, but also he was giving a commitment to protect formal elements of his own design, such as the spiral of buildings ending in the twisting Freedom Tower.[13] The iconic buildings would not be destroyed either by the far right or commercial pressures.

In early February the seven competitors were reduced by the LMDC to two and, most surprisingly given the polls and quality of his submission, one of them was not Norman Foster. The explanation given out on Channel 4 on British TV? He had listened *too* hard to what the developers wanted—new twin office towers—and not hard enough to all the other conflicting voices at Ground Zero. The shift of opinion among the power brokers was away from a better version of the Twin Towers toward something more ambiguous, many layered, and cultural, that is, toward Libeskind and the THINK team. These two finalists were then subjected to further corrections by the LMDC and tied more effectively into Lower Manhattan. As it affected the third largest downtown in the US (after midtown and Chicago), the scheme had to regenerate the stalled economy. As the destination for 300,000 people per day and a major transportation interchange between New Jersey and Long Island, it was to be a major center of economic movement, a second Grand Central Station. Potentially, it could hook up Newark and Kennedy airports in a single system and thus become the hub of the international scene, a global financial center ahead of the City of London. So, as LMDC had its twenty-two public hearings, as it banged together all the heads—bureaucratic,

CRITIC'S NOTEBOOK

Designers' Dreams, Tempered By Reality

By HERBERT MUSCHAMP

The decision on wh___
the World Trade___
pected to___
week___

___ have
___ plans at the
___ Manhattan De-
___ oration.

___ ibeskind plan originally
___ ried that most of the so-called
bathtub, the sunken area enclosed
within the concrete retaining walls of
the World Trade Center, be used for
a mix of cultural purposes. Much of
that area, however, has since b___
claimed by the Port Authori___
___ sion to build a major ___
hub within the ___
would leave ___
of the site to be___
team had plann___
stantially dimin___
tectural strength.

The most signif___
quired of the ele___ was the
reduction of the ele___ ed platforms
originally intended for cultural uses.
As now envisioned, a museum would
be between the 30th- and 35th-floor
levels of the two 110-story towers of

Less room in trough and towers for cultural uses.

steel lattice. Observation platforms
would be at the summits of the towers. The platforms originally designed for other cultural uses have
been eliminated, diminishing the
plan's vitality as a cultural center.
Officials of the development corporation said it would be impossible to
ensure construction on higher platforms after the museum was built.

Yet even the revised designs cannot be considered final. As is the case
with many competitions for major
building projects, the steering committee will be choosing a team of

The Night Before Judgement February 26, 2003

The Battle Of The Eyeglasses

Photographs by Joyce Dopkeen/The New York Times

Dan___ ___ for ground zero, talking to reporters.

Rafael Viñoly of the Think Team discussing its design after the finalists were announced.

Turning a Competition Into a Public Campaign

The Leak

The New York Times

Panel Supports 2 Tall T___

___ r and Governor ___ vor the Rival Proposal

By EDWARD WYATT

A key committee recommended ___
day that Lower Manhattan be re___
the lines of a plan that had___
favor, a proposal by th___
team for two soar___
the centerpi___
unexpec___
st___

___ ge E.
___ Bloomberg
___ ne other finalist
___ Libeskind, which fea-
___ ed pit on the site of the
___ d Trade Center towers.
___ The Associated Press reported yes-
___ erday that Mr. Pataki, when asked if he had
a favorite, said that he did, but then refused
to say what it was. "The mayor and I are
going to be talking about that this week,"
Mr. Pataki said. The final choice is to be
announced tomorrow.

The group that made the recommenda-
tion yesterday, the site planning committee
of the board of the Lower Manhattan Development Corporation, acted after a four-hour
meeting at which the seven committee
members reviewed the architects' revisions

Rebuilding officials challenge the politicians who appointed them.

4 STAR   QUEENS   FINAL

DAILY◉NEWS

www.nydailynews.c___   Thursday, February 2___

THE MEMORIAL MAN

INTERVIEW REBUILDING GROUND ZERO WILL BE A DELICATE BALANCING ACT, DANIEL LIBESKIND TELLS TOM DYCKHOFF

THE NEW WTC

The Win

INSPIRATION IN ITS EARLIEST STAGES

Libeskind initially developed his ideas using this series of sketches. In his final scheme the bathtub is shallower, and there are no sky gardens

"All the News That's Fit to Print"

The New Y___

VOL. CLII .... No. 52,408   Copyright © 2003 The New York Times   NEW YORK, FRIDA___

Daniel Libeskind, whose ___

PRACTIC___ FOR ___

Politics and Eco___
in Choice of Rene___

By EDWARD WYAT___

In the end, it was not so___
about architecture, about sole___
memorial pits or soaring gardens___
the sky. Instead, the decision announced yesterday to choose Daniel
Libeskind's design for the World
Trade Center site revolved mainly

O Brave **New Wor___**

___ n design the World Trade Center site is over. The winner is Daniel Libeskind. But how much of his powerful sche___

political, economic, and its own—the process clarified the issues. Voices still demanded contradictions—above all memorialization of the past and an economic rebirth for the future—but at least one could see now that one argument could not suppress another. All had to be accommodated, and memorial symbolism was just one important voice.

As it came down to the wire of February 27th, and the end of Act Three, the superficial differences of the two teams were sharpened. The Libeskinds hired not one but two public relations agents, and Daniel's thick, black Le Corbusier eyeglasses (and cowboy boots) were written up in consecutive Sunday Style sections of *The New York Times*.[14] Naturally, Viñoly countered by appearing on TV, and in other media, sporting double pairs of eyeglasses, one coming from the top of his head fully-blown like the emergence of the goddess Athena. On February 24th, both finalists appeared live, in a style and content scrap, on the *Oprah Winfrey Show*. Claims were made by zealous followers on each side that resembled the smear campaigns perfected by politicians. Just before the day of judgment there was a leak that Libeskind had *not* arrived on American shores seeing the Statue of Liberty, and, in the *Wall Street Journal*, that Viñoly had worked for Argentinian generals designing stadia and offices. Such allegations increased the feeding frenzy and the whole ritual became the ultimate media shoot-out in architectural history.

The leaked reports first favored Viñoly then Libeskind, making for a perfect photo-opportunity finish. Governor Pataki had appointed seven of the eleven members of the LMDC board, including its chairman. The day before the decision the board came out for the THINK team. The day of the decision, the two people who counted, the Mayor and Governor, overruled the board and picked Libeskind. Some claimed that the decision was influenced by the fact it would cost the government less money; others that it was Daniel's personal appeal to the sentiments of democracy, the families of the victims and New Yorkers' strong sense of pride.[15] All this mattered, but there was also a factor that illuminates the arguments of this book: the way those close to the tragedy interpreted the metaphors underlying both designs.

Libeskind's Strategy—Precise Denotations and Fuzzy Connotations

Much had been made of the way the design had to acknowledge September 11th and the question of how to do so. Viñoly allowed that Libeskind overplayed the sunken, memorial wall, the slurry wall or what was called a "bathtub" of structure that held back the Hudson River. This had remained as an icon resisting destruction on September 11th and therefore a natural symbol of standing firm, just the way Libeskind presented it. By contrast, the detractors, from Viñoly to Muschamp, could interpret the sunken concrete walls differently, as something inappropriate to New York dynamism: that is, a baleful "Wailing Wall" architecture. According to this reading, Libeskind's emphasis on memorialization had turned the area into a Trauma Theme Park, fixing the terrorists' attack for all time. "Al-Qaida wins twice," these critics put it. Double readings were possible with Viñoly's proposal as well. The two lattices in the sky, with elements placed between them, could be looked at positively, as Muschamp saw them, as "symbolic containers in which our hopes for the future can be crystallized by the uses that will be clustered within." Dynamic New York. Or, according to negative readings, they were "two skeletons" holding an incoming plane or dismembered bodies.[16] The horror. Obviously, neither architect intended their enigmatic signifiers to be read in derogatory ways, any more than Mrs. Malaprop meant to release superlative slips of her tongue. Yet, in the absence of any conventions and in the presence of many ambiguities, and a supercharged situation, little hints had big consequences. The Battle at Ground Zero, as it was framed, was influenced by such tiny, possible suggestions.

Governor Pataki insisted that family members of those killed preferred Libeskind's design. "The victims," he opined, "would be remembered by a symbol of strength—the slurry wall—rather than by what they characterized as a pair of skeletal towers that recalled how their loved ones had died." The skeleton metaphor became the deciding difference between the two designs. Since the Governor was the presiding judge at this inquisition of possible meaning, his opinion was the important one. But connotations with bones and carcasses, however fuzzy they might be, were plausible enough to persuade even those members of the jury who favored the THINK team. The U-turn in interpretation here was as extraordinary, and momentous, as Muschamp's had been.

Roland W. Betts, the chairman of the steering committee of the LMDC, President Bush's good friend since his student days at Yale,

RIGHT: Metaphors in the design include the crystal, the gesture in counterpoint to the Statue of Liberty, the six standing stones aiming at the Freedom Museum and the Wedge of Light—some precise denotations and possible connotations. Drawings by Madelon Vriesendorp.

was a strong defender of the Viñoly proposal. He may have been the source of the leak, the day before the decision, that the board favored Viñoly.[17] In any case, he ended up seeing the different solutions through Libeskind's eyes and metaphors. As he told the same reporter of *The New York Times*, Edward Wyatt, "What I didn't realize was that other people saw [the two lattices] as skeletons of the original towers and a constant reminder of the attack and of death."[18] So Betts suddenly reverses judgment when a rather fuzzy connotation is drawn across his vision.

Governor Pataki went on to reinforce the political message, as he did later, saying that the Freedom Tower created "an inspiring symbol that will reach into the sky and that will let the world know that the terrorists have failed." The *New York Post*, not giving up the bitter dispute even after the race was over, returned to the Wailing Wall connotations. The solution, they argued, was a graveyard, a ghoulish homage and a mausoleum with a minaret in the middle: "a blueprint so bizarre that it can't help but get better." In other words, the acrimonious process continued to amplify metaphorical interpretation, the connotations of form, and it continued to do so for some considerable time.

Who threw the first metaphorical barb is hard to say, but in his autobiography, *Breaking Ground*, Libeskind describes some of the vitriol. "Viñoly referred in the press to the bathtub as a 'death pit.' I responded by saying that his towers looked like skeletons. I also pointed out that the group's name was disturbing—THINK. Why the capitals? It seemed Orwellian, scary."[19]

Nothing demonstrates better the open nature of the enigmatic signifier and its role in the iconic building today. It invites, and when dramatic, provokes new readings, some of which may be aberrant or counter to the architect's intentions. An obvious reason Daniel Libeskind won the competition, aside from skilful lobbying and the fact that his scheme was more pragmatic than Viñoly's, is that he provided mixed signs and symbols that could be understood as both precise denotations and open-ended connotations. His Freedom Tower denoted the Statue of Liberty, 1776, the culmination of an open spiral of crystal skyscrapers embracing the memorial site. These signs were fairly accessible, once he had mentioned them, and the media had amplified his message. Moreover, he provided symbols of memorialization: the popular, sunken level below grade, the slurry wall, a literal sign of the tragedy that acted as a protective space of contemplation, and more esoteric but precise signs such as the "Wedge of Light." This is a triangle of space that defines the edge of sunlight on September 11th each year, at 8:46 when the first plane hit and 10:28 when the second tower fell. In other words he uses a natural element, as did Stonehenge the sun, to mark significant moments of time and connect earthly events with cosmic ones, a traditional mode of memorialization. This was one of the important icons of the masterplan that Libeskind, and Pataki, said they would preserve, but like all of them it came under renewed attack.

Shrinking the Icons

Act Four could be called "The Defence of the Icons by Strategic Retreat." Usually in American politics, after an election, the candidates shake hands and Al Gore and John Kerry go home and think again. The same is true of architectural competitions. Good losers accept defeat graciously and a new unity is declared. This was not to be the case with Ground Zero since a masterplan is never definitive and, in this case, no one knew who had the ultimate power—the public, the LMDC, the Port Authority that owned the site, or the developer who leased it. So it appeared that individuals and groups opposed to Libeskind's solution, of whom there were quite a few by now, could strip it of all the symbols, one by one. The signs looked to be the most arbitrary or ornamental aspects of his scheme. Invoking Robert Venturi's notion of the tacked-on symbol, they saw the chance to rip it off, and nothing seemed more strippable than the spire echoing the Statue of Liberty's outstretched arm.

When the judging was over Muschamp kept up the attack, getting ever more personal, excoriating Libeskind's masterplan by inverting its symbolism, "Forget Freedom Tower," he wrote with a venomous irony, "It should be renamed Straitjacket Tower. The guidelines are so rigid. . . . Expressionism has inspired many architects of Mr. Libeskind's generation to design projects that are antifascistic. But the Libeskind design flirts perilously with the ideology of its source."[20] The connection of Expressionism with the Nazis has been made many times, especially by those seeking to malign the artistic movement, but in the end it is no more successful than connecting classicism with Hitler, or for that matter, American democracy. But Libeskind could still be damaged, if not stopped altogether, by supporting the developer's architect, David Childs of SOM. So, in another turnabout based on the adage that the enemy of my enemy is my friend, Muschamp now embraced a kind of architecture he had spent the previous five years attacking: corporate modernism. Irony was twice ironized.

The tricky question in many people's minds, especially those of journalists and the victims' families, was what symbols would actually be built. What did Libeskind really win—a scheme, a sketch, a series of guidelines, a set of signs attached to buildings, a wedge of time marked in the ground, or everything? For the families of the victims it was the deep slurry walls, the building foundations that did not collapse on September 11th, that made the scheme the front runner. This solution kept the site open to memorialization and free from commerce. The Libeskinds listened hard to these people, and survivors, and were optimistic as usual that they could "protect the site" for them. Governor Pataki promised this as well.

Just after the announcement, on February 4th, 2004, Daniel Libeskind told *Channel 4 News* in Britain: "Not everything will be finished in four years. But the key components, the icon building, the 1776-foot tower, the Performing Arts Center, the museums around the Memorial and the Memorial itself and of course the Great Station [by Spanish architect Santiago Calatrava]: these icons will be built." He and Nina accepted that many things would change, but they said that the "cultural nexus" of the site was "non-negotiable." As she put it in an interview, "that includes the Wedge of Light, the Park of Heroes, the memorial site, the memorial museum flanking the site, and the iconic tower."[21]

Thus the I-word was again underlined and a list was given of non-negotiable icons; over time, it became a somewhat changing list. In one interview, on February 5th, 2003, Libeskind had characterized the most important element as the overall metaphor of "Memory Foundations," the way he was to refer to it from then on, with the massive slurry walls going down to minus 70 feet, to bedrock. "The walls are not just the footprint of the towers, which is something very abstract. It's a kind of sacred and spiritual area," Libeskind said. "They [the slurry walls] are really witnesses to the power of democracy— they withstood the attack. These indelible footprints really capture the dignity and profundity of the event."[22] By the time he won the final competition on February 27th, they had shrunk to minus 30 feet and, eleven months later when the memorial design was won by Michael Arad in January 2004, his Memorial Park had reached ground level— Ground Zero detractors would say, cynically.

Reflecting Absence—memorial design won by Michael Arad in early January 2004, and modified with Peter Walker, January 14, 2004. The Memorial Park is no longer sunken, but at ground level. The reflecting pools do descend 30 feet and a shaft, far left, goes down 70 feet to bedrock—traces of Libeskind's original intentions.

In spite of such setbacks, and Libeskind began referring to architecture as the "art of compromise," the "non-negotiable icons" were defended by appealing to the LMDC vote, to public opinion, the feelings of the victims' families, and votes on the world wide web. The sceptics would ask—well, how accurately were these feelings and votes registered, how democratically? It is fair to say that, after Foster was eliminated, Libeskind was most often favored in straw polls over the THINK team, but a popular vote was never fully conducted, nor if it had been was the LMDC under an obligation to follow it. In effect, the public was invited in on the spectacle to react, but never fully empowered.

If the process was never really democratic it is also true that Libeskind did provide a very important and missing element, a public persona to the scheme. During the next nine months, from Pataki's choice in late February to the presentation by Childs the following December, he personified the hopes and values invested in the site and became the only poetic voice that could be heard above the din. In the background, inevitably, there was a rumble of whispers, political platitudes, and vendettas. The new attack against him took a strange turn, especially for those who had previously questioned the icons. The detractors now claimed Libeskind was selling out, allowing the symbols of September 11th to be stripped from the plan, while, at the same time, they took an undisguised delight in this purgation. The crime now was compromise and, worse, fudging the evidence. The biggest offence was the supposed wedge of sunlight that marked the events of September 11th.

On May 1st, 2003, *The New York Times* carried the headline "Shadows to Fall, Literally, over 9/11 'Wedge of Light'."[23] This was a damaging claim. The architect of a building just to the east of the Wedge, Eli Attia, published a shadow study that showed that between 40 and 99 percent of the Wedge of Light would be in shadow cast by his Millennium Hilton Hotel during the all-important moments between 8:46 and 10:28. The fact that *direct* sun rays cannot be observed throughout the triangular piazza at these times, because of intervening skyscrapers, did something to undermine Libeskind's claims for a literal reading. But it did not destroy the symbolism altogether.

As Libeskind pointed out, when pressed, it was the general wedge of light that was most important—"the radiating light, the reflecting light, the atmosphere of light"—not the literal sun lines for the entire

Wedge of Light and Santiago Calatrava's Grand Station. The wedge is mostly in reflected light, though shafts break through the skyscraper void, according to Libeskind, at the key times. Calatrava's "bird" opens its backbone and lets light down three stories to the trains below—along the axis of 10:28.

hour and a half. Only at the edges to his new square does the light cut between skyscrapers to define the wedge. In other words, like so much solar symbolism (especially on cloudy days), it is a general lightness and openness that is at stake, not always direct light. The Wedge is written into the plan as an ideal, symbolic layout. Architects like Peter Eisenman and Richard Meier routinely incorporate such conceptual lines that are perceptual in only the most notional way.[24] There is a long tradition of diagrammatic architecture, starting with such buildings as the pyramids, extending through Palladio, and running unbroken to the present. Nonetheless, even supporters of Libeskind, such as Paul Goldberger, found his Wedge argument a bit of a fudge, and that "for the first time, [Libeskind] sounded as though he didn't know what he was talking about."[25]

This is a bit harsh. The Wedge is meant to be precise only on its edges where the morning light breaks through between towers. It defines a set of abstract radiating lines, like a partial sundial, and a public square on to which the grand station will open, literally. Calatrava's soaring bird wings will, in two minutes flat, open apart and allow light and air to penetrate down three stories into the black bowels of public transport. The cut-line this will create across the blue sky is oriented along the sun lines at 10:28. Thus September 11th will be dramatically marked when the roof is opened at that time, in memoriam. The other side of the skeletal bird (and Calatrava's bird flies through many of his schemes), the north canopy outer edge, marks the 8:46 moment. These markings, and the translation of symbolism into performing sculpture, are strong reasons why Libeskind supported the design, even though the layout modified his masterplan in several ways. It remains, of course, an open question whether these angles, edges, and real, direct sunlight will *actually* hit these key points of the structure and, if they don't, someone will have to take the blame for misleading the public.

Already and predictably, Muschamp aimed some metaphorical barbs at Libeskind as he praised Calatrava. Giving the latter plaudits for designing a "[peace] dove, released from the hands of a child," he tut-tutted the former. "No more secondhand Statues of Liberty here. . . . Rather, a prayer for peace."[26] No doubt the skeletal bird will be *the* iconic building at Ground Zero, because it is the building closest to the ground, a striking white sculpture of waving, steel needles and an exploding one-liner not to be missed. If it is built as designed the Iconic Wars may have their first clear victory with this showstopper. At the opening, on January 22nd, 2004, Mayor Bloomberg summed up what the whole building meant to him—"Wow."

Such stimulus-response to the icon is, perhaps, one of its intended functions, but on further reflection the explosion and bone metaphor may come back to haunt the design as it did Viñoly's skeletal towers. In any case, as Paul Goldberger put it, "Calatrava had all but usurped the role that Libeskind had hoped for as the shaper of iconic architecture at the site."[27] What is more, Goldberger, who is following the situation closely, claims that Libeskind was "horrified" when the jury selected the Arad design for the memorial and said that "the jury had undermined two years of his work." But then, backtracking and putting a brave, public face on the compromise, he claimed, apparently, that his bathtub, or slurry wall solution, was "never intended as anything more than 'a space that could be used and interpreted in any way the competitors chose to use it'."[28] Goldberger ends his piece summarizing the muddied lines of authority and the way this produces monstrous compromise, the "unnatural hybrid" such as the Freedom Tower: part Libeskind top spire, part wind farm designed by an engineer, and part Childs' bottom.

It has to be said that much of this was predictable and built into the quasi-democratic process. A masterplan is always very general, enforced *ad hoc* where it can be and compromised and fudged where it cannot. The fact that there were so many claimants to hallowed Ground Zero, including the Republican Party, meant architecture would always be subservient to politics. Finally, Libeskind has never built a project of this scale, and does not have the experience, or size of office, to oversee the construction of the sixteen-acre site nor the 10 million square feet of building. Indeed, even this figure has mission-creep written all over it. At one of the twenty-two public hearings that the LMDC oversaw, the most vociferous one that rejected the initial six plans in July 2002, it was decided "resoundingly," that 10 million square feet of building was too much, especially if half the site was now given over to the memorial.[29] The new figure, on which the seven competing architects worked, was "fixed" at 6.5 million. Yet that didn't last for long, and the amount has gone both down and up. For the moment, no one wants to work in high towers and downtown New York still has a glut of space but, in any case, the developer who has the lease wants the maximum. Where is the public in all this—after twenty-two meetings, three exhibitions attracting thousands per day, and 7 million hits on the LMDC website—where? It is just one more party to be consulted and played, like all the others, for what it's worth, in an open and unpredictable process.

The Incredible Shrinking Daniel Libeskind

By Independence Day 2004, July 4th, when the foundation stone of the Freedom Tower was laid at Ground Zero by Governor Pataki, journalists had made up their mind that the story to report was one of compromise, and the victory of Mammon over idealism. *The New York Times*, which read at times as if it were the moral arbiter of anything that happened on the site, featured a major story with a photo of a tiny Libeskind in black designer clothes striding across an empty white page casting an even tinier shadow, as if he were in a De Chirico piazza designed by Armani. The story reiterated the compromises: the rise up to Ground Zero of the previously sunken memorial floor, the loss of a 100-foot waterfall, the problems with the Wedge of Light and the Freedom Tower spire.[30] By mid-October 2004, Libeskind had suffered further setbacks as he failed to win the competition for the two cultural buildings at Ground Zero: they went to Frank Gehry and a Norwegian practice, Snøhetta.

But the only real news, in the media onslaught of July 4th, was that Libeskind was suing Mr. Silverstein for unpaid fees of $843,000—one battle he actually won in September, with an award of $370,000—and the fact that America's most upmarket newspaper was taking the side of its downmarket competitors. It even started quoting them to undermine the designer. "Libeskind's Luster Eclipsed by SOM," it ran, echoing a headline from the *New York Sun*, and it backed up the argument with further innuendo dredged from the *New York Daily News* and the *New York Post*. *The Times* of London followed this story slavishly, except where it misquoted Libeskind (without attribution) and turned the nuance of compromise into capitulation by him.[31] "One by one the key elements of the Libeskind plans have been abandoned," it asserted. "There will be no 'wedge of light' . . . the exposed slurry walls . . . will be covered up; square pits where the towers once stood . . . have been filled in with a garage for tourist buses; even Mr. Libeskind's central idea, the Freedom Tower, has been snatched from him to be designed by Mr. Childs."

Media half-truths were thus turned, once again, into nasty untruths. Libeskind answered these old exaggerations with a counter-claim: "The plan I designed is intact. In fact, it has been improved upon," and he went on to point out how his major symbols were still thriving. To

The New York Times, June 20th, 2004, defined the story with a tiny Libeskind set against a white background – their first use of the empty void.

cast more light on these and political points, I interviewed Libeskind when he came to London to open a small building in March 2004.

CJ: The critics first go after you because they don't like the icons, and then criticize you for having lost them!

DL: I believe in democratic not authoritarian design, and I have provided a matrix that could then be interpreted in many ways. I provided an entire range of possibilities; the bedrock, the excavation to thirty-five feet, and I left it up to the competition jury to decide how would they like to interpret them. Of course they selected the project that has many of the features. It goes to bedrock at some point, goes to thirty-five feet in the footprints and in doesn't in any way contradict my design. Many people thought what I had done was to design a memorial, but I never did design a memorial; I designed only the space in which a memorial would operate.

CJ: But even your defenders, like Paul Goldberger, think that you have compromised away certain essential parts of your icons, like the Memorial Park and Bathtub.

DL: People are free to think whatever they want. I believe in the democratic process, and not a single aspect of my plan has been compromised because I made the project in order to be able to develop it into full reality.

CJ: What about the Wedge of Light and the way Calatrava is on the 10.28 line when he opens the roof?

DL: I think it is a brilliant interpretation of an urbanistic idea, even stronger than what I expected because he created in more public space, decreased the shopping mall underneath and created a very dramatic central space along the Wedge of Light.

CJ: But it is going to be hard to see the Wedge of Light hit his building at 8.48 in the morning.

DL: No. At 8.48 it hits the northern site and at 10.28 it will hit centrally and will bisect the site and go all the way through the site up to the Freedom Tower. It is a very powerful urbanistic and internal expression.

CJ: In spite of the hotel casting a shadow, it will still go right down?

DL: Yes: that was a total red herring! It works exactly at those two times and at those times those planes and spaces will glow in light, if there is sunlight on September 11th.

In this and other interviews, Libeskind reiterates that the changes and the loss of space in the Bathtub and the Park of Heroes are not a

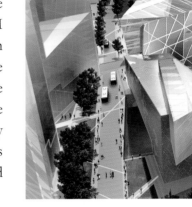

Libeskind's cultural icons set on a raised memorial park, framing the two footprints.

compromise, only a reinterpretation of his guidelines in a sympathetic way. Concerning the other accusations, he is adamant about the apolitical nature of his patriotic stance, and one can hear in his passionate defense of America the idealism and gratitude of an immigrant.

CJ: You know that, among architects in New York, you are not the most popular man in the world. They go after you for having wrapped yourself in the flag and displaying super-patriotism.

DL: Of course I know that. That is too bad, because I actually believe that patriotism does not belong to a political party. Patriotism, meaning the symbols (like the Statue of Liberty), belongs not to a rhetorical system; it belongs to experience. And I am fully behind what I say.

CJ: The conspiracy theory has you playing to the right wing and the Republicans—Mayor Bloomberg, Governor Pataki, and President Bush—and their great national convention coming up in New York. So, are you left wing or right wing, centrist or what?

DL: It is so absurd. I truly believe every word I say about the beauty of America, about the power of America and about what America means to me personally: liberties and freedom that I truly experience. Maybe Herbert Muschamp or Peter Eisenman don't experience them, but I do and I love them and love everything the country stands for and I am unashamed to say it. I was even asked by a journalist was I really an American patriot? What kind of question was that? I do love the country and love everything it stands for!

CJ: But nationalism is a problem: the nationalist looks to the future with idealism and the patriot to the past. In a nationalist situation today, with the Iraqi war, your building has become politically charged. You admit that but say that the right wing doesn't have a monopoly on these symbols or signs or icons. Is that your argument?

DL: It is not an argument. I believe in what I have done. I believe these things cannot be appropriated by the Right or the Left. The liberalist logic cannot wash over this. It is something fundamental and something that belongs to the site. I have always thought "Memory Foundations" is a cultural response to the terrorist events that befell New York. That is what it is about and that is how I developed it.

CJ: Well at least Nina is not on the Right, she is more on the Left with her relative Naomi Klein. Where do you see yourself—Right, Left, or Center?

DL: I never think in these categories. I think in what I really believe in and when it came to the project I just thought in a very pragmatic way:

What is the project about? What am I believing in? It is not a bunch of buildings made by architects to look trendy in the magazines. It is about the *meaning* of these buildings.

CJ: Yes, but you have been branded as right wing as a result of this. Are you going to distinguish yourself from that? Or not?

DL: No. People can call me any names they want. I am not a right-winger, people know I speak about social justice, and I would not just disassociate myself from the [rest of the] country and make the project into a partisan political project. That is, by the way, not how I saw it. I guess to your question about the right wing—do they call Blair right wing in England?

CJ: Well, they definitely see him in Bush's pocket. It is sad that, through guilt by association, you have been seen as right wing—I would defend your right to design this building in the way you have.

DL: Roland Betts, who was supporting Viñoly and the THINK team, is the closest friend of President Bush, so you cannot claim my partisanship here. It is about design and it's about what the design means and I am glad that most New Yorkers, and most Americans, actually have been very complimentary to my scheme and that is why it got selected. It did not get selected because of just the power of politics: the power of politics represented the public desire that the site should really be something beyond exercise of the ego of the architect.

The explicit denotation that helped win the argument.

In these exchanges, which continued in this way, Libeskind held to his basic point that his architectural and symbolic logic were above co-option by politics and he ended with an appeal to the people's judgement as more sound than his critics'.

DL: I *believe* in the design and I believe it is across party lines and does not belong to parties. It belongs to New York. Otherwise it would not have had a chance to be selected in a huge, unprecedented, participatory process, when 60 million people hit their websites, when the two last projects were on. So there was a lot of public awareness of the project. Just because some critics in New York are wishy-washy liberals does not disqualify me as an American, or an architect, with universal values.

Here is the architect and artist's eternal plea for poetic licence, the belief that a work of art has its own integrity and logic that transcends the market place, ideology and power politics.

The Subject of Icons—Emotional States

As Act Five opens, one that will be the longest and perhaps the bloodiest, as built compromises and a few good icons begin to take shape, what kind of interim judgement can be made?

At the very least, the process has illuminated the hidden tensions within architecture and forced important issues of the iconic building into the open. Given the horror and gravity of September 11th, and the way the media turned it into a ritualized, even sacred, event, the architecture had to face issues of symbolism. However much the Libeskind scheme may have been aggressively promoted, and exploited on a wartime footing, more than any other entry it did address the ambivalence of memorialization: the hope and tragedy, the mixture of heroism and rupture.[32] Libeskind's insistence on repeated visits to the site and thinking through the "Memory Foundations," as he called them, raised the poetic stakes very high. Whether his vision is built only as a trace or not, his voice has been inspirational. No doubt he has exaggerated the patriotism of some symbols, such as the 1776-foot spire, but his scheme addresses the key issues of life and death.

Furthermore, after two years, the process looks like it might produce three adequate memorial structures: the Freedom Tower, the two voids in the ground, and a fairly captivating Calatrava bird. While the media hype turns the first into "the largest building ever constructed" and the last into "wow," the realities are much more likely to be "OK, well done," something above damnation by faint praise but below the Bilbao Effect, the architectural engine behind much of this. My view is that the seven architects have acted quite well, given the low pay and the fact they were manipulated in a competition that called itself a non-competition. As a result of their participation, architecture itself was put on the world map, taken out of its ghetto in the real estate section to find recognition as serious cultural endeavor. And the public did play a role in shaping the architecture, even if a confused one.

Finally, as far as the iconic building is concerned, the saga of Ground Zero illustrates two emergent truths: the central place of ritual created by media amplification, and the important role of the enigmatic signifier. In a secular society, the media can ritualize an event such as September 11th so that it becomes a virtual religious drama. The outpouring of emotion after Princess Diana's death, her burial, and her subsequent cult show a similar role of media repetition and sanctification. Both events, and the response to them, bring up the quandary of our age.

If global society has no overriding beliefs, an ideological or religious direction in common, and yet at the same time commissions international superstars to fly around the world designing iconic buildings, then certain contradictions will come, inevitably, to the surface. Such things as death, catastrophe, and personal tragedy, all seen in the abstract, might take the place previously occupied by religious tropes and dogma. This would not be surprising since religions themselves are often founded on extreme suffering. People believe in trauma and pain as they do in nothing else. Witness the response to Mel Gibson's *The Passion of the Christ* (not to mention the previous 2000 years of storytelling and paintings depicting agony, spurting blood, mourning, weeping, and the torture of a body on a cross). In the first twelve days after opening in the US, the film grossed more than $200 million. September 11th, for Americans and much of the world, was a different kind of collective trauma, but it catalyzed experience in a similar way. The iconoclasm directed at the Twin Towers became a new icon for Western resistance.

Perhaps generalized emotional states will also come to be represented in iconic architecture, generic abstractions such as hope and sadness, progress and nature, and these might be expressed through enigmatic allusions. Faced with the necessity of "wow," and commercial agnosticism, what else can an architect do? Perhaps design a bit more than expressive, vague abstractions, and try to get closer to actual events and people's experience.

Libeskind won the competition, I believe, because he faced the symbolic and spiritual issues of the task both directly *and* through the enigmatic signifier. He appealed to specific signs of New York and September 11th, with some confidence and precision because of personal contact with survivors, victims' families, and the many stakeholders that have claims to the site. As preparation for the design, he told an enquiring student, he reread the Declaration of Independence, the Constitution, and the popular working-class literature of Whitman and Melville.[33] By contrast, the other architects were chary of engagement with the event of September 11th, as if any reference to it, no matter how oblique, would be both controversially ruinous for their entry and inadequate, either kitsch chauvinism or bathos. The result was that in the final competition of the seven most of them produced abstract references to other

Libeskind's crystalline grammar, evident in many of his schemes. Since Libeskind is now not designing any buildings at Ground Zero, the cosmic references are likely to be lost.

architectural solutions, that is, signs referring within the profession rather than provocative signifiers that reached outward.

In the battle of the final two, Viñoly's twin towers could be lampooned as "skeletons and hanging bodies," and this journalistic tag proved damaging. By contrast, Libeskind mixed suggestive abstractions with particular, denotative signs and his combination appears to have neutralized the counter-attack. His architectural grammar explicitly signified the crystalline growth of nature, rays of light, and, in particular, six shards or towers inflecting toward the museum at the heart of the scheme. It is a scheme that, if constructed, will carry a heavy symbolic and functional burden.

Somewhere in all this display of iconography, the rebuilding will have to address the reasons for the initial attack, the iconoclasm. After all, the old World Trade Center was targeted because it was so aggressively a symbol of the wrong kind of world trade, a smug dominance, a symbol, as the writer and critic Marina Warner reminds us, of overreaching, of the pillars of Hercules or, more simply, the two upright strokes of the dollar sign.[34] Money as power, twice affirmed. As it remained a few days after destruction, the smoldering wall fragments became completely different signs: of defiance, heroism, and tragedy. Whereas before, New Yorkers begrudgingly got used to the Twin Towers, after their collapse they started to love their memory. No one can fully control the meaning of architecture; its signification is both intended and fortuitous, but the worth of an architect designing iconic buildings can be seen in how well they handle the big issues of Ground Zero: power, life, death, and our relationship to the cosmos.

Iconic Dilemmas

ABOVE: Portrait of Rem Koolhaas.

Rem Koolhaas—The Flying Dutchman Goes East

For a short moment, on February 18th, 2004, while he was accepting the RIBA Gold Medal in London, the most prestigious prize in architecture except for the Pritzker Prize, the "Nobel of Architecture," which he had also won in 2000, Rem Koolhaas lost his noted cool. He had given four sell-out lectures over two days, sometimes to the same people who had come back hoping to figure out what he had said the first time. Journalists and the media followed his every move and many in the audience furiously took notes, surmising that, by writing it down, the message would clarify itself. Koolhaas, like Libeskind and Gehry, always plays to full houses around the world, enjoys the adulation up to a point, and depends on it for trying out difficult ideas, for enhancing his aura so that jobs continue to pour in, so that clients are sufficiently warmed to give into his black-humored charm. He circuits the world so much he is known as the Flying Dutchman.

But after four strenuous performances he had had enough. Summoning the ancient wrath of Achilles, he let out his heart to a journalist from *Building Design*, who reported the ire under the heading "Koolhaas Lambasts Idolatry." What he said shows the pressures on a famous architect fed up with the superstar system, with having to run so fast to stay ahead of his shadow.

> The idolatry of the market has drastically changed our legitimacy and status even though our status has never been higher. . . . It is really unbelievable what the market demands [from architecture] now. It demands recognition, it demands difference and it demands iconographic qualities.[1]

The marketplace does indeed demand recognition and iconographic qualities, relentlessly. One of Koolhaas' main commissions over the last few years was to re-brand the European Union. Its then leader, Romano Prodi, asked him to overcome the image of corporate dullness—of white men in black suits looking like so many accountants—that the role nations, unwilling to give up their sovereignty, wished on this conglomerate: Economic Man writ large. Its massive, pompous architecture in Brussels was a fitting symbol of

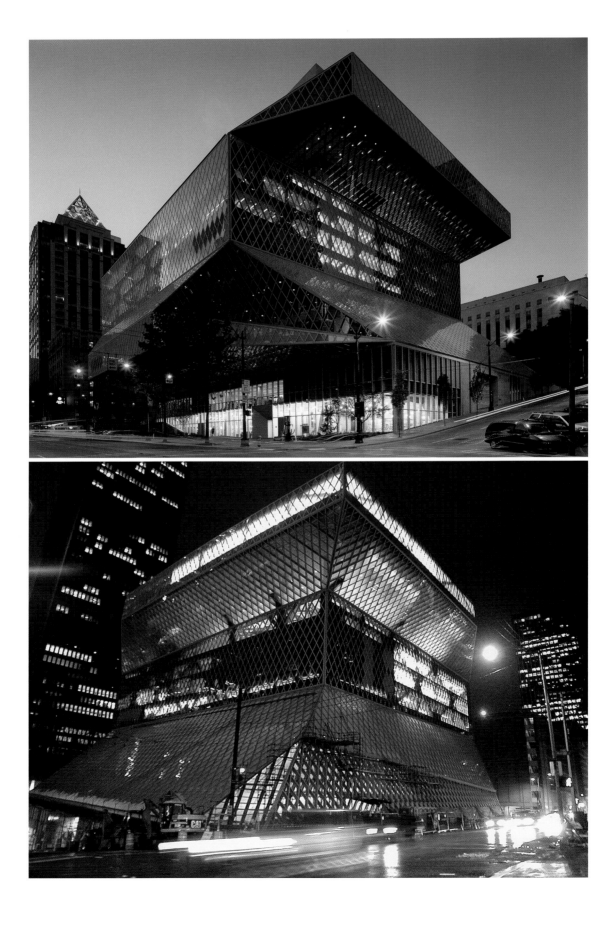

LEFT AND BELOW: Rem Koolhaas, Seattle Public Library, 2000–2004. A single skin wraps media at different levels and provides Seattle with an icon of reading set opposite Frank Gehry's icon of music, the Experience Music Project of the Millennium.

BOTTOM: Rem Koolhaas and Herzog & de Meuron, Sponge Model Hotel for New York, 2001. Tapering and deep, with punched-out windows, it is part cheese, part geology.

a corporate bigness going nowhere but bigger. As Henry Kissinger famously asked of this headless body in 1970, "Europe—what is its phone number?" Koolhaas, and his media group called AMO, echoed this in 2002 with "Europe—what is its sound bite?" And together they worked on some projects for a new identity, producing, among other things, a substitute for the blue European flag. This is suitably ordered like a clock, with twelve yellow stars marking the key points, a gilded Book of Hours, a perfect unintentional icon of time-watchers and cost-shavers. It also presented a false ideal of clockwork harmony, as if all national identity could be suppressed for blue-sky unity.

The flag and EU identity, however, had now been overtaken by growth and a new regionalism; it needed reconsidering. Koolhaas and AMO's answer to the problem was to take the twenty-five, and perhaps in the future thirty-five, national flags and turn them into thin vertical stripes organized in a horizontal rectangle. The design was an amazing, but prosaic, brand-image. Europe was no longer economic clockwork but now a checkout barcode. "E-conography," he called the facelift, and the barcode made the front pages of European capitals, and the *Independent* in Britain. The media reaction stopped work in his office for more than a week—the revenge of the icon.[2]

Yet re-branding could not change geo-political reality. On that hectoring round of four lectures, as the leader of *Building Design* went on to note, Koolhaas felt that, since September 11th and a loss of confidence in the European Union, the architectural center of gravity had moved away from the West. Koolhaas' advice? "Go East." That is how he phrased it for three hundred pages in his new publication, *Content*. "Go East," especially to China, where clients cared about the users and function of a building, and were not obsessed by whether it was iconic. Or that was the hope.

Koolhaas was also angry for personal reasons. He and Herzog & de Meuron, the other high-flying European office, had come together to create a dream team in order to work on several projects, among them a prestige hotel in New York commissioned by Ian Shrager. For twelve months they met in Basel, Rotterdam, and New York, cooking up the strangest of iconic hotels, which they called the "sponge model," a truncated obelisk full of irregular holes. It looked like a very interesting Gruyère cheese that had reached a perfect equilibrium between solid and void, what was left over and what had been eaten. Schrager lay down in a mock up of one room—a photo in *Content* shows his awkward posture on the hard bed—looked out of the weird-shaped hole that was a window and fired the architects. This was in December 2000.

In the next few years Koolhaas won two prime American commissions for museums, the Whitney in New York and LACMA in Los Angeles. Each of these proposals was a radical step in global architecture, part of the new paradigm that places emphasis on unusual, computer-generated solutions. Each breakthrough made the world anxious to see what Rem would do next; each was a step forward of the Bilbao Effect applied to the museum—the building type where architecture takes the greatest leaps forward. And, in a cumulative Great Leap Backwards, each was soon canceled.

"Go East."

Because of Enron, WorldCom, and the dotcom collapse, because of September 11th and the Bush national front, Koolhaas lost most of his big American jobs. His Guggenheim Museum in Las Vegas closed. The man who invented New York City as a euphoric condition—in his best-selling Delirious New York (1978)—wrote an angry new piece for his guest-edited issue of *Wired* in June 2003. It was called "Delirious No More" and it ended, not surprisingly, with September 11th. His conclusions were that Bush had captured the site and through "the alchemy of 9/11, the authoritarian [impulse in America] morphs imperceptibly into the totalitarian."[3]

This bleak assessment coupled with the loss of major American jobs—at one point attributed to "conservatism"—led Koolhaas away from the West and to some more black humor at his own expense. Never one to hide his own vulnerability, he tells the story under the heading "Saved by a Fortune Cookie."

> Early 2002—We received two invitations, one to apply to consider what should happen at Ground Zero, the other for the headquarters of China Central Television [CCTV] in Beijing. We discussed the choice over a Chinese meal. The life of the architect is so fraught with uncertainty and dilemmas that any clarification of the future, including astrology, is disproportionately welcome. My fortune cookie read, "Stunningly Omnipresent Masters make minced meat of memory."[4]

On the cover of the "bookazine" *Content*, a self-described hybrid of book and magazine with ads, one can decode his message to the West.

Content, 2003. Saddam/
Rambo with his icons versus
Bush/McDonald's sporting
his American Freedom
Fries—CCTV in the
background.

It is as funny, radical, and self-deprecating as anything Koolhaas has
done, in a long career of getting people to pay for being lampooned.
The barcode, in the lower right corner, is real this time. Saddam, with
machine-gun in hand, is given the body of a muscleman and the hair of
an ageing hippie (there are no barbers underground). Other
fundamentalists with arms, from the major power centers, surround
Dubya, who is looking stupider than usual. He leads his crusade with a
crucified and gagged Christ with a gun and has a hair-do made from
McDonalds obesity-chips. Multinationalism triumphant. Then a series
of diagonal slashes describe the interior contents (after all the
bookazine has to jump off the news-stand), while a yellow, radioactive
halo frames the main actors (magazines must feature the most famous
faces). His own triumph in China—CCTV—crowns the scene with the

largest slash in green: "Perverted Architecture." Is this the ultimate in masochism, or another trick of marketing?

Just as Andy Warhol traded on criticizing and promoting glamor at the same time, Koolhaas has perfected a double and opposite message. The reason for this? He is faced with the dilemma of the architect who must design iconic buildings, and become an icon in order to do it, but is hyper-aware of the downside. The wrath of Achilles. His angry face has appeared on so many covers, including *Wired*, the *Financial Times Weekend Magazine*, and *The New York Times Sunday Magazine*, that he received an offer from Hollywood to star as a killer-figure from the underworld.[5] He obviously loves and hates the situation of the iconic architect. So, if it is an inevitable part of the star system, why not turn the ambivalence into ironic comment?

CCTV

China Central Television is one of the most important public buildings in the New China. Its thirteen channels go out to 1.2 billion people, making it the largest single media voice in the world. Although it is ultimately controlled by the Communist Party, like everything undergoing exponential growth in the country, it is enjoying more and more autonomy. A series of graphs in *Content*, based on information from the World Bank, show the exponential growth looming upwards to the right, the Great Angle Forward. For countless years the economic landscape was a flat, slightly inclined plain. Then in the 1980s the GDP went up at twenty degrees and then, ever since the 1990s, at fifty degrees. Foreign investment, mostly from the US under Clinton in 1992–5, inclined at an angle of eighty degrees. Almost all the curves in China are now steep. In 2004, the economy, at almost $1.5 trillion, is the third largest in the world. The last ten years show greater growth than Japan in the 1960s: the Great Angle Forward.

Naturally, everyone is worried. Their litany of questions is repetitive. Can it be sustained? Is it real growth? Is it destroying ecology? Is it controlled by the Communists? Is it cowboy capitalism? Is it totalitarian? Will it pay fees? Will it bury the West? Will it swallow all jobs? The paranoia engendered by such power and paradox—Communist capitalism—made China an ideal destination for Koolhaas' philosophy "Go East." It also made it the target for large firms such as SOM, who, by late 2003, had thirty major Chinese projects underway. Like KPF, their major competitor Kohn Pedersen

Fox Associates, this became the secondary marketplace for their wares after America. As the *Asian Wall Street Journal* put the story, "Architects World-Wide Go East." It featured Lord Foster's Beijing airport terminal, at $2 billion, and the CCTV project, one of the biggest buildings in the world, at $738 million.[6]

Koolhaas gained the commission in July 2002, competing against eight large firms—including SOM, KPF, Philip Johnson, and a Hong Kong office, Toyo Ito, Dominic Perrault, and several Chinese firms. Since I was one of the few foreigners on the jury, along with Rocco Yim and Arata Isozaki, I should declare an interest and describe the situation.

The most important idea in the brief was that the building should be a "landmark," and the words clearly implied something approaching the stature of Gehry's Bilbao. Koolhaas grasped the logic involved, and in his presentation stressed the fact that if the future central business district of Beijing were to have 300 skyscrapers, then the 301st would certainly be a feint echo, not the desired landmark. The arguments were compelling, and perhaps his first shot in a new campaign to "Kill the Skyscraper": the idea that this old building type was not keeping pace with urban realities.[7] Many of the other entries failed, because they were obvious variants on the superannuated tower and not, like his, an extraordinary mutant.

It was also obvious that the building had to be huge and centralized. The size was clear from the brief, the volume of floor space needed and the way that bigness, in China today, equates with goodness. "To get rich is glorious," Deng had famously exhorted his comrades in 1978 and later, when they missed the message, he urged them to "get rich faster." This meant one thing for architecture: the richer the bigger. According to this logic, Koolhaas' entry was the most sophisticated, because while it was very big, at seventy stories, very bulky, as a kind of looped-tube shape, and very grand, as an echo of the triumphal arches in Paris—it was still not the 301st skyscraper.

I advocated the scheme for this reason and also because it was such a stunning iconic building, in the bloodline of enigmatic signifiers I had written about, stemming from Ronchamp and the Sydney Opera House.[8] Noting that their brief had specified a landmark building, it was obvious that Koolhaas' entry suggested both pertinent references to China and the media, as well as extraordinary overtones. A good icon has to work with opposite codes. As the accompanying sketches

TVCC 电视文化中心

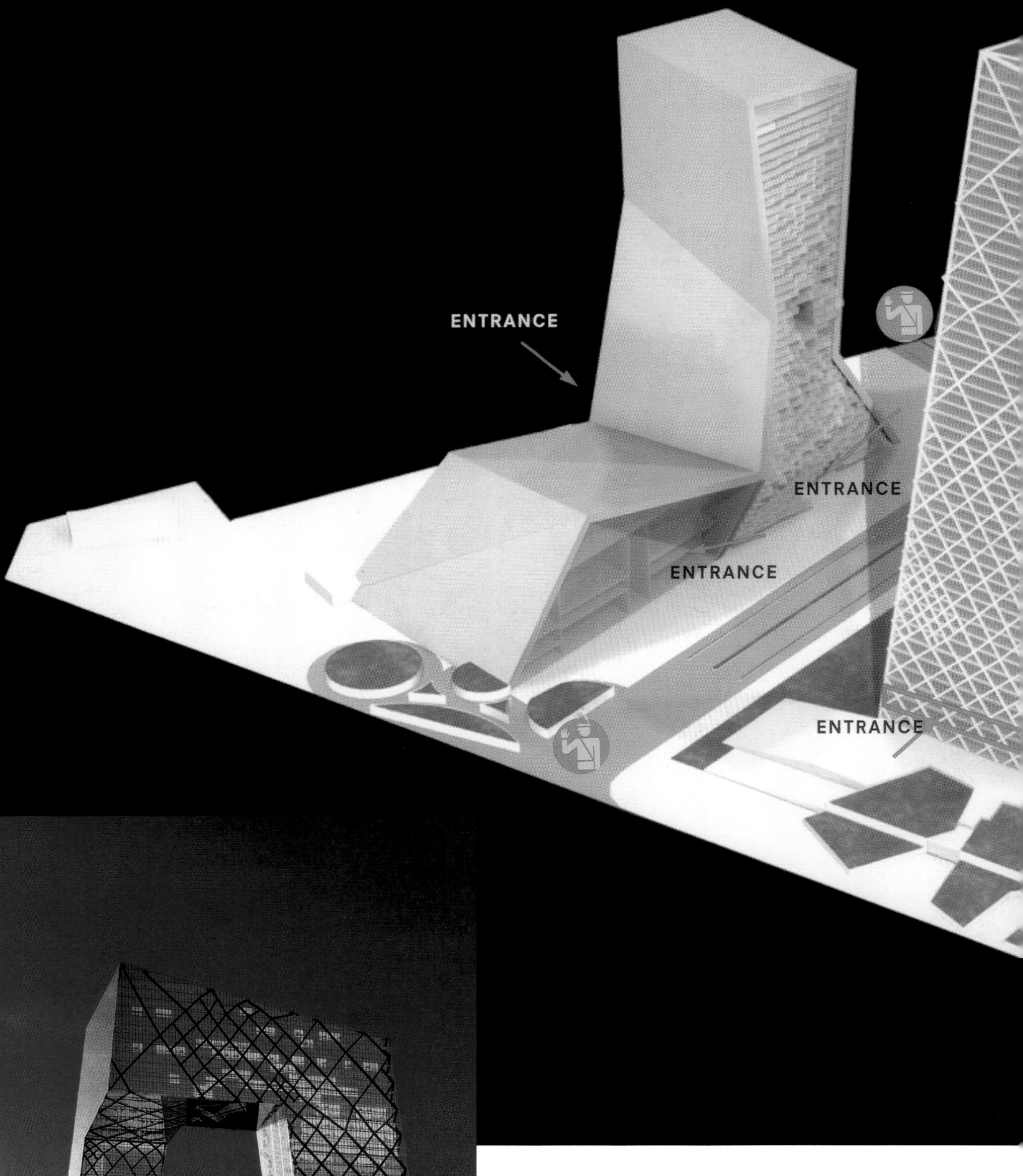

ENTRANCE

ENTRANCE

ENTRANCE

ENTRANCE

ABOVE: Rem Koolhaas, CCTV, original design with centralized TV in a loop-building juxtaposed with a vertical, truncated hotel.

LEFT: View of CCTV through the "moon gate" of the city and a new hotel.

RIGHT: Rem Koolhaas' comparison of his building to "world icons."

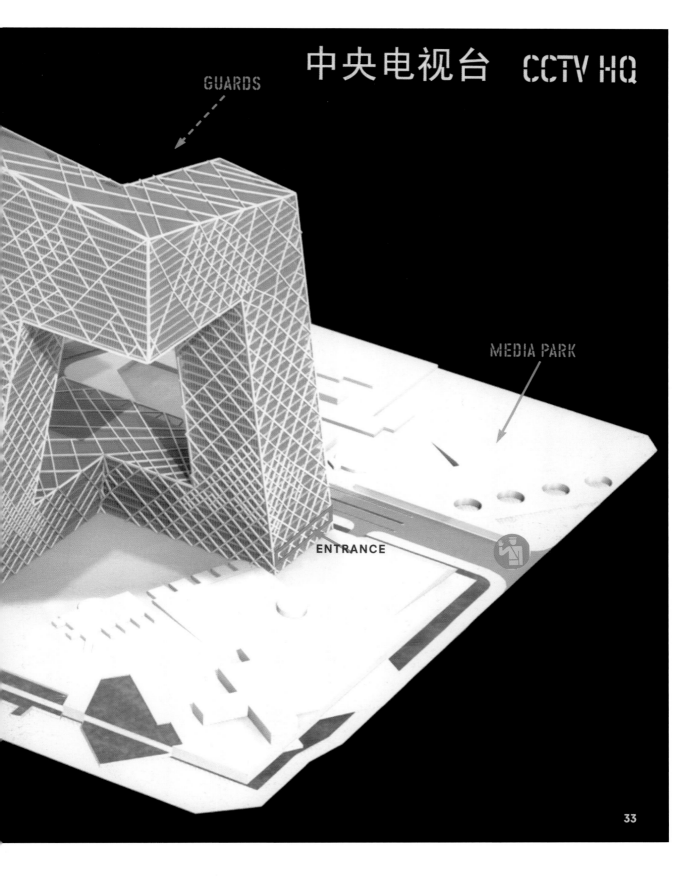

GUARDS

MEDIA PARK

ENTRANCE

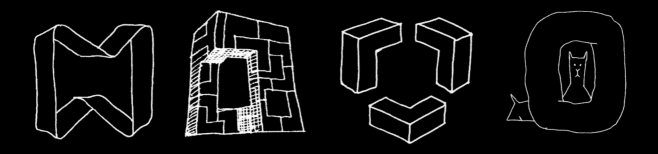
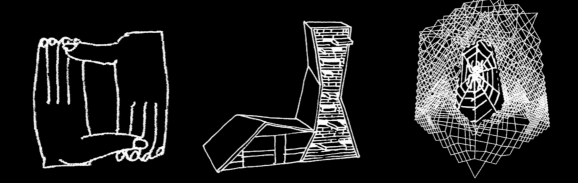
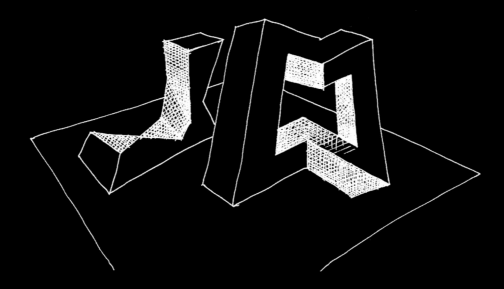

show, the distant view looks like a moon gate, the ornamental surround that punctuates every Chinese garden. This frame also bears resemblance to the pi-shape that goes back to the origins of China, a form that was normally made in bronze or jade. Even more suggestive is the exposed structure. This recalls the famous Chinese bracket construction, as well as the lattice windows that can be found in traditional homes. Others compared the structure and laminated glass-mesh skin to Chinese calligraphy. Koolhaas never mentioned these overtones, nor the bizarre but appealing Pop images.

In the loop that he emphasized, one could spy a donut being eyed by an upright dog, the pert hotel block in back. The opposition between these two iconic forms was charming and unique, a dialogue that the other entries lacked. Then there was a veritable spider's web of structure, a Chinese puzzle of interlocking "L"s, and, more esoterically, these can be conceived as a single, twisted Moebius strip. Perhaps more farfetched, but relevant, is the image of an "empty TV screen," something implied by the squarish void framing a blank monitor. According to this view, the city can be conceived as projected on to the screen, that is, literally being seen through the building.

My argument was that in a good enigmatic signifier these traditional, popular, and esoteric overtones are felt not named, suggested not explicit. Hinting but not stating a direction provokes the viewer to project into the puzzle certain codes or meanings. Essential to the success of these interpretations is the appearance of aesthetic and structural necessity, the suavity and assurance of the whole. Part of this is due to refinements—the six-degree tilt of the verticals, the way the diagonal structure expands and contracts in density to follow the actual loads. The engineer involved, Cecil Balmond, helped to realize these variable expressions of varying weight, a brilliant example of non-linear design applied to a leaning structure that is in torque.

Another part of the building's quality is also due to the creative insight, the basic hybrid—skyscraper-groundscraper—placed in the sea of towers. This new organizational type, the equivalent of a 180-story building, is wrapped together in six L-shaped or angled tubes, so that the CCTV workforce can both flow together smoothly and occupy differing urban spaces. The visual idea of a connected L-loop supports the functional notion of a continuous and connected operational process: TV production as an open loop or network.

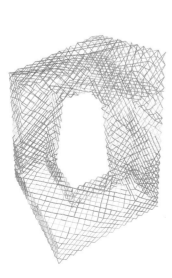

Koolhaas calls it "a single entity in which all parts are housed permanently—aware of each other's presence. A collective."[9]

For these and other reasons, Koolhaas won the initial competition. By comparison, Toyo Ito's scheme, Perrault's massive structure, and the Shanghai entry, the runners up, were less original and iconic. But there were structural risks in Koolhaas' design, and the question of expense, and so, over the next five months, Koolhaas had to re-win the argument again and again, and convince the Chinese hierarchy right up the ladder from the CCTV executives to the top. It was neither an easy process, nor one free of Western criticism. Designing such an organ of state power was likened to building a television station for Pinochet's Chile, though the comparison is a bit stretched.[10] For one thing, much of American investment is as we've noted already linked with China, and Europe is following suit, so why does it make sense to censure architects for this involvement? They are weak players in geo-politics. For another, Pinochet's Chile was more of a military regime.

Whether the new CCTV headquarters presages the New China, or just reinforces an old system, remains to be seen, but it is a key symbolic building, as important for China's self-image as the 2008 Olympics. The authors of the new Olympic stadium, Herzog & de Meuron, hope, inevitably, that they have designed "the most visible icon of contemporary China."[11] It resembles, like Koolhaas' syncopated net, a seemingly chaotic set of structural elements, a random basketwork, or "giant bird's nest" as it is called. So, in 2008 there will be an Olympic competition in architecture, to determine whose iconic filigree is the most enticing.

The rhetoric of the new has often been spread across an old power structure to re-brand it, and perhaps the only thing new today is that avant-garde architects are being used by governments instead of the usual suspects, the corporate architects. This is a hazard for creative designers, politically as well as architecturally. As with Libeskind's work at Ground Zero, there may be forces so great they cannot be overcome and the building might be compromised; but if these architects had not taken the risk, we would never know. Iconic building is a bet thrown on to a gambling table, and this comes with potential costs.

Herzog & de Meuron, Olympic Stadium for Beijing, 2004–8. Another basketwork icon, partly random, partly following the lines of force.

Enric Miralles—Great Building, Great Tragedy

Nothing illustrates better the potential and the hazards of the iconic building than the new Scottish Parliament. Designed by Enric Miralles in 1998, it finished first in a competition that seventy architects had entered. Like the Sydney Opera House thirty years previously, it became famous not only for being a great building but also for exceeding the original cost estimate by more than ten times—up from £40 to £431 million—and for generating a political controversy that raised fundamental questions about national identity. The controversy was further amplified, as it was in Australia, by the architect being a foreigner termed a "genius"—thus enjoying double immunity from one kind of attack while, at the same time, provoking local animosity. Finally, both iconic buildings suffered countless delays, and these simply added fuel to the other contentious issues; allegations of financial skulduggery, political horse-trading, avant-garde élitism, the old-boy's network, and most every sin to which a megaproject is prone.

Books have been written about the melodrama of the Sydney Opera House and books will be written about the Scottish version, with its name-play on the marvelous site of Holyrood: "Follyrood," it has been called, a madcap fiasco. On closer inspection, it resembles less a farce, and more a classical tragedy. As in a Greek drama, it is the minor flaws in major characters that drive the action, little mistakes which are magnified in importance and coupled with the unexpected emergence of that old demiurge, fate. Almost everyone is tarnished in this drama, as we will see, and yet a certain grandeur emerges at the end.

BELOW LEFT: Enric Miralles, Scottish Parliament, Edinburgh, competition design, 1998: the juxtaposition and blurring of styles, city and countryside.

BELOW: Enric Miralles and RMJM Team.

One of the main protagonists of the play was Donald Dewar, an upright Presbyterian and the *de facto* leader of the New Scotland. He, along with a jury of six worthies, picked the original design. With a sharp tongue and a compassionate but dour expression, the tall angular Scot epitomized all that was fresh and hopeful as the nation embarked on a difficult journey of devolution from Britain. His tricky brief was to keep alive continuities with the British past while gaining some independence from it—both for the design and for the New Scotland. External political relations, such as defense, would remain with Great Britain, while internal relations, and even some powers of taxation, would devolve to Scotland. Hence the politician Dewar put his reputation on the line in choosing an unconventional scheme by Miralles, the other main protagonist, a talented Catalan designer in the tradition of Antonio Gaudi. Dewar noted the risk when speaking of the early models:

> It's got that touch of vision, it's got that feel for Edinburgh, for Scotland's history. . . . It's the physical embodiment of an enormously exciting constitutional change. . . . It's not a traditional building but I think it's a sympathetic building that really sits happily with the Royal Mile, with the heritage and history of Scotland and yet will be very much for the twenty-first century.[12]

Through such constant support, and identifying his integrity with that of the architecture, an equation was made between Dewar's personality and that of the designer. Detractors called the building "Donald's Dome," after the Millennium Dome fiasco in London. But, have faith in my vision and judgement, Dewar said, even if the going gets tough, and added: "I've got some very skilful people in my own department who have wide experience and they are also playing a very significant part; so it is genuinely a joint effort." Dewar invoked these experts and the local, collaborating architects, RMJM, to consolidate public assent. It was very much his word that backed the "innovator" Miralles, and he had a credibility that is rare in politics. One reason for this trust was his candor and his readiness to admit vulnerability:

> I say this always nervously because I am quite sure at the end of the day there will be critics, the flak will fly and there may be occasions when I feel I ought to emigrate. But whatever happens I think it's been worthwhile. Whatever happens I will look back with enormous pleasure and maybe even allow myself a bit of pride.

A bit of pride, justified no doubt but dangerous. As the costs went up the flak did fly and the iconic building became the biggest political issue, and scandal, of the new democracy.[13]

New Metaphors of Democracy

In his candid remarks, Dewar also mentioned that many Scots might prefer classicism as the appropriate style for a government building. Greek architecture has a long association with democracy in Edinburgh—"the Athens of the North"—and countless columned porticoes and variations on the Parthenon suggested that this metaphor should continue. Yet neutral classicism, as much as abstract modernism, had probably become too predictable, even exhausted, to carry the message of a new parliament. Indeed, all historical styles seem anachronistic in the media age, where they are multiplied at will. So it was quite understandable when Miralles adopted an eclectic palette and blurred several formal types together.

It is revealing to contrast his design with that of the British Houses of Parliament of the 1830s, another vision of democracy that took a long time and a fortune to build, especially since it was dubbed, by Margaret Thatcher, "the Mother of all Democracies." Mother? What does that make the Scots' contribution to democracy, the Absent Father? Whereas the 19th-century London palace designed by Charles Barry and "the Goth" Augustus Welby Pugin, was a clear hybrid—Neo-Gothic finery covering a classical plan—Miralles' swarming forms are a more complex multifarious blend. Vernacular quotes are taken from 17th-century Edinburgh and bits of Art Nouveau, Modernism and Post-Modernism are fused together. Hints of these eras weave in and out of each other sometimes seamlessly, sometimes abruptly.

The seat of imperial English power is called the Palace of Westminster. It combines an urban iconography of religion, royalty, and history in a compromise, and this hybrid represents the trade-off necessary to a democracy. By contrast, the Scottish organ of government mixes unexpected images, a series of metaphorical allusions typical of the new iconic building. These come from the sea (upturned boats), nature (leaves and petals), and culture (the embracing amphitheater). One of the most popular paintings in Scotland—of the Reverend Robert Walker leaning forward on his ice-skates, by Sir Henry Raeburn—is taken up in the window-tilts and the black granite figures attached to the façades, often called a "trigger

BELOW: Raeburn's skater, one metaphor take up in the window tilts.

RIGHT: Metaphorical analyses showing the intended signifiers of "upturned boats," "petals," "inverted crowsteps," "Raeburn's skater," "merging of city and geology," and unintended overtones— "silvery fish." Drawings by Madelon Vriesendrop.

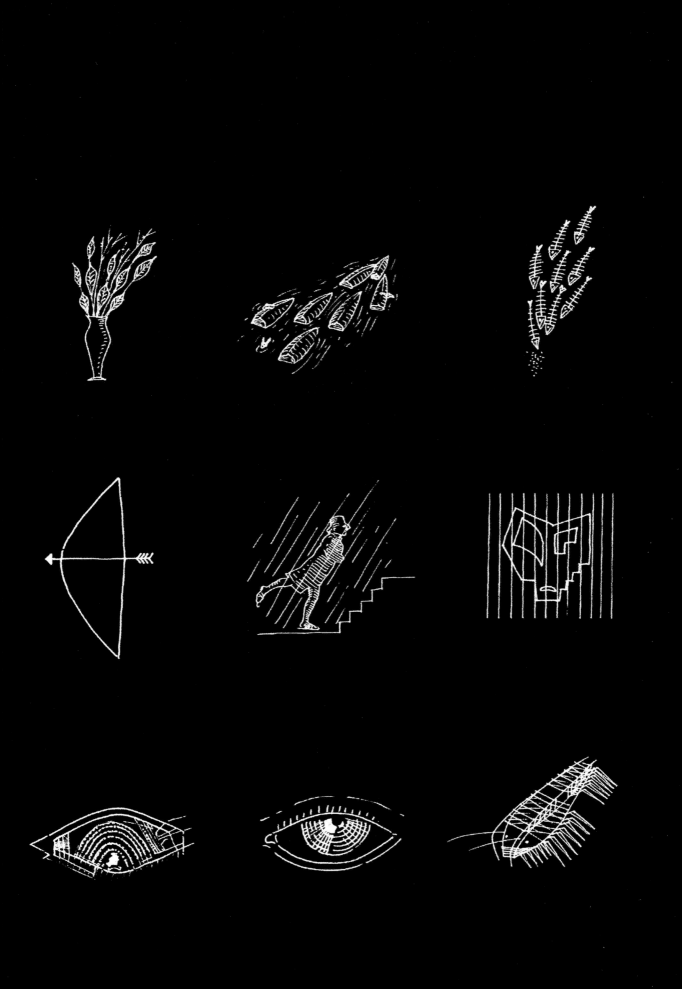

form," or "hair dryer." These might also represent politicians moving forward, dynamically, taking risks over thin ice, as everyone was to do.

Miralles and his wife Benedetta Tagliabue, who worked on the design, talked about "secrets," the overtones that are prompted by unusual forms. Indeed, as with Libeskind's provocative shapes, they denoted certain meanings; but also left open other connotations to be decoded by the viewer.

Finally, the building is conceived as city fabric wiggling into the countryside. This last metaphor is the most powerful. Miralles' building blends the Royal Mile of Edinburgh into the extraordinary remains of the extinct volcano known as Arthur's Seat. So the icon of democracy is more local, complex, and nature-oriented than its predecessor and, by law, more ecological as well. The fact that none of

BELOW: The study model shows the "leaf-grammar" of the rooftops, the Fifth Façade converging on the corner.

BOTTOM: View from Salisbury Crag showing the scheme as a tiny city nestling into the fragmented fabric, and then extending a long arm out to the extinct volcano from where this photo is taken. This "twig form", a turfed area with small pools, is meant for outdoor assemblies of up to 10,000, and is meant to relate to early Scottish democracy: the public meeting in hills and next to lochs.

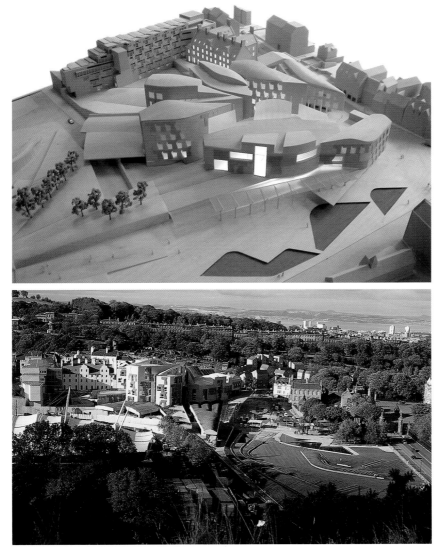

these metaphors is readily apparent, but all are felt lurking behind the forms, makes them typical enigmatic signifiers, suggestive overtones.

English tradition defined democracy as a conflict of opposed élites confronting each other across two sides of a chapel, so that truth would emerge through debate and loyal opposition. The new Parliament, however, stresses conciliation in its layout. The semi-circular debating chamber, with its gently sloping floor and the raked seats, encourages consensual exchange, or at least that is the idea. Hence, the shallow curve, or vesica shape, a form repeated elsewhere especially in the outdoor assembly. You could be sitting in a lecture theater with very grand seats, widely spaced. The generous mood is reinforced by the spiky dance of wood and steel overhead, another version of the vesica-shape. When debate becomes boring and pretentious, the other MSPs and onlookers only have to look up and stop listening to appreciate an interesting visual argument. How does this unusual structure hold the roof?

The airy truss, with compression members in golden oak and tension members in thin steel, jumps over the Presiding Officer's head in the most unexpected way to turn into a vast skylight that pours a yellow ambience over the entire room. That's worth deciphering, and so too are the diagonal compression struts that keep the whole structure from collapsing sideways like an accordion. Further interest is provided by the hundreds of hanging spotlights and not a few TV cameras. These glistening elements define a space like the underside of a tree canopy. All of this engages the imagination, as predictable rhetoric drones on, refreshing the MSP for a creative rejoinder.

Even more unusual is the way light spills in from the sides. Whereas in the London Parliament debate is closed off from the outside world, insulated, as it were, from reality, in Edinburgh the members are in visual contact with nature and geology, the deep metaphor that Scottish identity is wrapped up in its landscape. The openness and collegiality are reinforced by another contrast to the Anglo-Saxon view of government.

Whereas the English Palace stands out as an impressive object, even doubled in size by the water and with its Big Ben proclaiming national identity, the Scottish building takes up the protective coloration of its urban environment, the fragmented fabric of Cannongate, with its alleyways and broken roof lines. In this sense the scheme is a post-modern icon of inclusion, a meaning Miralles underlined when he called it "a gathering place." The site plan shows

The chamber interior with gently sloping floor, collegial layout, and extraordinary overhead truss of bones and tendons. The hammer- beam roof of the old 1639 Parliament is here transformed with laminated and steel reinforced oak beams spanning 100-foot space.

this metaphor: a loose congregation of similar shapes. Indeed, the BBC film of the building, overseen by the feisty television broadcaster Kirsty Wark, also titled it "The Gathering Place," a phrase that asserts the original intention of the building to become the symbol of reconciliation.

The London and Edinburgh parliaments share at least one important trait. They both have a neo-medieval atmosphere. Each has nooks and crannies where off-the-record conversations can occur, dark corridors of power, and little window-seats, inglenooks, and changes of level that make the structures more domestic than institutional. A valid criticism is that both buildings are too labyrinthine, too given over to the individual representative at the expense of collective democracy. Politics seems to be atomized here, like a monastery, as each monk-MSP faces the universe alone. Much of the work goes on in the six committee rooms located in the four towers. Yet, this idiosyncrasy and fragmentation are only a part of the building, as indeed are the dark, religious spaces.

Contrast is the key. The overwhelming feeling of the structure is one of generosity and light. One moves through dark areas to a series of complex, layered spaces that explode with light pouring in from

BELOW LEFT: Site plan showing the nestling together of elements, the repetition of fractal forms, versions of the vesica-shape. This shallow curve relates the four towers to the twelve skylights over the Garden Foyer, the Debating Chamber, the ponds, and the Outdoor Assembly.

BELOW: MSP offices and entrance vaults. A medieval, cave-like space is found at the public entrance, with a series of concrete vaults, and then again in the individual MSP office, with its "Think Pod" for meditation. Miralles intended the monastic and spiritual overtones and cast a primitive symbolism of Saltire crosses and personal signs into the concrete, even references to Scottish literature. Each seat focuses on Salisbury Crag and is shielded from sun and enquiring eyes by oak poles, a symbol of the twigs and leaves that won him the competition.

unexpected points. The richness and ambiguity are disarming at first and then, once one is oriented, profoundly moving. Nowhere is this more effective than in the Garden Lobby, another curved vesica-shape. Again, as Miralles pointed out, these relate to leaf-forms, the upturned boats found on many Scottish shores, and a shoal of fish—all three. These petals swim, or float, or nestle, according to preference, over the Lobby, celebrating one of the great processional routes in contemporary architecture. Light spills down the sides of the skylights creating a general reflected glow that is without precedent. They pull you up the slight incline of a grand stairway toward the debating chamber, another leaf-form, and a giant one.

Both British parliaments can be contrasted with Continental and American examples, which would never countenance such personal eccentricity in a public building. Like the Greeks and Romans, these Western nations value gravitas, impersonality, and the generic. Miralles' creation, to its great credit, commands humor, love, wonder, and surprise: feelings more usual to the theater and dinner party than to the debating chamber. Consider the way the petal-forms dance together overhead as skylights and then trail out toward Arthur's Seat, becoming contour lines of the landscape as they do so. This is a

sensuous geological metaphor, and very elevating to find as one sits down on the turf to have a political chat.

And here lies another innovation in Anglo-Saxon political practice, at least for the nation's capital: providing a place for public gathering. No agora, forum, or medieval piazza for the people—the foundation of European democracy—exists next to the organs of British and American government. Rather, suspicious of collective expression and the power of groups, all the people are allowed is a space captured through action and participation, such as Trafalgar Square in London, or the Lincoln Memorial in Washington DC. These places have become through a process of popular willpower the *de facto* public realm, wrested from the officials and now officially sanctioned. And why provide an agora or public area for 10,000? As Hannah Arendt, and other political philosophers have argued, when the public can no longer see itself as if in a mirror, in a single place—as it did on countless occasions in 1989 to bring about the collapse of Communism—then the people have lost control to their representatives.

So, Miralles, the Catalan, has given a new twist to the European idea of the agora; he has turned it into a soft, turfed place. Taking the same generic curves that he uses on the assembly, he creates an open amphitheater of steps and stairs and, in this way, sets up a clear equation between the people's debates and their representatives. Thus, it is all the more ironic that the process of building has generated conflict. Kirsty Wark was a member of the original jury, a friend and admirer of Donald Dewar, and, along with Professor Andy McMillan, one of the important supporters of the scheme. She also was pulled into the maelstrom when asked to testify at the public inquiry into the escalating costs.

This investigation was itself something of a folly. Led by Lord Fraser, it was set up in 2003, even before the building was finished, in order to judge whether the Scottish Parliament was "value for money." Determining the "value" of something before it exists takes a great deal of expertise, something in short supply since no architectural critics or historians, acquainted with the special genre of parliament buildings, were asked to testify. And the inquiry itself used up a considerable amount of money in its complicated ruminations. (Was it trying to echo the building?) Requested by Fraser to hand over documentary footage of interviews with Dewar and Miralles, the BBC and Wark resisted. They cited the precedent of withholding sources

PREVIOUS PAGES: The Garden Lobby, with its silvery fish-like skylights dipping into the space. Although a late addition to the design, this area has become the heart of the Parliament, and one co-opted by the media, particularly TV.

ABOVE: A landform of stepping turf for political chat, and possibly an assembly for 10,000 to see and hear themselves act.

until the date of transmission. The refusal only stirred up more suspicion and recrimination, now between judges, journalists, and broadcasters. The whole sorry mess became "The Gathering Place Dispersed," a tragedy twice compounded.

The Non-landmark Landmark

In spite of its ill-judged timing, the Fraser Inquiry did bring out some interesting truths, in particular, the widespread and variable use of the term "landmark building." In her testimony in November 2003, the broadcaster Kirsty Wark cited this notion as the major goal of the competition and Miralles' design as the undisputed winner in this category. "We wanted a designer who would deliver, and Donald's major concern was a landmark for Scotland." And, she added, panel members were "all of a mind about Miralles," because his design was the "most winning in all ways" (i.e. the way it carried on the conversation with the site and Scottishness, past and future).[14]

In fact, Donald Dewar was more specific about this, commending the design as what could be called a "Non-landmark Landmark." "Miralles," he said, "had ideas about how you put the building into the site that we found very sympathetic; he wasn't looking for a great landmark building, he wasn't trying to build the highest tower in the whole of central Scotland as a mark of importance of the Parliament. . . . What he was talking about was a building that grew out of that site, was not simply imposed on that site."[15] This idea, of growing organically out of the site, has a long pedigree in Italian architecture and that of Frank Lloyd Wright. Critics agree with Dewar in finding this the crucial point: "a landscape rather than a landmark building at the heart of Edinburgh," as Robert Booth puts it.[16]

The concept of a Non-landmark Landmark looms very large in the age of the iconic building. One architectural thinker, Aaron Betsky, devotes an entire book to prove the superiority, in a time of ecological stress, of what he calls landscrapers, buildings that nestle into the ground but nevertheless have a striking image.[17] Koolhaas' attempt to "kill the skyscraper" and Peter Eisenman's landform at Santiago de Compostela (see pages 162–9), also try to have it both ways. Miralles' parliament is very much part of this maverick trend, one that tries to invent the anti-icon icon (i.e. the bulding that is very visibly not there). The somewhat contradictory words of Donald Dewar and Kirsty Wark confirm this.

The Spiraling Cost of an Iconic Building

In September 2004, Lord Fraser published his inquiry and gave a press conference summarizing why and how the building costs had spiraled out of control. As many knew, there was more than one reason, and it is in this multiplication of risks that a lesson lies for the iconic building. It tempts fate on many levels at once, it invokes the infamous Murphy's Law that if something can go wrong, it will go wrong.

Firstly, Donald Dewar and his team, particularly the civil servants mediating the figures, radically underestimated them. The figure of £40 million, often mentioned in 1998 and later, was for a building on a green-field site and not an estimate of Miralles' design. Fraser cleared Dewar of intentionally misleading MSPs over the cost. The problem, he showed, was the form of contract, "construction management," where the taxpayer was the ultimate client who had to pay for changes. Fraser said he found it "astonishing" that civil servants had not told ministers about the financial estimate of risk coming from "construction management"—and the MSPs didn't ask. Many newspapers concluded that this silence amounted to collusion. According to Scotland's Auditor General, Robert Black, the main cause of the problem was that there were never clear lines of control, a situation that often arises with a new parliament building, especially when politics enters the equation.

Secondly, the politicians themselves expanded the brief considerably, adding more requirements and room to the initial design. The area increased from 250,000 square feet to 320,000 square feet, and the people to be accommodated increased from 300 to more than 1,200. Thirdly, the terrorism of September 11th added £30 million to security features. Fourthly, Enric Miralles' design was so complex that, it is said, four out of five details had to be worked out on site; and, while it was under construction, he changed the shape of the debating chamber. Indeed, 15,000 design changes were made, and the windows costing £17,000 apiece did not fit.[18] Fifthly, and returning to the first point, the premise was that the best building must be built as quickly as possible, before it became a political headache. This combination of high quality and speed ruled out cost-cutting, and thus produced the official final cost of £431 million.

All this would be enough to make any budget look ridiculous, but sixthly, and most unpredictably of all, just as the building was getting out of the ground, the two protagonists suddenly died, Enric Miralles in July 2000 and Donald Dewar in October of that year. If both had lived, and taken control of what became a runaway project, the costs I believe might have been halved. Why? Because the death of the two outstanding and creative individuals behind the design left everyone else in a perplexing double-bind. Consider the role of the collaborating architects, RMJM, the team that had to turn the design into a building. They would be damned if they did not keep such things as the integrity of the curves and finishes, the sixty-foot concrete cantilever, and the idiosyncratic windows, the beautiful dovetailing of sycamore, oak, granite, and stainless steel. Thanks to RMJM, the finishes are stunning. The Scottish Parliament is the largest crafted building since Antonio Gaudi's Sagrada Familia in Barcelona, and that cathedral of the 1890s is still not finished. How could RMJM not carry through the work of a "genius," once he had died? And yet, how could they not be blamed for getting paid an ever-increasing amount to carry on the job? Actually, the fees for all the consultants were not exorbitant, a bit more than 15 percent, acceptable for such a complex scheme and the kind of thing one expects with a house.[19] Finally, it is never cheap to build the work of a great, dead architect.

The MSPs were also in a double-bind because of Dewar's reputation of rectitude, that they would not tarnish, and their own inattention to the cost overruns. Yet, after his death, no leader took up the defense of the building. Instead, an inquiry was called and, as the press of the time noted, "the game of name and shame." An understandable, but tragic situation. Consider the way, as Shakespeare would have dramatized, everybody is embroiled. In June 2003, the

BELOW, LEFT AND RIGHT: Window and furniture details of a Committee Room, one of six. The handling of the elements and space give a spiritual dimension to politics. Indeed, the interior of Ronchamp was here one model for Miralles.

First Minister, Jack McConnell appoints an inquiry into why the Holyrood Parliament is two and a half years late and costs ten times the original estimate. By March the next year, McConnell, who signed the cheques and prepared the decision in 1999 to go forward with the building, has escaped from testifying in front of the inquisition he has set up. The Fraser Inquiry proceeds; Brian Stewart, the RMJM boss, is humiliated in tears; the contractor's integrity is impugned; Presiding Officer Sir David Steel is accused of misleading Parliament; the MSPs are themselves accused of causing delays and cost increases; Lord Fraser makes more than £150,000 out of the inquiry; the people of Scotland fume; their representatives prove they can not govern themselves, let alone an emergent nation. So, "The Gathering Place" is called into being . . . and a hellish time is had by all. It would have been very different had Dewar and Miralles lived.

And yet, a little historical perspective, and appreciation of tragedy, gives a different reading of the whole Affaire Ecosse. Many, let us say most, iconic buildings of government have missed deadlines and had huge overruns. Even the best architects are guilty. Le Corbusier in Chandigarh, Oscar Niemeyer in Brasilia, Mitchell and Giurgola at the Canberra Parliament House, Lord Foster at the Berlin Chancellery, Michael Hopkins at London's New Parliamentary Building, Richard Rogers at the Welsh Assembly in Cardiff—to name but a few. And, most of the citizens of these countries would argue that the resultant architecture justified the cost.

The London Parliament, rebuilt after a fire, and a competition that Barry and Pugin won in 1835, was estimated at £865,000 and a six-year building program. Seventeen years later, when partly completed, the cost had risen to £2.4 million. By 1860 the Victoria Tower was completed and not until 1928, and the fitting out of St. Stephen's Hall, was the architects' work done. Dan Cruickshank, the architectural historian who supplied me with these figures, told me the delays were partly due "to massive interest—and interference—in the project" by Prince Albert, various politicians, and "growing costs [causing] massive problems and cut-backs." As a consequence, the architects were asked to cut their fees to unconscionable levels.[20] The blame and shame game sounds familiar.

Yet compare. The Scottish Parliament was designed in a competition of 1998 and finished in 2004—a mere six years. Depending on what one takes as the London figures, the northerners' speed of building exceeded the southerners' by three to fifteen times. Of course, given the difference in century and style, the whole comparison is slightly ludicrous; but it is the kind of defense one is forced to make when a public inquiry takes the accountants'-eye-view of things. Architecture has to be defended against intimidation by the ignorant.

With this sort of perspective on parliamentary buildings, one might conclude that the Scottish iconic building is not very wasteful of time or money. It is, however, tragically true that the two protagonists made some mistakes, which were then amplified by their unexpected deaths. It is also true that Scottish hopes for a fledgling democracy were set back by what the media portrayed as duplicity. But with time, as these sad facts slip into the background and the power of the building and landscape emerge into the foreground, the whole saga may be revisited as that rare genre: the tragedy with a happy ending. The strengths of the building are bound to show through.

RIGHT: A fractal grammar, reminiscent of Gehry's Bilbao, and also carried through in glistening skin, becomes the Fifth Façade. Here the Committee Room Blocks can be seen swimming around their focus, the big fish of the General Assembly (courtesy BBC Scotland.)

Renzo Piano—Function Stymies Form

Beyond the high cost and long delays that may strike the iconic building, is the specter of the misfired metaphor. The provocative creation may rebound on the creator, become an unintended signifier of exactly the wrong things, an architectural slip of the tongue. This failing is always a possibility even with the best designers, as we have seen on two prominent occasions with Norman Foster and Rafael Viñoly. Since it is becoming ever more common, it may be invidious to single out examples and hold them up to inspection. And yet there is a type of mistake that has general causes and therefore contains important lessons for the age of the iconic building.

The botch typifies the case of an architect, not especially trained as an artist, who intends to make a grand sculptural gesture that has never been seen before and yet still make something functional. Caught between opposite requirements, pushed by celebrity culture one way and pulled by a utilitarian philosophy the other, he may be blind to the emergent blooper and fail to see that function plus unlikely gesture equals a screw-up. These bloopers are becoming common enough to constitute a class in themselves and, like all dominant genres, not something merely to be suffered or inveighed against, but also to be relished, like Mrs. Malaprop's wonderful circumloquotations.

Renzo Piano's concert hall complex, the new Parco della Musica in Rome, is a case in point. Started in 1994, the building suffered the usual Roman delays because various ancient artefacts were found on the site, and so it was not completed until late in 2002. Three concert halls rotate around a central amphitheater and are placed at ninety degrees to each other. They are sheathed in a common, gray unit of lead that repeats itself like both shingle and the shell of a tortoise. The

BELOW LEFT: Renzo Piano, Parco della Musica, Rome, 1994–2002. These concert halls, with capacities of 700, 1273, and 2756, surround an open piazza.

BELOW: Concert Hall interior, with its vineyards of people and polished cherrywood reflectors resembling seats and pillboxes.

RIGHT: Metaphorical analysis showing the organic overtones—from the carrot to the rat—and the unintended mechanistic signifiers.

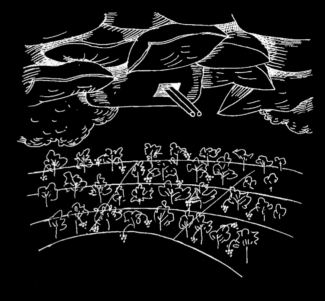

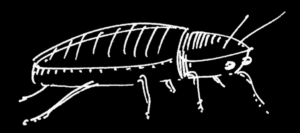
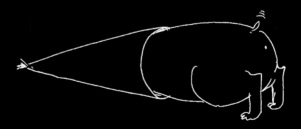
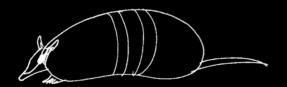

problem is that this heavy, functional material is too stained, and rectangular, to sustain the organic comparison and the bulges look like distended blobs. Piano likens them to what he calls "lutes," metaphors for the music heard within, while critics compare them to half-peeled onions, scarabs, armadillos, insect carapace, and Japanese armor, among many other things.[21] No doubt all these metaphors have some validity, but it is the bulk, the stains, the graceless curves that push readings in a less propitious direction.

Because Piano has derived his curves functionally from a mathematical curve (a torus), kept their sweep to a minimum, and broken them (for gutters) one-third of the way along the volume, they emerge as surprising figures, three animals with heads feeding at a common trough. Pigs, rats, armadillos, or maybe well-behaved whales; it's a sombre meal, no feeding frenzy here. In some views the organic metaphors are irresistible and friendly. The curves look like bottoms and carrot ends, pleasant to touch and nice to taste. The segmented lead sections, nipped and tucked around each other, could be folds of skin. All of this is empathetic and to be welcomed and yet, in the end, it's all so bulky and inert. Moreover, the inside has similar problems. The metaphor of "vineyards of listeners," a standard for auditoria since Hans Scharoun's work in Berlin in the 1960s, is seen by the architect in another way. He likens the acoustic ceiling "to an upturned vessel"; but again these wooden reflectors have less savory overtones, being seen by one critic as "like the internal organs of some giant living creature—kidneys maybe," and upturned pillboxes.[22] Once more the misfired metaphor seems to stem from the contrary impulses operating on Piano, his desire to produce a unique and strong image and wrap it in a minimal and economical shape. The requirement to celebrate a concert hall pushes him, as it does Gehry with the Disney Hall (see pages 170–83), toward the expressive equivalent of frozen music, but his training as an engineer dampens the sound and mutes the melody. Piano may be one of the world's renowned architects and a recipient of the Pritzker Prize but, like many an architect trained in functionalism, an internal censure has cut short his heavenward flight.

Lead volumes protrude on to the main square.

Cancellation

Another dilemma facing the would-be icon is the way it can be canceled out, or upstaged, by competitors. The architectural critic Deyan Sudjic, no friend of the genre, makes this failing his telling point. Recalling Nikolaus Pevsner's stance in the 1960s against the

emergence of iconic buildings, he aims his scorn at the vanity of a city trying to put itself on the map with a landmark when, at the same time, every other region is trying to get in on the Bilbao Effect. The result is the mutual cancellation of effect through architectural inflation. As he says of attention-grabbing structures:

> This is the way to an architecture of diminishing returns in which every sensational new building must attempt to eclipse the last one. It leads to a kind of hyperinflation, the architectural equivalent of the Weimar Republic's debauching of its currency.[23]

Sudjic, like Pevsner, cannot help himself censoring these one-liners in his weekly *Observer* column, damning each building's faults while at the same time amplifying its celebrity. We are back here in the moralistic world of a journalism that tut-tuts the Page 3 nudes while taking a certain satisfaction, and economic interest, in poring over the evidence. Sudjic's main target is the Spanish-born Santiago Calatrava, whom he never tires of shooting for his sins of "blatant exhibitionism." While this kind of journalism, having it both ways, is as much a cause of the problem as the solution—after all celebrity culture is created by media hype—Sudjic is also right that hyperinflation of expression devalues urban currency and is in danger of turning world cities into world fairs.

The Las Vegasization of the city is a real danger, as pointed out at the beginning of this book, and it could result in an urban context in which any gesture is overwhelmed by all the gesticulation. And yet it has also resulted, where competition is extreme but also regulated, in such marvels as Venice. There, too, every palazzo tried to upstage the preceding one, every nouveau riche tried to add an illegal obelisk to his Baroque cornice—and sometimes got away with the crime. Only a spoilsport would wish Venice to sink into oblivion, which it is destined to do; but its example should remind us that the dark side of iconic building should not obscure its potential for pleasure and invention. So it is important to look at the two architects who provoke Sudjic's censure to see how really bad, or valuable, they are, and at others who are challenging Frank Gehry for the crown as *the* iconic architect.

The Challengers

Calatrava Looks to Nature

Two architects have self-consciously sought to create iconic buildings, and they could not be more different in temperament and appearance: Will Alsop, an Englishman, and Santiago Calatrava, a Spaniard. Both designers, in their mid-fifties, also contradict their national stereotypes. Alsop is blowsy, open and outspoken, apt to have a drink in one hand, a cigar in the other, and wearing a welcoming grin— rather Spanish. His buildings are as unconventional, un-English, and gregarious as they come. Calatrava, by contrast, is serious, reserved, businesslike in deportment, and as soft-spoken in authority as the classical English gent. Only his structures go way beyond anything seen outside an architectural school.

As mentioned, Deyan Sudjic reserves his most withering comments for the Spanish engineer, who understates his words the more to overstate his buildings. At their worst, Sudjic writes, Calatrava's structures "topple over the edge of kitsch to create a world that seems remarkably like the set for a 1950s science fiction film, prefabricated Gaudi, extruded from a toothpaste tube by the yard."[1] This criticism of his work in Valencia has some truth, as we will see, though Sudjic's recurrent accusations of kitsch, repeated like a mantra since 1992, are questionable, and the characterization of the scheme as a film set points to one of its strengths. Calatrava's work succeeds, when it does, through consistency, high finish, and theatrical performance. The landmarks do not suffer, as Renzo Piano's do, from inner doubt.

BELOW: Portrait of Santiago Calatrava by Dennis Sharp.

BELOW RIGHT: Santiago Calatrava, Lyon Airport Station, 1989–94, based on one of his favorite structural images, the wing/bird, an image also developed in his sculpture and, characteristically, accentuated with strong Op Art repetitions.

Calatrava trained first as an architect in his hometown of Valencia and then went on to get a Ph.D. in engineering at the famous ETH in Zurich, where he started his practice. His 1981 thesis was "Concerning the Foldability of Space Frames," revealing an interest in unfolding structures and moving skeletal bones that characterizes all his subsequent work. What keeps Calatrava's engineering from becoming kitsch resides in such inventions, some of which resemble an unfolding umbrella, others the rippling backbone of an animal, the struts of a fan, or the layered wing of a bird. As these metaphors suggest, Calatrava works through natural and physical analogies. He takes a few simple structural ideas from the living world, perfects their outlines, repeats them as startling white members and then has them built with loving care. It is the extraordinary quality of construction that, again, lifts the work above the censure of the K-word—for kitsch is a form of degraded rubbish and no one can accuse Calatrava of skimping on the finish or the details. Some of his landmarks, such as those at Tenerife and Valencia, have taken more than ten years to construct.

Calatrava sees himself as the inheritor of Gaudi, Charles Rennie Mackintosh, and Frank Lloyd Wright, and his early love of Le Corbusier's Ronchamp—*the* standard for the iconic building—is well documented in his many drawings. The fact that he places himself in such an august bloodline is revealing and, as Sudjic also notes, his website refers immodestly to the aristocratic origins of his name. Clearly he intends to challenge the great tradition of architecture. His most avid supporter, the critic Alexander Tzonis, unblushingly compares him to many others in the tradition of the *Homo universalis*, among them Leonardo, Spinoza, Goethe, and Buckminster Fuller. Thus, in spite of his modest appearance, there is no doubt that he intends to challenge all contemporary architects as *the* iconic architect.

Sometimes this ambition overwhelms his better judgement. A case in point is the concert hall for Santa Cruz on the island of Tenerife. This is meant to do for that port city what iconic architecture did for the ports of Sydney and Bilbao—transform the economy—and it has resulted in one of the biggest empty gestures in architectural history. A favorite bird-shape of his, reworked in several buildings and sculptures, sends its upper beak, or wing, or whole body (depending on your view) swooping over the concert hall below, an answer to the swoosh logo of Nike, or the front end of Saarinen's bird for TWA. One problem here is that this covering gesture doesn't cover or contain anything except itself—it is literally empty. Another problem

ABOVE: Santiago Calatrava, Concert Hall, Santa Cruz, Tenerife, 1990–2003. A "breaking wave," 60 metres high, sails over the main concert hall that is cupped within two conical sections

MIDDLE: White broken ceramic tiles and nautical imagery hold up this predatory and fascinating shape.

BELOW: The section showing the hidden V-truss that is supported from the apex of the main hall, an auditorium that has a marvelous fan of folded petals, a palm-frond shape.

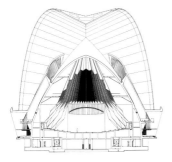

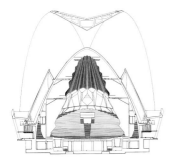

is that while it pretends to cantilever the whole way as a thin shell, it actually conceals a V-truss behind its swoop and this rests on a nearly invisible point about half-way up the curve. This slight of hand might be forgivable if the swoop did anything important for the rest of the building, and Calatrava did not invoke Frank Lloyd Wright in insisting on his "truth against the world." "I am with him," he said of the Fountainhead architect, "when he says that, with truth on his side, he is ready to take on the world. I believe there is truth in my structures."[2] Maybe in most of his structures, but not here in Tenerife.

Lastly, while the architect intends the swoosh to be the metaphor of a wave breaking, as they do near by, his mounts up 200 feet high and 300 feet long—a veritable tidal wave and, to those unsympathetic critics, also a predatory pterodactyl. Sudjic finds it looking like 1950s hair-styling, "a teddy boy quiff."[3] Mrs. Malaprop again, the iconic building finds another victim. And yet this early work (Calatrava was only forty when he designed it) has some marvelous interior spaces and a superlative finish, and these aspects help to rescue the scheme from complete bathos.

It is apparent from his work as a whole that Calatrava strains after effect and affect. He challenges the masters of modern architecture and his favorite, Gaudi, by working within the bounds of structural expressionism, that is, accentuating the lines of structural force and constructional reality, but something in him always pushes beyond this basic poetry, exaggerating a cantilever a bit too far, tapering a concrete section just a little too elegantly, repeating a structural unit once too often.

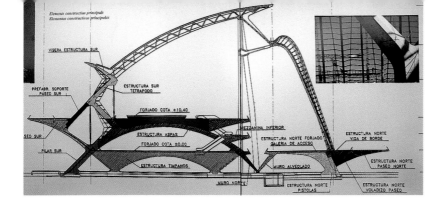

If, as Jean Cocteau remarked, tact is knowing how far too far you can go, then Calatrava sometimes goes one step further. This is why, as Sudjic constantly reminds us, he is not particularly admired by his peers. The censure hurts; but then Calatrava knows it will happen; he realizes he drives other architects mad with jealousy of the virtuoso. "Why can't *we* get away with such outlandish expressionism?" is their unvoiced query, followed quickly by the implicit response: "Because we don't have the guts and skill?" Maddening.

Perhaps a more favorable way of considering the bravura is to tone it down, to put it in its historical context, to show how it derives from many predecessors and is therefore not a threat: the sculpture of Brancusi and Kenneth Snelson and the late 1950s architecture of Eero Saarinen, Oscar Niemeyer, and Kenzo Tange. Like all these figures Calatrava experiments with structural energies, then turns up the rheostats. The results are not, as Tzonis argues, some breakthrough to a new paradigm, nor as Sudjic claims, "perilously close to kitsch," but, rather, a media-driven engineering that appeals more to the public than to those interested in a complex architecture. Calatrava is like Felix Candela, an architect-engineer he knew and admired, someone who strains against the tectonics of shell construction to discover its latent beauty, or Gustav Eiffel, an engineer who also was spurned by architects but caught the public's imagination. Approached with these predecessors in mind, his structures and spaces actually look quite sophisticated. Compared to Saarinen or Tange's work, they are extraordinary light-boxes that bounce and articulate light and shadow in captivating ways. Surfaces that radiate, glow, and reflect make his buildings look like veritable insects of luminosity. A case in point is the City of Arts and Sciences in Valencia, the £2 billion project that took fifteen years to complete, in 2005.

Placed in a dried-up riverbed, this white "city" reflects its brilliant exoskeleton in a shallow basin of continuously cleaned water. Purity, sparkle, and the sound of fountains counteract the strong sunlight, as they do in many Spanish gardens. This feeling of freshness and pleasure is helped by the tapering and modulated forms of white concrete that are impeccably made. The continuous finish is a consequence not only of Calatrava's design but the patience and skill of the local industrial workers. They spend much time polishing the interior of the formwork, smoothing out any joints so that the final cast comes out looking like a new version of shining marble, or a

LEFT AND RIGHT: Santiago Calatrava, City of Arts and Sciences, Valencia, 1991–2002. A spectacular urban landscape sunk in the old Turia River is open to the public night and day, a white jewel against a blue sky and green pool. The heart of the scheme, a half-ovoid, becomes a whole blinking eye when reflected in the pool and when the canopy rises and lowers. It holds an IMAX cinema and planetarium. External walkways and leaning buttresses pulsate to filter the light. The white concrete structure is everywhere sculpted with curves that profile the play of forces, and it is constructed without blemish as a large sculpture.

superior form of plastic. In this sense it epitomizes every architect's dream: to find one, continuous, perfected material that can be used for everything—floor, walls, roof, structure, and joints. The result is an all-over Brancusi in which one can perambulate, a dream space.

At its heart is the planetarium, "the eye of wisdom," that blinks its eyelid on electronic command. Reflected in the still water, the oval and retina become complete, and when the canopy is half closed the planetarium seems to squint and stare. The metaphor is a bit corny, but at the same time convincingly carried through, and even appropriate for the role of cosmology today. The universe looks back at the eye it has created, us, looking at it. Some critics see this work as epitomizing the biotechnical aspect of the new paradigm.[4]

The largest structure, at 130 feet high, is the science museum. Like the Natural History Museum in London a hundred years before, it employs the cathedral metaphor to house and domesticate emergent knowledge, there Darwinism, here DNA. A new type of flying buttress leans into this spikey form and it results in another metaphor that probably was intended but is no less surreal for that. At night, thirty rigid eyes pop open as light shines out from between triangular eyelids. By day thirty rigid beaks snap out against the blue sky. They are eye-beaks, improbable though that sounds. These forms and associations stem from Antonio Gaudi's windows at the Colonia Guell, a building well known to Calatrava and a reason that Sudjic finds the building an unfortunate echo of the past. But it is the new sense of space and light that is more apparent, not the quotations from history. Every view in this airy cathedral of science becomes a dazzling optical illusion of filtered light. Indeed the strength of Calatrava's work here is the way it modulates light, breaks down the glare, and cuts it up like a Op Art trellis.

Reflected in the shallow pools and cut across by walkways and floating tubs of cypress trees, Calatrava has created a water garden inspired by the great Mughal works of the past. Urban theater is put to public use both day and night since much of the site remains open, and dramatically lit. One can traverse it several ways, like the city-garden of Fatehpur Sikri, and curiously in the dark find the buildings turned inside-out. At night, the forms that modulated sunlight during the day now become giant chandeliers and lamps, the epitome of the art-light industry, a staple of the iconic building in its tourist mode.

One may object to all this rhetoric, as does Sudjic, for being a garish show-off but then, as mentioned, by that token one would

The City of Arts and Sciences at night—a lighting expert's dreamscape.

have to consign Venice, not to mention the Baroque, Rococo, and Art Nouveau periods to the dust-bin. This he is quick to do, as he ends his attack on iconic buildings with the summation: "Perhaps, like Art Nouveau which flourished briefly at the end of the nineteenth century, the icon has become ubiquitous just as it is about to vanish."[5]

The opinion, and view of history, is again reminiscent of Nikolaus Pevsner, who also termed Art Nouveau "a short interlude" and Gaudi "a freak and fantast."[6] Critics, like historians, are not above hoping their prejudices will become self-fulfilling prophecies. But Gaudi has well outlasted Pevsner's censure to become, along with Michelangelo and Le Corbusier, one of the most celebrated European architects. The iconic building is not a nine-day wonder, but a future condition that has deep causes. These we leave to the conclusion, but suffice it to say here that, while it is true Calatrava has a propensity to overstatement, his work will go on to exert influence because it is skillfully carried through and because it relates to a long-term interest in nature and a cosmic iconography. Seen against the clear blue sky of the dry climate of Valencia the white city comes alive as shimmering filigree in bones and thin tendons. The body metaphor is extended as the flexing eye and made strange by entanglement with the beak of a bird and the skeleton of an insect. The natural metaphors do not amount to a program that is thought through in any philosophical sense, but they have an artistic and structural consistency that is developed in subsequent projects, not something to be easily dismissed as kitsch.

Will Alsop Pursues Difference

Will Alsop has self-consciously pursued the iconic building as a goal in itself, and done so since the 1990s when he designed Le Grand Bleu for the municipal government in Marseilles. This extraordinary civic landmark captures the deep Mediterranean blue of the sea and sky and takes it one shade deeper. It surrounds the public place within with metallic curves—an early built example of the blob architecture that became fashionable somewhat later. Alsop, aware that his iconic building was in the same city as Le Corbusier's much earlier Unité sees no problem with the idea of grand expressive gestures. For him, rather, they open up the field of architecture to artistic possibilities.

In addition to the blob, his expressive themes include the all-over surface, the pixilated surface, the flat horizontal box on splayed stilts. He favors shapes that are as form-less as possible set against ones that are highly identifiable, even proposing a building in the shape of a fat teddy bear for one of his regeneration schemes. Several provincial cities in Britain have come to him to bring economic recovery, the Bilbao Effect, with an unlikely iconic building. Among those seeking renewal through architectural re-branding are Barnsley (with multi-colored blobs and boxes on stilts and a halo), Middlehaven (with faceted structures, hillocks, and a teddy bear), Bradford (with pier buildings on an artificial lake, with donut and wiggle shapes), and Liverpool (with a "squashed donuts on stilts," as Alsop dubbed it).

This last structure won a competition in December 2002, against top British contenders Norman Foster, Richard Rogers, and Edward Cullinan, and did so because it was explicitly more of an iconic building than the other entries. Both the jury and Alsop confirmed this point.[7] What made it superior on this score? Whereas the other entries for the pier site were more impressive as landmarks, they referred to previous architecture. Like the other competitors, Alsop was

ABOVE: Portrait of Will Alsop.

BELOW LEFT: Will Alsop, Hotel du Departement, Le Grand Bleu, Marseilles, 1993–5. Several linear blob-shapes, in dark Mediterranean blue steel, house the local municipal government.

BELOW: Will Alsop, Middlehaven Masterplan, a "landscape of icons" from the "form-less" blob, left, to the corn-on-the-cob center, hills, and teddy bear, right.

asked to design a "Fourth Grace" to set alongside the three existing Edwardian monuments on the Liverpool waterfront. His solution won because it was "blob-like," "form-less," "a lump of material"—perhaps a faceted "rough diamond"—and, most extraordinary of all given the sobriquet, graceless. But it had the advantage of recalling nothing specific and in that sense was more provocative than the others. His search for the perverse and the uncanny is, of course, highly self-conscious and based on such things as Freud's investigation into the unconscious and the power of paranoia. Alsop understands that an iconic building must inspire fear and loathing yet, like the mascots now designed for every Olympics, also be cuddly and cute. In short, it must send contradictory messages.

Thus his first design for the Fourth Grace, resembles a Dalek, the friendly English robot-figure that became a sci-fi icon in the 1960s. According to other paranoid readings, it also resembles a fat banker with a cigar, a sparkling multi-colored gem on a ring, the collapsing donuts he mentioned, and other uncanny images assimilated to science fiction such as the stereotypical UFO. The difference between a bug-eyed monster and an Olympic mascot is not that great, and since Olympic cities demand a new blobby logo every four years to personify their unique status it isn't altogether surprising they should also ask architects to give them a blobby landmark.

Significantly, of the four competing schemes, the public warmed to Alsop's entry the least, giving it only 19 percent in a vote compared with Norman Foster's 30 percent. The explanation for this, according to one architect in Alsop's office, brings out a distinction between the iconic building and the landmark: "If you propose any icon the instant response is negative because it challenges perception: it is the nature of an icon. None of the other schemes were icons. They were landmarks."[8]

In other words, the landmark makes an impact but a familiar one, while the icon is always strange and challenging, disturbing and new. There is some truth in this, as we have seen with Pevsner and Sudjic's negative response to the iconic building. For Alsop it is a primary point, and we debated whether the iconic building really has to go beyond the accepted bounds of good taste and architectural history. He, like Gehry, admits to the shock-value of the unknown.

WA: Liverpool was definitely looking for an iconic building. It was only at the second stage of the competition that I realized our scheme was not yet iconic, and so we started all over again and went on to win.

LEFT: The Fourth Grace, Liverpool, first scheme 2002, sits as a multi-colored jewel on an open plaza with the Third Grace to the left.

RIGHT: Metaphorical analysis showing the Grace as Dalek, squashed donut, shower cap, gem, and fat man.

BELOW, FAR RIGHT: Will Alsop, Barnsley Masterplan, 2003. Form-less and unexpected shapes surprise the English vernacular.

While you could give Foster's and Rogers' schemes an architectural lineage, you could not do that with ours.

CJ: So where did it fit?

WA: We were very aware that the "Three Graces," the existing Edwardian buildings, were invented in those terms by the client especially for the competition. So we were then asked to invent the "Fourth Grace"—they actually called it that in the brief.

CJ: So you were under pressure to design a graceful, feminine building? What are the enigmatic overtones of the Fourth Grace— perhaps, blob-like?

WA: Maybe for other people. What interests me is to try to make something "form-less" in some way. This interest started when I was teaching at St. Martins in London, and a sculptor suddenly emerged with this piece of art, or lump of material, to be turned into art. It was very engaging and I thought, how extraordinary, you couldn't tell what it was. These sculptures looked completely random, with only a hint that the material was purposely manipulated. They were very flexible. And with the Fourth Grace, one could add bits, inflate, or deform the shape and it would not make any difference.

CJ: This reminds me of Rosalind Krauss' exhibition at the Pompidou Center in Paris in 1996: L'Informe. She collected those artists of the 1960s who wanted to make things formless—there's a genealogy.

WA: But that is an *art* genealogy, not an architectural one. Frank Gehry's designs are known as being blob-like but they are more to do

with planes. "Blob" is so meaningless, and derogatory, whereas the Fourth Grace is more a faceted, form-less thing.

CJ: Some see the facets as "gem-like."

WA: Not a precious gem, a rough diamond—more an industrial diamond. I'm happy with bits of rust, the melange of materials. That is deliberate, and contrasts with High-Tech architects interested in the beauty of details.

CJ: If you squint at your Liverpool design you can see a generic "fat face." English people will map it on to other familiar forms, such as the outer space robots, the Daleks.

WA: We are thinking of using hairy panels on the façade—using fibre optics—so that they move about in what is a windy place. They would appear to be out of focus. I hadn't thought of the Daleks, but that metaphor wouldn't upset me. The Atlanta Olympics invented a similar creature by consulting a computer to make something that would appeal to as many people as possible—a blur. This goes exactly with my notion of the form-less building that appears to be out of focus and always moving.

CJ: The Olympic mascot is an icon designed anew every four years for each city. It has to be unexpected but loveable.

WA: I have to admit to a link between what we did and a particular computer program where I can sketch and turn things around. It's called "Lightwave." You can skin the building, and then take the skin off and see the bones, the structure, and do it very quickly—faster than sketching. Paintings can give the notion of potential form, which you can then explore on the computer. I don't know how Frank Gehry works, but I tend to do all that design by myself. Then

I can sit down with the engineers and say that I know this scheme is going to work.

The Fourth Grace is held by two legs and the black ones on the side; it's a cantilever that is propped, with a garden inside. The whole structure is a kind of "scribble," which I am very interested in because it is an indefinite form. With the computer, we are able to deform the forms and get Piranesian endless space, the notion of not knowing where the internal space is going. And it would contain a five-star hotel, a public office maybe for Apple, a museum, and public garden for picnics at the top, all of which is free and inviting for all sorts of different reasons.

CJ: How would you describe the structural net, the deformed net?

WA: The structure is also the basis for the volume, it creates the volume. One of the considerations is to make it not look like an "inflated structure." Some of the late work of Henry Moore looks inflated because he did not make it himself. As architects using these types of form, you have exactly the same problem. If you are untrue to the material you are actually using, it is easy for it to become something else. Then it wants to be truly inflated!

CJ: As a deformed network, it relates to two other iconic buildings under way, one is Rem Koolhaas' building for CCTV and the other is Herzog & de Meuron's building for the Olympics in China.

WA: The stadium in China is a completely different structural principle while Rem's CCTV building is a more rectilinear, bent form.

CJ: Well, the structural expression of the members, like yours, is a series of faceted triangular, irregular points that are generated by the structure.

WA: OK, but Koolhaas is not using it to make such an expressive structure in a more curvilinear way. His is much more rectilinear form. If you take Rem's library building in Seattle—which I think is beautiful—it has rectilinear forms, with gaps in between, and is slightly rotated. He used the glazing bars to give what looks like stretch marks, which look beautiful because it is "unexpected." When the people of Seattle first saw it they did not know what to say about it or make of it and asked the question "What is it?" Curiously enough in Liverpool, apart from the critics, the good old Liverpudlians on the whole have not asked that sort of question—"What is it?"

CJ: What has been the hostile criticism?

WA: The usual comments. Do we need it? Is this another Dome? Will it cost a lot of money? Give us a hospital. Usual things. It comes from unfamiliarity, which is the disadvantage of competitions.

The Fourth Grace in its pier context, next to the Third Grace, left.

CJ: But, it's built into your statement that beauty *has to be* unexpected.

WA: Yes, but outside of competition, as for example in the English towns of Barnsley or Bradford, you start with a clean sheet of paper and work with the people alongside. When you get them engaged in the project and able to contribute and become part of it, then the question is never asked. I find that really intriguing. The big dilemma with a big competition is that it is more likely to create hostility.

CJ: Yes, but you cannot deny public the right to be hostile. It is an important part of the iconic building. It's a tradition that engenders a necessary paranoia—otherwise it lacks an electric charge.

WA: I agree, but you can actually get people in line beside you, creating that charge, if you are not in a competition. That is the nature of competitions and, by implication, the nature of planning committees. They have protected people and on the wrong assumption that the public does not want to know what we, as architects, can do. Now we begin to see that the people do want something extraordinary and "landmark" buildings, and new architectural tourism begins to emerge. Particularly in Liverpool where the extraordinary new is acceptable, alongside the extraordinary old as well.

Alsop, like Calatrava, has been influenced by Brancusi and applauds the way this sculptor separated himself off from the world, went outside the gallery system to fashion hermetic works, such as *The Kiss* and *The Table of Silence*. These went beyond the aesthetic codes and understanding of the time. By comparison Alsop's own works are form-less and unfinished but, he hopes, equally alien.

Once again we have reached the point where architecture approaches the condition of contemporary art and demands the surreal and unfathomable. Some people of Liverpool have rejected this extension of architecture saying that, unlike a work of avant-garde art, they will have to live with the graceless Grace forever. It is this kind of argument that Deyan Sudjic mounts against the scheme. Calling it "lurid" and a "liver-colored tottering spiral, propped up on spindly legs, ambushing the imperial Edwardian relics of Liverpool's past like something out of *The War of the Worlds*," he goes on to summon the usual objections. The proposal has no pressing need to exist, apart from regenerating the city; it will soon be an out-of-date gesture and fade as quickly as Art Nouveau; and it shows a lack of cultural confidence.[9]

There are good reasons for the "lack of cultural confidence" today. We are living through a period of cultural pluralism, in the West post-

Christianity, where conventions of value and architecture have given way to the open-ended signifier and people are indeed confused by these shifts. That does not mean there are no distinctions to be made or that anything goes, but rather that new, comparative standards are to be set.

In any case, in a failure of nerve that is typical when the iconic building is at its early stages, Alsop's Fourth Grace was canceled by Liverpool City Council and the other public funding bodies. Their claims were the usual ones: spiraling costs and the danger of a "Millennium Dome Mark II," that is, a public fiasco. Both claims could be challenged, as they were by Alsop; but whatever the truths there is also the question of ethical behavior. Liverpool won the award as the European City of Culture 2008, against many competitors including Birmingham and Newcastle, and it did so featuring the Fourth Grace in its publicity and promotion. This was worth quite a lot of money, as it had been to Graz in Austria, a city that also used an iconic building to garner the award. Once having won this designation using the design as a major focus you would have thought the City's Fathers owed the architect some commitment, or good manners—or, at least, an apology. Instead, the first Alsop heard of being fired was when he read the press release, a shabby evasion that speaks volumes about loss of nerve.

Seen in this light, Alsop's forays into the unknown are something like Calatrava's: a challenge for the tradition of the iconic building but not its ultimate expression. Take, for instance, his "flying tabletop" icons, one produced as a library for a deprived area of London, another for a College of Art & Design in Ontario. The latter pre-empted a Frank Gehry icon across the street, and Alsop, assuming it would be curvilinear, adopted the ultimate contrast.

Designing "boxes on stilts" was the accusation against Le Corbusier seventy years ago. Here, the box are much more boxy and the stilts are much more spindly. Their odd angles and multi-colors make the whole image, hovering over the existing Design School, more precarious. It looks exactly like the kind of project design critics used to trash in an architectural jury by snapping off the supports. "Unsubstantial," "too thin," they would say, and "not architecture!" Precisely; and therefore for Alsop a candidate for iconicity.

But, and this is what gives the building greater resonance, the flying tabletop makes intelligent functional sense. Its nine-story-high canopy allows in a lot of light to the older art school below, and it

ABOVE: Will Alsop, Peckham Public Library, London, 1999–2000, the first of several flying tabletops on canted stilts.

BELOW AND OVERLEAF: Will Alsop, Ontario College of Art & Design, Toronto, 2001–4. The all-over white surface, pixelated with black squares, sits atop the old design school on skewed, multi-colored legs.

opens street life to the public park that was cut off from local passage. The urban park had suffered problems typical to an underused green space—drug use and crime—and by providing a covered transitional area, Alsop has effectively added the extra use needed. Jane Jacobs, an inhabitant of Toronto, has insisted for many years that streets and parks have to be heavily used to be safe, and self-policed, so it's fitting that this architectural move should be made in her own back yard.

How the art and architecture students in Ontario are to be taught the rules of breaking the rules remains to be seen but, as an uncanny object raised on spilikins, it is hard to beat. The metaphors? "Computer punch card?" "Pixilated box sending an alien message in a code of black squares?" "All-over white cheese with deep window-holes?" "Le Corbusier done with multi-colored cocktails sticks?" Or simply, as it is known, the "flying tabletop."

LEFT: Will Alsop, Middlehaven Masterplan, the grid seen from above, bursting in color out of the gray urban utilitarianism.

RIGHT: Will Alsop, Shanghai Kiss, 2005. Viewing pods on a continuous loop are a big wheel or moving Eiffel Tower, a new icon to eye Shanghai.

Any one of these enigmatic signifiers may have shock value, and with Gehry's Museum next door, a dialogue will take place between the rectilinear and the curved. But to see what a whole landscape of Alsopian icons might look like, one has to examine his urban schemes. The Middlehaven proposal for regeneration shows a riotous assemblage of colors and shapes dropped between two walls of rectilinear infrastructure: in effect it's the world fair as urban strategy. Here Sudjic's objections are proven right, each gesture overwhelms the next. The result of simultaneous exclamation is white noise, not significance.

Yet, from a realist point of view, this cacophony is just a projection of the forces of late capitalism at work, precisely the goal that Shanghai and Las Vegas are setting themselves, the idea that every large corporation should have its large icon. "Chacun pour soi," as the French say of the marketplace, "et Dieu pour tous," except that now the hidden hand of God produces not harmony but monolithic cliché. Late-capitalism, producing naturally its large chunks of competitive real estate, is not known for its subtlety, or urban coherence. In this sense, Alsop's world fairs at least have the advantage of being unlikely. Like Claes Oldenburg's giant Pop icons, these urban gestures bend existing trends away from Main Street towards the commerce of the art gallery, and are all the more more interesting for that.

Zaha Hadid—Icons of Fluidity

Yet one of the artistic problems with Alsop's proposals is that they do not usually convey that sense of inevitability on which art thrives, its expression of internal logic. They feel somewhat alien and contrived—as he intends—and thereby what they gain in surprise, they loose in necessity. That is not true of Zaha Hadid's work. She is another contender for the mantle of *the* iconic architect, not only with fluid buildings based on her graphic work and paintings, but also in her persona as *the* architectural diva. She is often seen decked out in a spreading tent of Issey Miyake pleats, a monument of statuesque femininity, as concerned as Frank Lloyd Wright was with cutting an image as the implacable architect. La Zaha, as she is sometimes known, is inevitability itself.

Born in Bagdad in 1950 and trained at the test bed of experimental architecture, London's Architectural Association, she has suffered a few humiliations: for being an Iraqi, a strong personality, and a woman who stands out, with a swear-word or two. Having won the competition for the Welsh Opera House in Cardiff in 1994, she saw the commission slowly dissolve away after a campaign of innuendo about her competence and fear about the amazing style of flying beams. Her buildings seem to rush off the ground like rockets leaving at twenty degrees from a tilted launch pad. At least in her drawings, paintings, models, and computerized images they take off, and it is these four graphic media that have won her the fame. With Hadid, more than any other iconic architect, you have to see the graphics—at least in the back of your mind—while walking through the building, because they are an essential part of the message.

She models the space, light, and surface through the four media; she turns these representations into works of art themselves, and then sells the results, or exhibits them. Her work thus ends up in museums, as well as becoming the museums that house them. Six years after graduating from the AA in London, she had a major retrospective in her school! The architect as avant-garde artist, a road that many have traveled but few have taken very far, has led her to New York's Guggenheim Museum, San Francisco's MoMA, and countless other national galleries. It has even translated her iconicity into a major publishing enterprise, and she has had major glossy monographs produced by the key outlets, above all Japan's *GA Architect* and Spain's *El Croquis*. These two enterprises will publish twenty pages of multi-colored images on a single building with hardly a word of comment—

ABOVE: Portrait of Zaha Hadid by Steve Double.

RIGHT: Zaha Hadid, Rosenthal Center for Contemporary Art, Cincinnati, 1999-2003. The master of architectural representation, exploiting four different media for their utmost dramatic presentation of her idea of movement and anti-gravitation, Hadid has also used them to invent a complex space. (South-east corner sequence; perspex model study; cross-section rendering; computer painting of "Urban Carpet" and back wall; longitudinal section model of movement.)

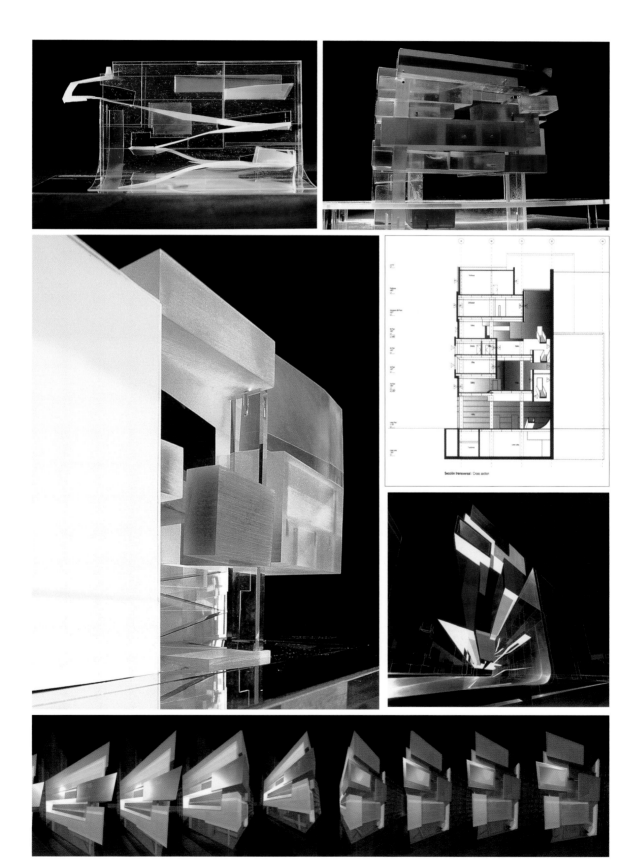

architecture as pure representation. If ever an architect knew how to feed the media frenzy for daring, glamorous imagery, it is La Zaha, and her "anti-gravitational architecture." With only a handful of buildings completed by 2004, it brought her the Pritzker Prize, a recognition that the image of the idea, in the age of the icon, is part of the idea.

This approach works out very well with her Car Park outside Strasbourg and her Ski Jump in Innsbruck, cases where frozen movement makes obvious sense. It also works for museums or galleries that need windowless volumes, and with this building type she has also won several competitions. A contemporary arts center in Cincinnati is a masterful display of interlocking volumes frozen in mid-flight. On the south side of a busy street, horizontal tubes of space in concrete, metal, and glass slide past and over each other, looking both like the Constructivist designs that inspired them and a series of stacked vehicles accelerating in traffic. At the east end they bundle closely together like stacked logs. One has to imagine these volumes as in her models, partly transparent and interlocking in section, providing a complex spatial route. It is the moving architectural promenade she dramatizes—as did Le Corbusier—with surprising punched-out voids set on a continuous path. "The lobby positions itself on the pedestrian level of the city as a fluid continuum of existing public paths," she writes, as if it were inevitable, "making a kind of public square . . . making the back wall a continuous surface." Or, as she calls it, "an Urban Carpet."[10]

"Urban Carpet" is pure AA-speak for a tough, reverberant swoosh of continuous hard surface leaping over bridges, traveling up escalators, zooming into cut-out voids, wrapping around atria, and shooting up on that back wall, eight stories, into outer space. "Urban Carpet!" There is not a piece of fabric the whole way. It doesn't matter because, like her graphics, Zaha's words, when she underlines them with a deep Iraqi rasp are utterly inevitable. Authoritative, decisive.

By the late 1990s, her winning competitions also became fairly predictable, as her reputation matured and clients became aware that she was an iconic architect and had suffered an injustice with the Cardiff scheme. Curiously, now the fact that she was an Iraqi woman who had been mistreated played in her favor. Her loss of Cardiff also helped other avant-garde architects win competitions, such as Daniel Libeskind with his entry for the Victoria & Albert Museum in London. By this time, and because of Bilbao, there was a general feeling that every city had to have the unexpected landmark, and

ABOVE: Zaha Hadid, Ski Jump, Innsbruck, competition first prize 1999, built 2002. A "landmark on a mountain for the Olympics," the ultimate commission for the architect of frozen movement. Sometimes the right architect gets the right job.

RIGHT: Zaha Hadid, Rosenthal Center for Contemporary Art, Cincinnati, 1999-2003. The temporary exhibition gallery, located at a busy urban intersection, becomes a new way to turn the corner in architecture, and one of the few convincing iconic buildings after Bilbao. Photographs by Helene Binet.

Hadid was one beneficiary of this change in mood. She won the competition for the Contemporary Arts Center, Rome, in 1999, and that for the Science Center in Wolfsburg, Germany, in 2000.

Here, as she says, "a mysterious object [gives] rise to curiosity and discovery . . . a degree of complexity and strangeness"—absolutely necessary for the iconic building—and then, just as inevitably, "however [it] is ruled by a very specific system." Of course, mystery *and* system—what could be more canonic to the iconic building? It makes one realize that to succeed, this type of object *must* be an oxymoron. And so the Science Center is partly a series of odd-shaped funnel-cones and partly a large-scale horizontal sculpture, predictably in scale with the other monoliths near by. Mystery and system continue in the spaces—a "crater landscape" with "wormholes" as she describes it—and then a set of normal entrances, lectures halls, and exhibition spaces (albeit in the shape of funnel-cones). The same oxymoron continues in the lighting—dramatic and dark but with illuminated focal points that pull you through—and the materials—reinforced concrete along the usual waffle method of structure and void, but now bent on the axes of movement.

If ever movement was frozen solid it is here in this horizontal concrete slab—a mighty bulwark of cantilevered triangles that looks like the proverbial spaceship hovering over the ground, except so heavily carried through that it is more a monument to the end of space travel than a harbinger of the future of featherweight travel. It is, however, an icon to the glories of this area, one that put the Volkswagen on the map, and a worthy successor to the former monuments of Aalto, Scharoun, and Schweger in the same city. It is meant to be seen as continuing the enlightened patronage of the company town, and does so with Hadid's consummate force.

More than any other iconic architect, she succeeds through consistent self-reference; her works carry the conviction of all art that gives the appearance of necessity, the coherence of an internal aesthetic system. Inevitable.

LEFT AND RIGHT: Zaha Hadid, Science Center, Wolfsburg, Germany, 2000–2004. A large slab, in scale with the surrounding blocks of late capitalism, hovers over the ground with an uncanny mixture of opposite qualities: heavy lightness, lightened darkness, bent waffles, and rationalized warps: the iconic building as oxymoron.

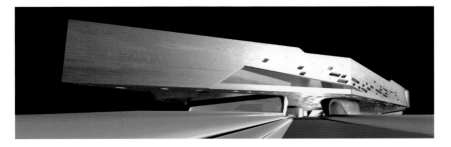

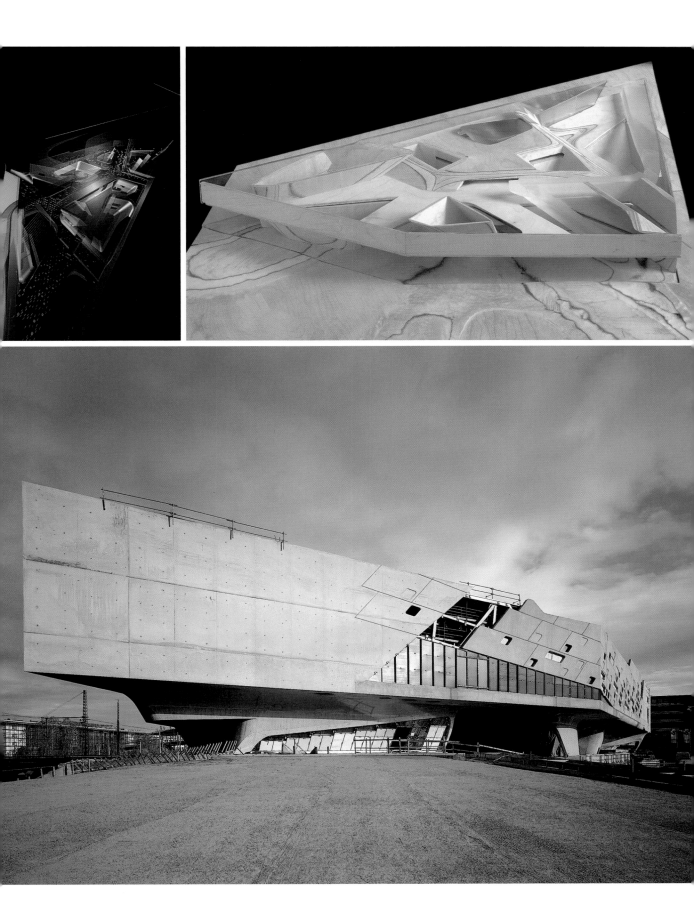

U R Feeling the Intellectual Icon

Peter Eisenman, like Miralles and a few other designers of an intellectual bent, pursues that paradox of the anti-icon icon. Being a contrarian has always interested this maverick, both for philosophical and social reasons. Born in Newark, New Jersey, in 1932, he has always worn his Jewish status in a forthright manner, sometimes using it to question the assumptions of a WASP society, sometimes using it to question assumptions about depictions of the Holocaust. Like Warren Buffett going against the stock market the more to beat it, Eisenman works systematically through the ideas of modern architecture the more to be non-modern. In a way, taking heart from the Deconstructionists, he tries to be non-everything, placing a "de-" a "dis-" or an "un-" before a cherished value of our time. This is amusing, especially since the tactic also can suddenly make him seem quite the reverse of the position he is questioning; that is, "ultra-" "hyper-" or "super-". Hence, when considering his anti-icon icons, it is profitable to ask whether they are not more "pro-pro." Who is to say?

He has designed several works that look as if an earthquake has struck them, one in Japan, which is not particularly fond of the metaphor. More cogently, he has used this formal system of deconstruction to create a new set of fractal buildings and, in an important way, he is the father of computer design because he was one of the first to understand its potential for generating emergent grammars. Whereas most early work in CAD (computer-aided design) used the tool to produce a building already worked out beforehand, Eisenman grasped the deeper point that it allowed us to think about multiple determinants differently. Codes of architecture could be programmed, run separately, and then conjoined to see what novel results could be thrown up. Mostly designers fed technical and morphological information into their machine; Eisenman also gave it semantic and philosophical data to chew on. An early case is a university building in Cincinnati that fractures and reassembles the old modern grammar of the structure to which it is attached. The result is a new form of contextualism, a fractal version, which also refers to the movement of tectonic plates, the earth as a moving body of material substance always self-organizing under our feet. The code is inanimate matter animated. But the structure that, more than any other, is an anti-icon icon, is his large landform for Santiago de Compostela, a non-building with an opera house, museum, and libraries. This was the focus of one of our many conversations.

TOP: Portrait of Peter Eisenman.

ABOVE AND RIGHT: Peter Eisenman, Memorial to the Murdered Jews of Europe, Berlin, 1998–2005. A grid of 2,751 concrete pillars is closely packed so individuals only can traverse them following a chaotic route to nowhere. "In this monument there is no goal, no end, no working one's way in or out."

Peter Eisenman, Aronoff Center for Design and Art, University of Cincinnati, 1989–96. Metaphors of tectonic plates, fractal nature, and the zigzags of the building to which it is attached.

CJ: You won the design for this "City of Culture" in 1999 and told me then it was only possible because of the "Bilbao Effect," a term you coined.

PE: Yes on both counts. Santiago wanted to produce a secular tourist attraction, other than the religious one they have, and they saw how successful Bilbao was for the economy of the Pays Basque. They wanted an alternative to the figural object of Gehry, so we gave them a landscape—a project totally "other" than Bilbao.

CJ: Your great attractor is 185 miles from Bilbao so it has to compete with it for tourists, but you said: "I'm a great beneficiary of Bilbao, they would have never picked me beforehand, or anything as radical."

PE: That's correct.

CJ: For me the design is important because of the way it mixes different qualities. Not only is it a landform building in the manner of Rem Koolhaas and the Dutch, but it is in a more literal sense because the landscape begins to come over it. Also, semantically, it merges several different codes. As well as the generative ones of deforming spatial grids, it refers to the Coquille St. Jacques—the scallop shell of St. James, which is the symbol of the city—and also it relates to the medieval city plan. It folds those diagrams into its generation.

PE: There's another code that you don't probably know about, and the idea of the ley-lines. The whole project is developed along these sort of Druidic ley-lines which led the people from France to Santiago. What we did was to extrapolate them. All of the deformations internal to the building are based on the deformations of these ley-lines.

CJ: Are the texts explicit, or are they only operative from a helicopter, or from your diagrams?

PE: No, no. They're explicit, affective physically. They're three-dimensional.

CJ: Will people be able to see when they're on a ley-line, or be given a map?

PE: No.

CJ: Will they ever see a scallop shell?

PE: No.

CJ: Would they ever know it's the old plan of the city?

PE: No.

CJ: But they will feel in the alleyways that they're in a kind of medieval situation in the present day.

PE: Yes. They will feel in the alleyways something, but it's not quite medieval and it's not quite modern. It's something else. In other words, my whole idea of affect is that you experience something, you feel something, you see something but you can't quite explain it. It has an Ur-dimension to it.

CJ: I call that the enigmatic signifier.

PE: Well, I'm glad you've got a term for it—I call it the blurred signifier.

CJ: OK. The enigmatic signifier starts in recent history with Ronchamp, and it comes through the Sydney Opera House and a whole lot of buildings up through Bilbao to your Santiago. You call it a what? An "Ur-"?

PE: An Ur-feeling. Something between understanding and not, let's say.

CJ: That's "U R feeling"?

PE: U R feeling. Some deep immanent sense that it's not quite what you know it to be.

"You are" feeling, a typical Eisenman pun on letters and a clever way to characterize how the enigmatic signifier works somewhere between understanding and sensing. This is an important point and his City of Culture is an important confirmation that the successful iconic building mixes different codes, that is languages and meanings from different walks of life—not just architectural or technical references. In Santiago it mixes codes from five discourses: the scallop shell, a traditional sign of pilgrimage and religion; the Cartesian city grid deformed, which is an architectural code; the ley-lines of prehistoric cultures; the medieval city plan; and the morphology of the existing hillside into which it is all carved, that is, nature. Having layered these

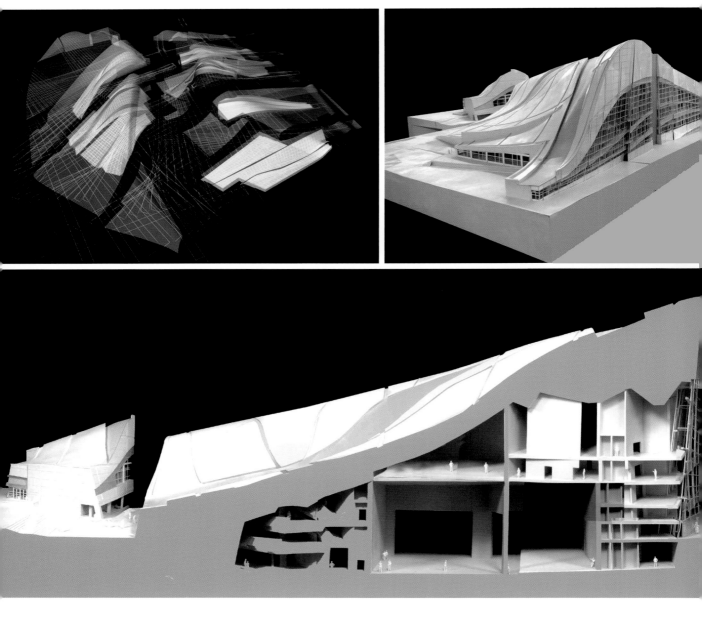

Peter Eisenman, City of Culture, Santiago de Compostela, 1999–2005, a landform comprising six buildings conceived in three pairs. The Museum of Galician History and the New Technology Center are one pair; the Music Theater and Central Administration Building are a second; and the Galician Library and Periodicals Archive are a third. The pairs are intermixed to "further complicate and enrich one's experience ... a rare opportunity to develop the interstitial space of the site."

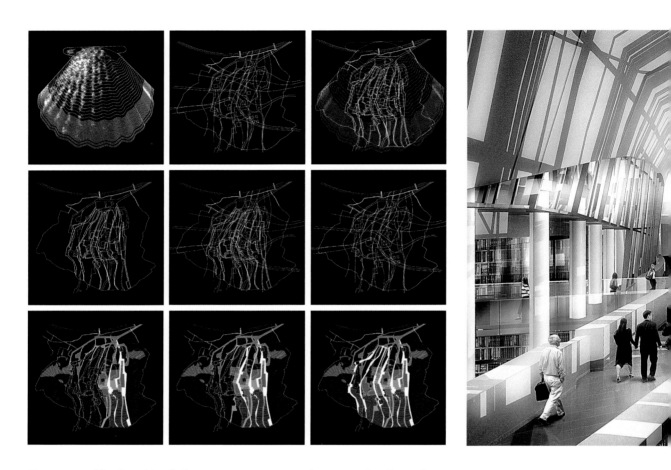

diagrams with the aid of the computer, a new language is allowed to emerge, which Eisenman then articulates. The resultant landform is thus biomimetic in some respects, and cultural and contingent in others, a cross-coding that is richer and metaphysically more convincing than one based on a single discourse.

With this building, unfinished at the time of writing, we have another contender for *the* anti-icon icon, a real hybrid of landscape and architecture. Eisenman is that rare breed of person who probably could design iconic buildings as convincingly as anyone, if he wanted to, but for reasons of temperament and belief chooses to put himself on the sharp edge of critical practice where the idea and gesture behind the building is often more important than the finished product. In the end there are few completely convincing iconic buildings that can sustain the kind of reading of a Ronchamp and a Bilbao, the standards for the emergent genre.

ABOVE LEFT: Diagrams of the scallop shell, old Santiago, ley-lines, and the site intermixed to produce interstitial space.

ABOVE: Interior linear atrium with its movement systems and overlapping functions.

Two Winners

Successful and Failed Icons

It is obvious, from the previous chapters, that one can generalize about iconic architecture, clarify the difference between successful and failed versions of the genre and write some of the rules for this method of rule-breaking design. I raised these points with Frank Gehry in the interview quoted at the outset, on the Bilbao Effect, and one can see from his words as much as his practice that he is fully conscious of the emergent tradition, although he is not without contradictions. On the one hand, I asked him what the difference is between a good and bad iconic building—and whether fish can inspire such architecture. "No," he answered, denying fish inspiration, "for me the building has to grow from the inside. I call this 'playing close to the bone.' The bone being the budget, the program, the context, and the culture it's in. If you ignore all of that and just make a thing, I think that is not a good icon."

On the other hand, I asked him the question in a historical way, pointing out how his curved buildings derived from a little whale-shaped room he had done in the early 1980s for an advertising agency. I got an interesting admission that clarifies a crucial point about how and when new grammars of architecture arrive. Was the Chiat-Day whale-room, I asked, where he really pushed the curved architecture?

FG: Absolutely, it is where I started and it was intuitive. What I was looking for, from the beginning, was a way to express movement with materials, and trying to get that into architecture. Accidentally, playing around with the fish-shapes got me there, very accidentally. The first was the big kitsch fish made of wood for a fashion house, thirty-five feet long, made of wood, with eyes, a fin, and a tail.

CJ: In the early 1980s you designed fish lights, for the company Formica, and then you built that Japanese fish restaurant.

FG: That was horrible, a super piece of kitsch.

CJ: It may have been horrible, but it opened up your experiments with the shape.

FG: Exactly; if I hadn't done those, I couldn't have done Bilbao.

CJ: Then the outdoor structure in Barcelona, which was a more abstracted fish.

FG: That is where I used the computer to perfect the building for the first time. And it was playing with the fish and getting the structure built in Barcelona. That fish opened the door and from then on, I had the beginning of a language that I could play with and build.

CJ: I am trying to get the difference between a good and bad icon . . .

FG: It ultimately comes down to the talent of the person who creates it. My experience with art, and here you are getting into the realms of art and sculpture, is that when I see something that I really don't like, I find that if I give it more time and see more examples of that person's work and if they are any good, I turn around quite strongly in their favor. You have to learn their language. If somebody puts a new language on the table, it has got to be disconnected in the first instance, it has to be shocking in a way, but not intentionally. I build a logic system for my work that seems careful. It looks like something that scares people and then after they see it for a while and they see other examples, then they begin to understand it. It is like you get trained in the new language, over time. So, it's what holds up over time that proves whether it is good or bad.

CJ: Well, the Psalms are right, with the new architecture you "have to taste and see." It is like wine-tasting, you have to grow your own new sensitivities.

In other words, the new language and metaphors—such as fish architecture—must be worked through again and again, over time and also in the same building, so that the grammar re-codes experience, educates a new taste. The good poet, as Wordsworth wrote, creates the audience by whom he is judged, and it is never easy nor without risk. We touched on some recent failures, and he expressed unease—

CJ: Do you feel there are questions of decorum and appropriateness —or does anything go?

FG: Not for me, no.

CJ: But, look what is happening today.

FG: Well, maybe that's where people are turning that corner. I do not feel comfortable with that.

CJ: There is Calatrava's Opera House, just opened in Tenerife, which has this great bird-like protuberance that people associate with a quiff of hair, architecture as hair-styling. This quiff serves no function except to be a huge icon for the city, and certainly it functions well in the travel advertisements.

FG: I like Calatrava a lot, but I'd have to go and see it. The same thing

Frank Gehry, Walt Disney Concert Hall, Los Angeles, 1988–2003. Acoustic diagrams also generate the exterior.

happens in Milwaukee where he creates a museum which is not really a museum. He just makes a big "thing."

CJ: It's an entrance to a museum.

FG: It becomes a gateway to the city. I haven't crossed that line, in spite of what people might think—but I certainly don't believe it. Disney Hall, for instance, grew from the inside out. It came from the requirements needed, and the acoustic interior that I wanted to express on the outside.

CJ: You're giving the classic architectural position, Frank, the functionalist and contextual argument.

FG: You know I'm an old guy. I haven't been able to cross that line.

CJ: Although many people think you're being tempted across it.

FG: I am having a hard time.

Hard time or not, it is obviously true that the success of Gehry's Disney Hall, equal to that of Bilbao, comes both from designing from the inside out and his having mastered the grammar of fish.

The Shape of Music

The Walt Disney Concert Hall in Los Angeles opened in October 2003, six years after Gehry's New Guggenheim. Winner of a competition in 1988, it thus took fifteen years to emerge through a tortuous process of changes in design, fallings out with and between the clients, and two recessions, in the early 1990s and after September 11th, 2001. In a way the building is a giant metaphor of this battle-scarred process and the riots of 1993 that marked this strife-torn city of minorities, a fitting image of sprawling pluralism. If LA is the ultimate heteropolis, the apogee of the melting pot and boiling pot, then it is appropriate that its crowning symbol floats, dances, and explodes at the top of its downtown acropolis. Architecture is frozen music, according to the cliché, but the sounds are not always harmonious or what the audience wants to hear.

It was hoped, by client and designer alike, to pull together this diverse and fragmenting city, to be a unifying force for the conurbation as a whole—"a living room for the city," as Gehry called it—and something that would galvanize the downtown economy and create ethnic peace. Never in LA history has so much civic idealism, and money, been invested in a prime piece of architecture. After Gehry's success at Bilbao, the stakes were increased. Everyone concerned felt the pressure, not least Gehry, who feared that the result, which had actually been designed before Bilbao, would be considered a pale imitation or something worse. The commercial implication? The sequel, coming before the original, was in danger of killing it. As the most self-conscious iconic building in the world, in the capital of glitz, its ostensible task was to change the local economy and architecture, once again. Nothing less. Out with that old cardboard icon of the Hollywood sign, in with the new shiny sculpture on the hill, Bunker Hill, the place where high-rise LA stops and monuments to culture and religion start, the site of Oscar ceremonies and empty boulevards.

To most people's surprise, even Gehry's, the original was as good as the sequel and, some critics claimed, even better.

That a work of architecture should have so much emotion and

Disney Hall, the sparkling city crown at the top of Bunker Hill.

money invested in it—the official figure is $274 million—is a sign of the times. Where a cathedral might have served such unifying functions in the past, Disney Hall was meant to reconcile an ethnically fractious community and provide a spiritual home to a spread-out population. The opening events bear this out. The adjacent boulevard was turned into a giant transparent enclosure for dining and civic celebration. From here fireworks could be seen exploding over the city, brilliantly deformed and enhanced in the stainless steel reflections. In contemporary terms this symbolized the communal campfire, with citizens gathering around, uniting building and city with the desert cosmos overhead, in a new theophony. Music, architecture, and a well-tuned universe, according to the Pythagorean tradition, are audible and visible manifestations of the divine.

This sounds portentous, but such thoughts are provoked by the building, and the fact that a demonstrative Catholic cathedral, designed by Rafael Moneo, opened on the LA acropolis at the same time. This was another enigmatic signifier and, given their close proximity, there was bound to be a comparison as to which one was the more spiritually convincing. Gehry's building shows that one does not have to believe in any scripture, or superior being, to relate to nature in its transcendent garb. Great music and architecture are enough.

If one compares the initial design with the final one, the centrality of music in the scheme becomes apparent. In the first design the glazed city "living room" dominates and the volumes are relatively inert. Then, after constructing thirty study models, along with the

BELOW AND OVERLEAF: Opening fireworks visually amplified in steel.

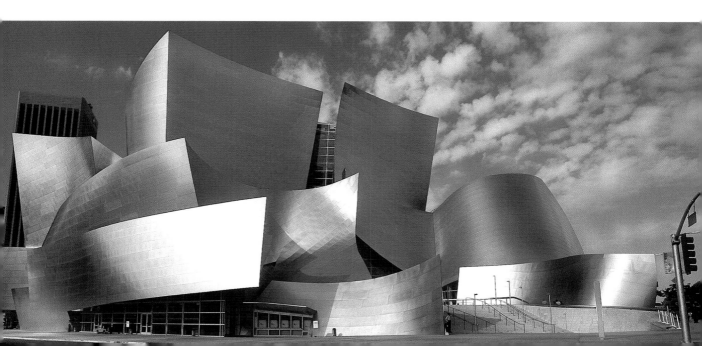

acousticians Yasuhisa Toyota and Minoru Nagata, Gehry designed the flowing curves literally from the inside out. The exterior is an icon of that acoustic interior. So, when the conductor Salonen wrote him a dedication "To the composer of the most beautiful frozen music of our time," he was referring to more than the standard cliché. The interior shapes have been likened not only to musical themes, but also to other metaphors that had become commonly applied to his work, such as "billowing clouds" and "furling sails." These images are apt, as is the comparison to the interior of some giant animal or whale.

The Douglas fir that is stretched over most of the surfaces, giving them a common golden hue, is also bent inward at the listener to reflect sound waves. This gives a gentle compression, a feeling enhanced by the fact that seats are stacked very steeply to make everyone as close as possible to the stage. The model is Hans Sharoun's Philharmonic Hall in Berlin and its steeply raked "vineyards of people." Gehry took the idea and compressed it even more, so there is not an acoustically dead seat in the house. As if to compensate for an inwardness that might have been claustrophobic, he has broken the space on its long axis and, unique for a building of this type, allowed in natural light and distant views. This release is welcome both emotionally and imaginatively: when listening to music one wants not just a sea of faces but a connection to the outside, the beyond.

Critics resonated appreciatively to the sensitive acoustics. "One could feel," Martin Filler writes in the *New York Review of Books*, "the thrumming bass line through the soles of one's feet." The effect

BELOW LEFT: Billowing acoustic clouds in the belly of a whale.

BELOW RIGHT: Organ pipes as "French fries" or "flying hosannas."

RIGHT: The space is compresssed, but released to light spilling in at the ends, rare in a concert hall.

BELOW: The Raised Garden, on two sides of the public, gives the downtown a public green, sheltered from traffic.

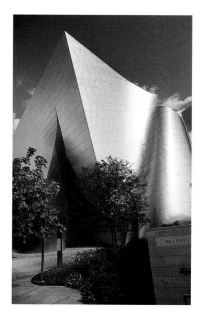

prompted Salonen to remark that the orchestra had a "newly discovered bass octave." Filler is also transported by the organ pipes as they "fly up like the hosannas ascending from the mouths of singing angels in Flemish Primitive paintings."[1] Another critic, Herbert Muschamp of *The New York Times*, compared them to "the bursting gilded rays of an altarpiece by Bernini."[2] To a third critic they recalled "French fries." We are back here in the world of metaphorical overkill, proof that we are again in the presence of an enigmatic signifier.

Verbal Evidence

As usual, the successful iconic building detonates a burst of verbal pyrotechnics, a beautiful logorrhea, as if the writer had to equal the structure with overflowing words. This was evident when Disney Hall was first unveiled to the public. Los Angeles journalists immediately responded to the welcoming presence of the huge glass foyer, the LA communal room that has now shrunk into the building, but also re-emerged on the side as a luscious garden in the air. They felt the generosity, as Gehry described it, "of a living room for the city . . . creating the kind of public architecture that is easy to walk into off the street, and in tune with the relaxed sensibility of Los Angeles." It has a relaxed, even populist air, but not a condescending or conventional informality. The entrance steps, for instance, flow easily and in great width up to the stainless steel curves that are then parted by glass facets to welcome you in. It's impressive but not monumental.

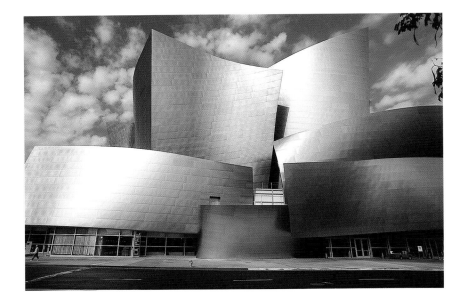

Leon Whiteson, writing for the *Los Angeles Times* in 1991, saw the early design in this positive light and in ways that were to become standard metaphors. He called it "a galleon in full sail . . . a cluster of superbly orchestrated eccentric shapes . . . and the interior, a giant wooden boat Gehry once dubbed 'Noah's Ark'."[3] Nautical images are the norm not only because the stainless steel billows out, but also because Gehry enjoys sailing, and likes making the comparison of stretched steel to taut sails. Here the wrinkles of Bilbao are ironed flat and visible joints are tucked out of sight. Thus a heavy galleon in full sail becomes the metaphor of choice for those conducting the guided tours.

Some of the early populist reaction was extremely negative. In fact, given the conflict in a city of minorities, the unusual forms were bound to spark a response counter to Whiteson. It was published in the letters column under the heading "Disney Hall: Work of Art or Wet Cardboard?" The galleon's curves were far from "superbly orchestrated" as he had claimed, but "ugly," what one writer called "deconstructionist trash," or "cardboard boxes inhabited by the homeless." The rage that an enigmatic signifier inspires equals the praise in hyperbole. Another writer saw the "joyful shapes" as too infantile, as "a playful child with tongue stuck out"; a third critic denounced the forms as "a fortune cookie gone beserk"; a fourth as "a clump of trash in the gutter"; a fifth as "a pile of broken crockery from an archaeological dig"; a sixth as "a rain-soaked cardboard dumped unceremoniously from a trash truck'; a seventh, again, as "an emptied waste basket." Such negative metaphors took the wind out of

LEFT: Glass facets of the public space burst through the waves of steel to welcome visitors up the steps.

RIGHT: Metaphorical analysis of a few of the critics' comments. Drawings by Madelon Vriesendorp.

Whiteson's "billowing sails." Then Gehry's supporters rallied with countervailing images, and attacks on the Philistines, who responded with yet more critical images—"a tornado," "a wax building left in the sun," and "Downtown after the Big One."

The war of metaphors simmered on for ten years with "Earthquake LA" battling it out in the mind's eye with "Marilyn's Skirt."

The hyperbole of 1991 was equalled at the opening in 2003, except now it shifted in a positive direction, as critics pole-vaulted over each other in ecstasy. The building was seen by Herbert Muschamp in delirious ways, as "a Moon Palace for the Hollywood Dream," "a luminous crescent," a series of "drive-in movie screens," "ships prows," "a flowering cabbage," and as "the Rust Belt before the Rust." As he observed, "If you're unwilling to mix your metaphors you've come to the wrong place."[4] How true, and the London critic Marcus Binney added his "French fries" to the bouillabaisse and, in order not to be outdone, stirred in "an inverted armadillo" and "kinetic painting."

The verbal evidence again supports the argument that the enigmatic signifier provokes an emotional response—positive and negative—rather like a religious icon, except that now there is no preexisting referent to the signifier and no doctrine to uphold. If the building is seen in this light, as a shrine or place of pilgrimage to an unknown religion, and if many thousands pass through it listening to the guides and wondering about the strange comparisons that pop into their mind, it makes sense to ask the basic question: just what is it that the successful iconic building is doing? At a minimum, with its sensuous materials and mixed metaphors, it is heightening experience. Beyond this it is playing on positive natural overtones and paranoid comparisons—both codes of natural creation (animal and vegetable) and destruction (explosion and deformation). When coherently aligned with metaphors of music—the deeper meaning of the concert hall—these codes guide interpretation along very general paths and are not just random associations. The transformation of similar shapes gives this coherence.

The ultimate meaning of the iconic building may be partially open—and that is the point of the open work in our time—but it is consistent enough to provoke the pilgrim, or tourist, to try to decipher the icons. The successful building is, in effect, a giant iconostasis asking to be decoded, which is why people come back again and again to try to fathom the meaning.

RIGHT: The Founders Room: billowing skirts in polished stainless steel, and shown as 5 on the plan, below.

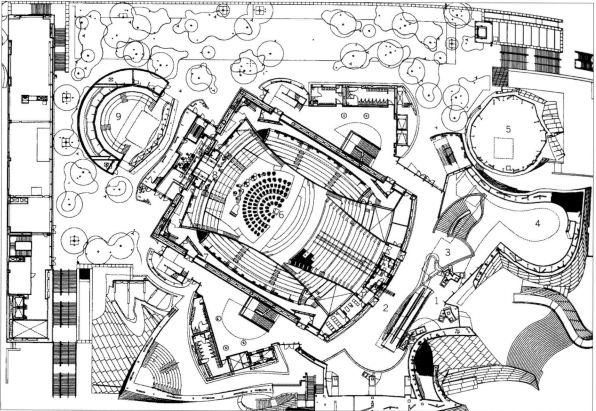

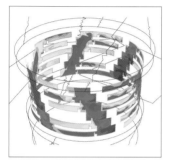

LEFT: Norman Foster, Swiss Re headquarters (30 St. Mary Axe), London 2000–2004. A swelling curve, smaller at the base and sharper at the top, like the beautiful entasis of a Corinthian column.

TOP: Portrait of Norman Foster by Carolyn Djanogly.

ABOVE: Atria twist up the outside pulling the air up six floors and naturally ventilating the skycourts, one of several ecological goals.

The Cosmic Skyscraper

The iconic building need not be freeform, nor completely unusual. Norman Foster's bullet-shaped tower in London is a case of the successful icon actually being a rational, well-functioning building. It is also the most original and elegant skyscraper ever produced in Britain. It has all the hallmarks of the iconic building—the reduction to a striking image, a prime site, and a riot of visual connotations. When first unveiled it was nicknamed "the gherkin," not because it looks much like an edible, green pickle, but in order for British understatement to triumph over phallic overstatement. It is popular with the media, and indeed the public, for the other obvious reason that it breaks the skyscraper straitjacket. It's not the usual flat floor upon floor—all the same—but a curved spiral of ascending skycourts. These elegantly punctuate the repetitions and afford wonderful diagonal views across six floors: "villages" as Foster quaintly calls the clusters of vertical space.

Critics again responded to the visual stimulation with a roll call of comparisons. For Jonathan Glancey of the *Guardian*, the tower is a "dirigible" with an "airship profile" or a "space rocket" and its top floor is a "glamorous restaurant with a James Bond" touch.[5] That is, mechanical images of control, levitation, futurism, and power dominate. For Deyan Sudjic of the *Observer* it is "a muscular steel basket sheathed in a smooth glass skin . . . wearing giant argyle socks"—the diagonal facets dominate.[6] Other critics likened it to a torpedo, a baguette loaf, and, negatively, a fat banker in a stocking suit. Actually the design of the Swiss Re headquarters started off life as a "stretched blob" conceived as a city landmark.

The first model had an egg shape and then, after wind and structural studies, re-emerged as other natural metaphors—not only the farfetched gherkin of the tabloids, but a more plausible and welcoming pinecone and pineapple. It shares its diagonal close packing with these plants and it is this organic quality which probably makes it so inviting to the public. The iconic shapes, that is, the inherent similarities of form, strike a balance between threatening and friendly images, the organic and the mechanistic. As nasty machine it is a rocket, a screw, and a bullet; yet as a familiar body part it is a penis, a brain, and a finger. Or is the comparison a pinecone, a Russian doll, or a cigar? The metaphorical overkill, as usual with the visual icon, is essential. Similarities abound, contradictions are pulled together, and it has just the right mixture to inspire a bit of paranoia. New and threatening it is, but in familiar ways.

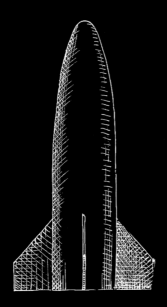
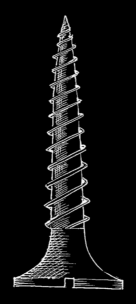

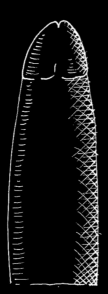
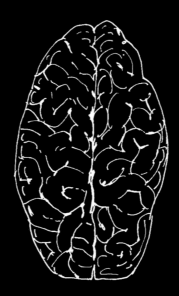

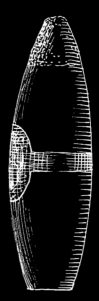

To explore this further, I talked to Norman Foster about the way this supercharged symbolism challenged that of St. Paul's Cathedral, and is deepened by everyday functional considerations. Especially interesting was the way Foster justified his curved skyscraper with many ecological determinants.

CJ: As a modern architect, I suppose you have a deep suspicion of the monument—especially in the 19th-century sense—and a wariness of images that are self-consciously imposed. So you would hate designing Swiss Re as a "gherkin," as it's been mis-labeled, and you don't usually design with iconic shapes.

NF: I think you search for as many anchors as you can find. Anybody who is trying to optimize on a design opportunity is simultaneously thinking of the problems from many different vantage-points.

CJ: But, in the way that the architect Jörn Utzon used orange peels to generate the Sydney Opera House, you have used the egg as a model. His is the most iconic building in Sydney, the symbol of its renewal, and your Swiss Re will be iconic in London. So I ask you *how* you see its symbolism? Although the gherkin reading is fun, and shows it's a pop building, how would you want it to be read, publicly?

NF: Well, the "gherkin" label has a dismissive element, journalistically, but it's interesting that the design captures the imagination, whether critically or otherwise. The one-liner also reflects the little Englander context; such a comment would be unthinkable in, say, Spain. I think the building comes out of very considered responses to the perceived needs of the building in the space of the City of London, the context of the City, on that particular site.

CJ: You're talking about the view in, the way it's seen curving from the outside so as to lessen its volume. Its bulk looks much smaller than its half a million square feet. Also, versus the flat skyscraper, the curves lessen the wind pressure at the base—so it doesn't create those horrible gusts.

NF: I'm talking about the way the building is seen from the outside and the wind, yes, and the way that the building is generated internally.

CJ: Also the green agenda?

NF: Yes, the whole ecological issue, the way in which it can create a more benign interior environment. We've developed the idea from the Hong Kong Bank in 1986 and the Commerzbank Headquarters in Frankfurt in 1997. With Swiss Re the six-story-high gardens that spiral up, all nine of them, change their vegetation depending on the

LEFT: Metaphorical analysis of a few comparisons. Drawings by Madelon Vriesendorp.

BELOW: Wind diagrams helped to generate the building. The streamlined shape means that, compared with a rectilinear tower, there is less downdraft at the bottom. What is more, the diagonal skycourts with differing air pressure further aerate the building.

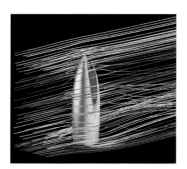

direction that they face—we hope there will be the so-called Asian garden, the North American garden, the Mediterranean garden—all visually interconnected.

CJ: So you see it as a *green* spiral—that's your answer to the gherkin. Public symbolism, if it is so explicit an icon, demands a content worthy of being expressed.

NF: But also it is a question of satisfying a very conservative, institutional market that wants a traditional type of accommodation. The way in which you create these relatively shallow spaces for an institution that is essentially European—not an American-based company, not with that different tradition of the deep-floor-plate—is by creating these green lungs and then shifting them so they become continuous spirals. Those become the means of the climate modifiers, the means that reduce the energy and also produce a more acceptable internal environment where the population of the building can have an involvement and a control over it. That's only one part of the story. I could describe it from other directions, in terms of its slippery shape.

CJ: You're saying that the symbol grows from the inside out, and *that* gives it integrity.

NF: I'm also aware that, unlike Manhattan, which is gridded and ninety degrees, the City of London is a different animal. The site is located away from all those so-called protected view-cones of the historic core, of St. Paul's Cathedral. This area has what is the closest London has ever got to a cluster of tall buildings, and one can create a breathing space, a kind of lung in the City, and it is arguably better, doing something that is relatively narrow at its base which will swell out as it goes up.

CJ: You *do* have multiple determinants and they are well resolved. Swiss Re is going to be the most important skyscraper in London for some time—the building type at which it has never excelled. It's almost as tall as the other big building near by?

NF: It's ten feet shorter than the NatWest Tower.

Foster was extremely proud of the way this tower was 50 percent more energy-efficient than comparable buildings in London and also how, with its serrated spirals in plan, it afforded more perimeter views for the many inside, not just the privileged few on the edge. As a designer associated with High-Tech and super-efficiency, Foster always has a list of requirements solved, ready to overwhelm the

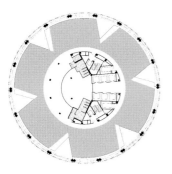

ABOVE: The serrated plan gives more people more perimeter views, natural ventilation and light.

OVERLEAF: In a square city, the towering pointed dome becomes as exceptional as St. Paul's. A spectacular 360-degree panorama over the city ends in a small, cosmic domelet. Like John Soane, Foster inverts the Pantheon convention for signifying the heavens. Instead of a solid masonry support, the domelet is held by light-filled mullions.

audience. He is the coiled spring of functionalism set to burst open at the first doubt and, like many English Protestants, he is a believer in pragmatic truth. This means his work, like that of Renzo Piano and Richard Rogers, may be less cogent at the symbolic and sculptural level, so I questioned him on these points.

CJ: Like the Reichstag, the tower's crown will become a beacon at night. I may be wrong, but presently the top looks a bit weak and is *not* open to the public. Let me put the symbolic issue crudely like the public newspapers and, I suppose, the Dean of St. Paul's. This building will be, since St. Paul's Cathedral, the most important curved landmark, or "dome," in London. Because it's so provocative and well done it will become a secular symbol and here its cosmic and ecological meanings are important. They provide fitting orientations for the 21st century. The sun, the wind, the spectacular view, the cosmos become the protagonists and, let's say, *sotto voce*, that this orientation is what the Church used to be about. This is the answer to St. Paul's dome—a cosmic dome.

NF: It has been difficult enough to hang on to the idea that the top is transparent and inhabited and not the kind of plant room usually put there. In recent meetings I've had with the client, we've been concentrating energies at improving the bottom of the building— which has been under a lot of threat in terms of subleases for commercial space. We have fought these battles successfully and I think we've generally calmed that down. I think we need a convincing proposal for the top. The client is adventurous enough, as a point of principle, to really want to do this building. I can't think of any such British client who could have handled this project, hung on in there, and, at a very strong political level, have said: "We're not going to Canary Wharf; we're not doing anything else. This is the building we want, and we want it there. If we can't have that, then we'll go somewhere else. Thank you very much." They also have a very strong eco-morality. I think we can probably eventually target them on the top of the building.

This conversation occurred in 2001, when the building was under construction, and Foster did manage to persuade the client that the top floors be usable and celebrate the panoramic view and sky. The pity is it turned out to be a private restaurant, not a public cosmic observatory along the lines of Hadrian's Pantheon, and there is no

reason not to demand such a historical standard for this kind of space, if it is going to challenge St. Pauls Cathedral and become *the* iconic building of London. This is the double-bind of the genre. The better the building gets and the greater its civic importance, the higher the measure goes. With all its ecological innovations and striking shape, it has set one benchmark for the skyscraper to meet; it is not a complete realization of the cosmic symbolism inherent in its genesis, but is certainly a step in that direction.

Architectural Virtue

Other, more purely architectural qualities, also make it a significant step in skyscraper development. Aesthetically it has surprising, emergent virtues, whether intentional or not. The diagonal facets—the "Argyle socks," according to one reading—occasionally look like stacked diamonds. This is quite unexpected, since one normally reads such a spiraling shape on the diagonal, and it provides added interest. When the sun strikes these facets and they are reflected on to the city pavements or in offices across the street, the old expressionist dream of a crystalline city of towers becomes just imaginable. Equally fascinating are the number of readings of the skin, structure, and interiors. They are layered in such a way that silver and black diagonals alternate with a horizontal grid of glazed space behind and contrast with the heavy, white, structural V-shapes. There is much visual ambiguity to enjoy here, as much variety as the various metaphors.

But what clinches the building in architectural history is its place in a line of centrally planned towers. Every type of skyscraper has its inherent form of beauty—whether in the shape of a needle, a slab, or a cluster—and Swiss Re puts itself very much in the first category of needle or spire. The Seagram Building and CBS in New York have jointly, and for long, held the honor of being contenders for the most elegant shaft, but they are both rectilinear. Their square geometry not only created anomalies on the corner, which Swiss Re avoids, but inconsistencies in structural loading, that the circular layout also overcomes. Are these geometrical innovations merely of academic interest? No more so than refinements in any art. Just as most visitors to the Parthenon enjoy the entasis of the columns—the way they swell out toward the middle and taper near the top—so too most people will perceive the entasis of Foster's creation, the way it curves gently out and then rushes inward toward the nose-cone. These

The diagonal facets give many surprising readings, since they are flat sheets of glass set in a curved profile. View down one of the hanging gardens.

refinements were carefully correlated by computer for their multiple implications in terms of cost, wind pressure, and visual delicacy. They are not accidents, but the result of selective pressures, the competition of an in-house beauty contest.

In effect, the tower is an example of propositional beauty, the fulfilment of an architectural idea, the round, centrally planned skyscraper. No one had built it before, especially with entasis, and so, like a mathematical proof that zeroes in on a single answer, we have here the rare case of elegant harmony that comes from solving a problem that had never been put this way. While Swiss Re is an iconic building with bizarre associations necessary to the unusual shape, it is also something that seems quite inevitable, as do all propositions clearly put.

Surprising Conclusions

BELOW LEFT: Colin Fournier and Peter Cook, Modern Art Museum, Graz, 2001–2003. "The friendly alien," as Fournier characterizes it, or "an animal with its back hugging a chair," as Cook calls it, is "a blue bubble," according to the local inhabitants, a blob building grafted on to the historic center. The City Fathers' hope: "It is meant to do for this city what the Guggenheim Museum did for Bilbao."

BELOW RIGHT: The section, plan and structure of the blob show how it nestles efficiently into its right-angled environment of setbacks.

A New Era?

There are basic questions posed by all these iconic buildings. Do they usher in a new era of architectural creativity and freedom, or are they, as Deyan Sudjic hopes, like the extraordinary blooms of Art Nouveau, a flowering that indicates imminent death?[1] My view, supported by examples since Ronchamp and the early 1950s, reveals that there is a long-term global trend, which has deep and irreversible reasons for existing: commercial and spiritual. These are amplified by the decline of conventional religions and historical iconographies. The iconic building is not going to go away, and may indeed increase in volume, as long as these widespread forces continue. Art, and the museum as a building type, have not so much replaced religion and the cathedral, as they have just moved into positions formerly occupied by them. Absence of strong belief in any metanarrative, ideology, or religion has characterized post-modern culture for several decades and is a strong motivation for the iconic building to become an enigma.

The drawings in the preceding pages vividly depict the emergent zoo of contemporary architecture, an extraordinary liberation of the imagination unprecedented in its scale and virtuosity (and lack of taste). It's a wonderful sight, and—admittedly—a horrible one. As I have pointed out, the genre seeks to provoke that strange combination of admiration and disgust, delight and paranoia. The

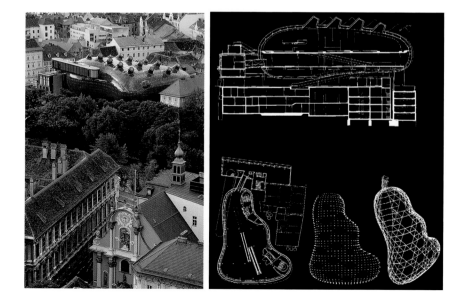

mixture is over-determined. Given the desire of society and architects to have great icons and yet not to agree on any iconography, they will inevitably produce enigmatic signifiers of varying quality.

While the iconic building is relatively recent and special to our time, it is only one of five or six important trends of contemporary architecture. It is certainly the most visible shift in what I have called the "new paradigm" in architecture but, from the point of view of underlying movements, not necessarily the most profound.[2] The move to a complexity paradigm, stemming from the new sciences of fractals, chaos, and self-organizing systems, is *the* seismic shift going on beneath the surface. It, and computer-aided design, may often facilitate the iconic building, but they are very long-term—virtually a one-way shift.

To gain perspective on the iconic building it is worth returning to the historical situation, when it emerged from the crisis of the monument, a condition that continues to create it.

Louis-Philippe Stumbles on the Enigmatic Signifier

Most monuments built today suffer a predictable ignominy. Except for the rare case, such as the Vietnam War Memorial in Washington DC, the grand civic building or sculpture is not dedicated to an event that people can long remember or find significant. After a few years the very artefact that is meant to stimulate memory becomes invisible and forgotten, or worse. When styles and ideology change the wrong symbol just reminds people of previous folly and execrable taste.

This perplexity became apparent in late 18th-century France with three transformations: fast and revolutionary political change, a commercial culture based on the turnover of products, and the growth of pluralism and agnosticism. All three forces worked together to make the idea of a permanent monument look very doubtful. One can find this skeptical mood emerging where least expected, in the layout of commemorative royal squares in Paris. In 1749, the main focal point that now connects the Louvre with the Arc de Triomphe, today called the Place de la Concorde, was designated the Place Louis XV to memorialize the permanence of monarchy. In 1757 the magistrates commissioned a bronze statue of the King on a horse, a triumphant figure like that of Marcus Aurelius in Rome. But the name, usage, and symbolism did not last for very long. During a marriage celebration of the King's son, in 1770, a panic during the

ABOVE: Fountain in the Place de la Concorde, Paris, on the site where the guillotine did its work on Louis XVI. The imagery, designed by Hittorf with dolphins and nautical themes, memorializes not the events that changed France, but the naval ministry opposite and, to obfuscate further, uses Roman symbolism to do so. The triumph of piety and beauty over truth.

RIGHT: The Obelisk of Luxor, a monolith of pink syenite 75 feet high and weighing 250 tons, was presented to Louis-Philippe in 1831 and erected in the square. The hieroglyphs commemorate the deeds of Rameses II (13th century BC).

fireworks left 133 dead. This was a bad omen, as often in history events restructured the meaning of architecture and public squares. After the Revolution of 1789, the statue of Louis XV was pulled down. The King, like Saddam Hussein, was publicly de-monumentalized and replaced by a giant figure of Liberty. By 1792, the name of the square was changed to Place de la Revolution. This was the first of several aliases.[3] In the same year a guillotine was set up in the square, and the next year it started claiming its victims: King Louis XVI and his wife, Marie-Antionette, who had been married in the same place more than twenty years previously. Then, among others, Danton, Robespierre, and Mme Roland, who observed ruefully of the symbolism: "O liberté, que de crimes on commet en ton nom."

Between 1795 and 1815 the square became "Place de la Concorde"; then, with the Restoration it was resurrected as "Place Louis XV," briefly. Then, with a change of monarchical symbolism in the 1820s it was designated "Place Louis XVI," to acknowledge the regicide. Finally in the 1830s, it was re-christened "Place de la Concorde"—although Discorde would have been more to the point.

All of this impermanent permanence was not lost on the then King Louis, Louis-Philippe. He pondered the implications of his regal predicament and its symbolic niceties. By previous tradition a square should have the name and statue of a royal personage, yet after the Revolution this system of unification became its reverse: divisive. What to do? A visit by the Muslim ruler, Mohammed Ali, fortuitously provided a solution. He had given the Christian British an obelisk, Cleopatra's Needle, and now he donated another one, borrowed from Luxor and etched with hieroglyphs, to the Christian French. Conveniently, the messages carved by the ancient Egyptians, referring to the deeds of Rameses II, signified little to the Muslims and Christians, except the connotations of mysterious power. Louis-Philippe had thus stumbled on the answer to the eternal question: how to make a monument that remains permanent. By making it enigmatic, but in several particular ways. He underlined the virtues of this obelisk to his Prefect. "It would not recall a single political event," he remarked and, he might have continued, 'but it *will* signify royal power in general."

What a brilliant insight, and an evasive action, at one and the same time. Let us call it the Obelisk Solution. It is one intelligent response to the present predicament of the monument, because for a clear iconography that will be destroyed by changes in politics and culture, it substitutes both unfathomable overtones and precise meanings. We have seen that Daniel Libeskind used a variant of this strategy in winning the competition at Ground Zero; his design used precise denotations and fuzzy connotations (see pages 84–6). The Obelisk Solution is more than abstraction, the modernist method of dealing with the monument, because of its appropriate suggestive overtones, but abstraction does play an important role.

Eiffel Adds a New Experience

We can see this with the most important monument ever constructed in France, the Eiffel Tower. Designed by the engineer Gustav Eiffel for the Universal Exhibition celebrating the hundred-year anniversary of the French Revolution, it was first of all just an abstract structure of metal, something utilitarian to ascend. Secondly, and by association, it was an abstract bridge tilted vertically. Eiffel was already famous for cantilevering bridge sections from one side of an open gorge to the other so that they would meet miraculously in the center and come to the most proficient structural stability. Here the bridge was cantilevered, as it were, from the earth straight up at the moon to meet its other half in fantasy—the "ultimate Tower of Babel," as it was termed in the press, and then mercilessly attacked.

At 300 meters (980 feet) it would be the tallest tower ever built, the equivalent of today's 100-story skyscraper, and it was obviously meant to be the last word in iconic building (though the term was not then in use). This height became itself a paranoid symbol, and so by a bizarre logic the Committee of Three Hundred was formed to fight it every meter of the way. Three hundred artists, scientists, and statesmen wrote a denunciation in *Le Temps*. They included the painter Bouguereau, the architect Charles Garnier, and many famous writers such as Alexandre Dumas. They protested at "the useless and monstrous Eiffel Tower." "Is Paris going to be associated with the grotesque, mercantile imaginings of a constructor of machines," they asked rhetorically, "to be irreparably defaced and dishonored?"[4]

And then, with a clinching sneer against Yankee greed and philistinism, the case was completed. "For the Eiffel Tower, which American commercialism itself would not want, is, without any doubt, the dishonor of Paris. Everyone knows it, everyone says it, everyone is deeply afflicted by it, and we are only a feeble echo of universal opinion."

Gustav Eiffel, Eiffel Tower, Paris, 1887–9. A utilitarian structure without an original use, this icon of Paris has become the ultimate Rorshach Test, meaning everything and nothing for countless Parisians—both the triumph of Modernism and Nihilism. Conceptually, it is four lattice columns swooping into the

sky, cantilevered against wind pressure. It is tied together at the base by a classical lattice arch, another visual gesture that works well in counterpoint to the swoops, but it is the contrast with Paris and the experience of ascension that mark it as one of the first successful iconic buildings.

"Universal opinion?" The tower *was* ugly, utilitarian, overweening, useless, without iconographic intent, except to become the biggest thing in the world (that well-known aspiration of the iconic building). That is, it was all these things from the viewpoint of the past, the previously reigning codes of classicism. But, to Eiffel the engineer, it was something else, created by following inventive structural logic wherever it might lead:

> I think, myself, the tower will be beautiful. . . . The first principle of architectural aesthetics is that the essential lines of a monument are determined by its perfect accord with its purpose. Of what factor have I had to be aware, above all, in my tower? Of wind resistance. Well, I maintain that the curves of the four edges of the monument [the four arches], which my calculations have furnished me, will give an impression of beauty, for they will reveal to the eyes the daring of my conception.[5]

It was disingenuous, of course, to hide behind his calculations, as if their iron logic had forced the solution on him and not the old, indeed classical, solution of the four arches at the base (these curves are much more visual than they are functional). And Eiffel, as the critics said, made a pile of money, from the concession granted him to run the whole tourist enterprise. Thus, among other things, greed rather than necessary function was indeed the motive. The "hatpin," as it was dubbed, only gained a purpose as a broadcasting tower fifteen years later. But the four visual swoops to the top, at a scale no one had seen before, gave an external appearance that was uniquely powerful; and an internal traveling experience that no one had ever had before. It was this experience that transformed the useless structure into becoming *the* symbol of Paris, and for the world, France.

Being wise after the event, we recount the struggle Eiffel had as the classic story of his Modernist daring versus reactionary taste, and congratulate ourselves inwardly that we wouldn't be as stupid as the academics and artists who rejected this, the most famous innovation of the 19th century. We would be out there with the captains of capitalist society, leading the enlightened taste forward, with the engineers, the Cubists, Futurists, and Dadaists, and art dealers, and tourist agencies.

The Eiffel Effect, like the later Bilbao Effect, was invoked to justify not only some great individual works of innovation, but also the exploitation of the Parisian suburbs by a Modernist ideology allowed free reign. The deeper meaning of the Eiffel Tower is not its space-time aesthetic celebrated by historians such as Sigfried Giedion, but its leap into the unknown, a gamble that paid off. Equally, of course, it might have failed. The designer was gifted and well experienced, but the innovative biggest building in the world might well have resulted in the image of a utilitarian prison, like the area of La Defense, the 1960s development north of the Arc de Triomphe. The modernist reflex is as unpredictable as the traditionalist. With the open work, open to innovation and new interpretation, there are no guarantees of outcome either way; there is only the framework of similar attempts we can bring to bear in judging the design.

De Chirico Names the Enigma Variations

The confusions in taste and outlook that typified the time of Eiffel are key for understanding the iconic building today. The prevailing orientation was disorientation. By the early 20th century, the artist, architect, and writer faced a double loss: the disappearance of a traditional audience and the erosion of public symbolism. The twin declines—in faith and the cultivated public—were accompanied by the extraordinary success, and domination, of the market system. This led to an increase in competitive differentiation and, in the artistic world, the emergence of a bewildering set of new "isms." Like changing products in the market, they were in danger of becoming "wasms."

In literature this transition, and feeling of loss, is marked in the early 1920s with T.S. Eliot's *The Waste Land* and James Joyce's *Ulysses*. Both writers were Christians and they responded to the crisis in their worldview with a superabundance of arcane and historical allusions. Their ironic look at religion both accepted and denied faith in the same breath—it was an early version of today's "negative theology"—and they both hoped to substitute the idea of a new tradition for the rupture of the old one. The Modern tradition of Eliot and Joyce thus meant the continuity of a spiritual outlook by shifting the burden of religion to the role of culture as a whole—a complex mixture of high and low tastes, Dante and music hall comedy, or their own characters, Prufrock and Bloom.

James Joyce remarked about *Ulysses*, half jokingly as usual, "I've put in so many enigmas and puzzles that it will keep the professors busy for centuries arguing over what I meant, and that's the only way of ensuring immortality." He was successful beyond his own hilarity.

Giorgio de Chirico, *The Uncertainty of the Poet*, 1913. Familiar objects are made enigmatic by distortion, strange juxtapositions and long shadows. The train in the background threatens the classical and organic worlds in the foreground, the metaphysics of one age replacing another.

There is now an academic industry devoted to explicating every difficult passage, and also the very streets of Dublin that Leopold Bloom walked as the modern Ulysses. The tourist business of Dublin now regularly cashes in every June 16th, Bloomsday, on the same benefits of enigma.

In the 1910s, the Italian artist Giorgio de Chirico, faced with similar perplexities of the age, was asked what he painted and replied, "the enigma." The phrase recurred in a series of paintings, *The Enigma of an Autumn Afternoon*, *The Enigma of the Oracle*, etc., that conveyed a strange mood of melancholy, dissociation, and historical loss. Typically the subject had an urban and architectural background, often an Italian piazza seen at six in the morning, when there are few people and many shadows. The place looks like an historical stage set after the actors have gone home, with some uncanny objects demanding attention. What is that outsize torso supposed to be, headless and legless? Not quite a classical quote, it is engaged with a bunch of bananas in casting more long, doleful shadows. The feeling in all this Metaphysical Painting is not only melancholic, but also threatening, and yet full of possibilities.

Describing the genesis of these metaphysical landscapes—he painted fifty-seven "piazza d'Italia" over a long life—de Chirico emphasized that even he didn't understand their uncanny meaning.

> One clear autumnal afternoon I was sitting on a bench in the middle of the Piazza Santa Croce in Florence. It was not the first time I had seen this square. I had just come out of a long and painful intestinal illness, and I was in a nearly morbid state of sensitivity . . . I had the strange impression that I was looking at [the piazza] for the first time, and the composition of the picture came into my mind's eye . . . The moment is an enigma to me, for it is inexplicable. And I like also to call the work which sprang from it an enigma.[6]

Like the Surrealists and Dadaists, who followed in these footsteps of obscurity, the trick was to make the familiar surprising, as if seen for the first time. In the painting *The Uncertainty of the Poet*, the juxtaposition of ordinary bananas and unusual scale, sensual body parts, and unforgiving architecture set up tensions that are enhanced by the distorted perspective. At a metaphysical level, it is the loss of collective and spiritual life that is represented by the haunted piazza, one further menaced by suburban development in the distance, and a passing train. In Italy the piazza is traditionally the center of city life, the place where the iconic mother church and father palazzo share the stage, whereas in these renditions, the city fathers have lost control, the deity is absent, and the machine age and pollution are taking over.

Illogical juxtaposition, de Chirico said, was invented by Nietzsche, who demonstrated how absurd Western life became when subtracted of its central faith. The Metaphysical Painters, he further asserted, "were the first to teach what a profound meaning the non-sense of life has," painter-philosophers "who have overcome philosophy."[7] Thus, like Eliot, Joyce, and a host of other artists and writers of this time, de Chirico turned loss, confusion, progress, and the strange contradictions of contemporary life into a new poetry.

The Lesson for Architecture: The Successful Landmark

The various arts expressed similar ideas, but it took another eighty years before they could be translated into mainstream architecture and urbanism, and paid for by hard-headed clients. Several things had to happen. First, the tenets and exemplars of Modernism had to become part of mass culture. James Joyce's fabricated enigma did not have to be understood by the public, *Ulysses* did not have to be read by the tourists who flocked in their hundreds of thousands to Dublin on Bloomsday, but everybody did have to know about the ritual, and find it important. In effect, like the Battle at Ground Zero, it had to become a media ritual before it could be absorbed into conventional society and the business world.

Secondly, the clients had to be vaguely acquainted with the tenets of Metaphysical Painting, Surrealism, and many of their offshoots, or, at least, affected by the assumptions behind them, ideas and feelings that had widespread currency in the West, especially in the world of advertisement. It is one thing for a painting, poem, or ad to express an unconventional image and idea, but quite another when a municipal body, such as those in Beijing, New York, or Edinburgh, has to spend half a billion dollars on an enigmatic signifier and justify it all down the line, maybe even to the taxpayers. Recall the explanation of why Warhol and Rothko had become "the hot labels" at the Sotheby's auction that night in November 2003. As the director of contemporary art said, they are "iconic postwar works." And, as the Miami collector clarified the situation, "it's the kids who studied art at a younger age, they're the ones who are supporting the bottom of the market." The kids know their de Chirico, they are now grown up in a

Frank Gehry's Disney Hall "galleon" grows out of the seating and acoustic requirements; the first flare the shape, the second lower the center. Drawing by Madelon Vriesendorp.

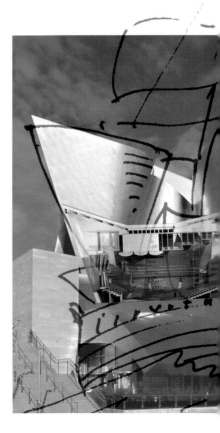

way, and they not only buy the most expensive contemporary art but also commission the landmark buildings.

Thirdly, and to reiterate, they want to create monuments without knowing exactly what to monumentalize. They demand iconic buildings to put themselves or their brand on the map, without specifying a collective iconography, and they thereby put the architect in a perplexing position: "étonnez-moi ou vamoose"—amaze me or you're fired. Moreover, they have learned the lessons of Louis-Phillipe and de Chirico: that, in an agnostic age, monuments can be divisive at first, and then ignominiously forgotten.

And, fourthly, what the architects in this book have discovered is a way around this double humiliation. The successful landmark has to be both enigmatic and expressive, it must suggest much more than it names, and leave the final interpretation, if it ever comes, up to the critics, the public, and the detectives of mystery. These few lucky buildings are good examples of what Umberto Eco has called "the open work," those creations that allow completion by the viewer, those that elicit multiple interpretation along coherent but unchartered lines. The structure of the open work may channel understanding along certain avenues, but it does not force those in search of the meaning down a single or one-way alley. As we have seen repeatedly, and Frank Gehry confirmed in his words on the Disney Hall, the successful iconic building grows from the inside to the outside, and takes up its new metaphors from this growth. Its requirements, context, and function direct the open work along broad boulevards of possibilities. As Zaha Hadid's work shows, the coherence of the architect's aesthetic further guides the understanding. Thus the iconic building is open to new interpretation, but in a controlled way.

Emergent Meaning: Nature and Cosmogenesis

However positive, this is a somewhat agnostic conclusion. As we have seen in the first chapter, almost any building type can produce an icon, there is no overriding direction to global culture, the market prevails and demands continuous differentiation. Religions, and their substitute metanarratives, are in decline. Communism has lost its adherents. Conversely, the belief in economic and technological progress, even the faith in late capitalism, like that in democracy, gets, in E.M. Forster's words, only "two cheers—they are quite enough." And this absence of a deeply held metanarrative is a problem, for if

SHADOW HORN

BECOMES BREAST AND ARM

shotgun
oo
infinity

SYNTHESIZED

nostrils
merge
B & B
infinity

Profile of Ronchamp

BREAST
ARMS AND
BUTTOCKS

ABOVE: Le Corbusier, Ronchamp Church, 1950–5, with its metaphorical relationships to the animal, the body and alchemical signs of the cosmos.

nature abhors a vacuum, then the iconic building gets absolutely hyperventilated without some important justification. On the one hand, this void in belief drives the architect every-which-way in search of credible alibis that could legitimate great cost and fearsome gesture— functional, ecological, urban, and technical. The High-Tech movement in architecture, as in other fields, reveals this frantic search for legitimacy, but has ultimately been as fruitless in finding it as the other "isms" that became "wasms." On the other hand, it pushes the architect, in Frank Gehry's words, "over the edge" into new creative territory.

Ceaseless searching, amazing inventions, and extraordinary, and sometimes horrible, results in architecture—all that would be one fair conclusion to this story. There is no question that, like nature herself, culture now shows endless and superfluous variety—experiment—as its deepest truth, but is that all the new iconic building reveals? Looked at selectively, I believe, the evidence also shows two very important and related themes. These buildings nearly always refer to or imply a greater nature, and the idea of an unfolding cosmos, cosmogenesis.

Recall the iconic overtones of the prime examples. Le Corbusier's Ronchamp was implicitly a "temple to nature" and based on many alchemical signs. The architect incorporated in it prow-forms and allusions to the body.[8] Its metaphors of praying hands, nun's cowl, and mother and children were generally spiritual if not doctrinally directed. What could be more natural than these human and body images? Our continuity with nature is further apparent in other images that generated the forms. They include a duck, and a shell found on a beach in Long Island (this generated the famous upturned roof). As for the cosmic overtones, they are quite apparent in the stained glass. It bathes the inside surfaces with colored icons celebrating the sun, moon and stars, the clouds, and sand. Le Corbusier was drawing and painting these natural and cosmic icons for his iconostasis, the art work that he said was a key to his philosophy, *The Poem to the Right Angle*, and we can find them repeated in many other contexts, such as the doors and tapestry of the General Assembly in Chandigarh.

Think back to the Sydney Opera House and its multifarious overtones of nature: waves in the harbor, fish eating each other, turtles making love, and above all the shell forms—orange peels that generated the design and sea shells that relate to the context. Overall, the building is an exploding flower of white petals reaching out in two

RIGHT: Jörn Utzon, Sydney Opera House, 1956–73. Glistening tiles shield petal shapes that unfold to the sea and sun, metaphors of natural growth.

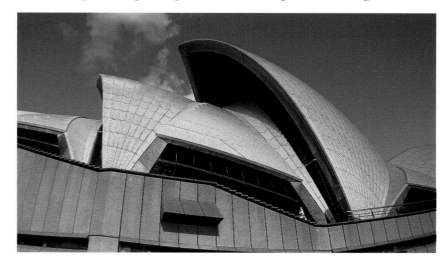

directions. All these images of nature bursting out are appropriate to a cultural institution furthering growth, natural metaphors of music and animal pleasure. Yes, there *are* many other non-natural overtones—boats in the Sydney harbor, a car accident with no survivors—and there isn't a single iconographic script. But as one wanders through this building it is hard to miss the way it celebrates the sea, sky, and sun, all glistening in its highly reflective tiles. Implicitly, it's another object inviting us to share in the free pleasures of the cosmos.

Frank Gehry's two successful landmark buildings are, like Calatrava's best work, solar performers. His language of curved metal has many natural overtones—the scales of a fish, the body of a mermaid, and the burgeoning of plant-form. Disney Hall is a swirl of clouds and billowing leaves, but what it and Bilbao celebrate most strongly is the sun and the changing weather that dramatizes light. I have seen both buildings over several years in the rain, fog, and the setting sun and, most memorably, at Bilbao, during the lull in a storm when the angled sun broke through the clouds, and the building burst into several contrasting shades of silver, yellow, white, green, and black—all at once! Reflected in the adjacent river, which also turns different tints of blue, brown, and green, the building becomes the mirror of nature. It looks as if Gehry, like Le Corbusier, is involved in some unspoken sun- and weather-worship. His many model studies, exploring the space and structure of architecture, are also worked out, like Baroque churches, as light-catchers and light-enhancers. This is not Egyptian sun god worship, nor a New Age equivalent, but it *is* architecture as the celebrant of nature.

Today there are many architects pursuing similar goals: they may be ecologically motivated, they may use biomimicry as a design tool, they may, as several books and exhibitions are called, follow a *Zoomorphic* or *Biomorphic Architecture*.[9] The trend is widespread and deep. Both of the aforementioned publications show more than forty buildings of nature-based work that recently have been constructed. Probably, on a global scale, there are over a hundred such biomimetic landmarks, many of them zany or unconvincing, but enough to speak of a recognizable movement. And this is the point. One should regard these metaphors as revealing, not only a double crisis in ecology and iconography, but as markers of a tendency that is increasing. Nature, Mother Nature, and biology as an efficient designer, are all becoming implicit goals of a new architecture. They may be partial motives, and

BELOW: Emilio Ambasz, Fukuoka Prefectural International Hall, Japan, 1990. The completed building became an icon of ecology, a set of garden terraces on top of a governmental office. These hanging gardens returned to the city the parkland that the building took away.

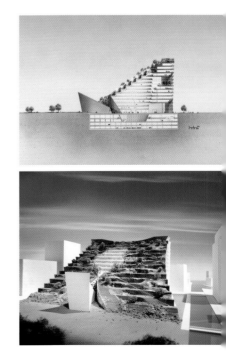

RIGHT: Frank Gehry, New Guggenheim, Bilbao, 1993–7. The building is extremely sensitive to changes in the Nervion River and the weather—here shown in the rain as the sun catches the titanium. The atrium opens on views of the surrounding hills, river, and city and folds the sun into its structure.

in most buildings only a trace of them can be found, but scratch any iconic building hard today and it will bleed nature metaphors.

Metaphors are labile and open to idiosyncratic interpretation, but they have to be taken seriously as the primary way architecture communicates in the age of uncertain iconography. As this book demonstrates, they dominate the iconic building. The Battle at Ground Zero was won ultimately by Daniel Libeskind because his "Wedge of Light," "Freedom Tower," and series of crystal analogies of growth were more cogent than what came to be seen as "skeletons in the sky." Rem Koolhaas won the CCTV competition because his entry had Chinese overtones—"moon gate," "Chinese puzzle," "pi-shape"—and naturalistic analogies with a spider web and an animal. Enric Miralles won the competition for the Scottish Parliament with his mixed metaphors of leaf-fish and upturned boat. Whether one finds them appealing or not, the body metaphors of Birmingham's Selfridges and the rodent images of Rome's new concert halls have struck the popular imagination and put these buildings on the map. Again, in all of this work there are traces of nature imagery.

Equally, Calatrava's naturalistic structures, with the overtones of birds and exoskeletons, continue to dominate the mass media, and the formless yet organic blobs proposed by Will Alsop outrage and delight our mediated culture, in equal measure. In this summary, and roll call, of iconic architects, Zaha Hadid and Peter Eisenman are most resistant to naturalistic and identifiable imagery; they usually confine themselves within the languages of architecture. But even their grammars tend to organic fluidity, and the rolling fractals of landforms.

With Frank Gehry and Norman Foster, very different designers, the naturalistic and cosmic imagery is both explicit and veiled. Gehry's transformation of the fish and snake scale into an architectural language was a well-advertised pun of the late-1980s. His vermiform grammar and wave-forms derived from rolling metal sheeting were not particular to any species, but they were analogues of wave-forms pervasive in nature, and as I've just pointed out, their glistening reflections celebrate the changing face of nature. Similarly, Norman Foster's recent work is derived from curved geometries, of a more limited palette, that have overtones of the body, pine-cone, and spiral found throughout natural growth. He recalls the cosmic architecture of the Pantheon with his domed geometries, at the Reichstag and Swiss Re Tower, and there are traces of DNA, Fibonacci Series, and other organizational forms of nature in his structures.

Frank Gehry, Fish and Snake Light, 1984. The grammar of complex curves in architecture was derived from such investigations of nature translated into hard Formica chips.

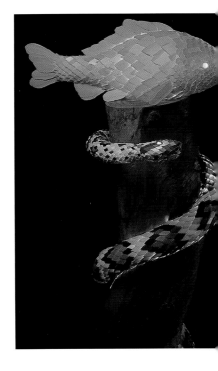

A summary of these naturalistic and cosmic metaphors makes the point: they vary from the hidden to the explicit sign, from connotation to denotation, an indication of where iconic architecture is headed when it is partly decoded. Architecture, like the other arts, can refer to anything today, including nothing and its own abstract systems. This profligate pluralism will continue, but it seems to me a question that has to be posed by each generation is how we relate to the rest of the world, and the universe, its laws, changing moods, and continuous creation. This is fundamentally a spiritual and metaphysical question, entailing a grounding in science and the material world of our bodies and technology. Previously, for maybe 25,000 years, it was a question answered by a communal tradition passed on from generation to generation, and the building of primitive houses, graves, and such things as stone circles and pyramids. Then, with the organized religions and for roughly 5,000 years, it became a question on which theology, scripture, and the priest thought to lead. With the waning of belief and the increase in secularization, the focus has shifted again.

Today we understand that the universe is not, as Einstein thought, an eternal cosmos, but rather a process of cosmogenesis, that is, an expansion and complexification. It was born approximately 13.7 billion years ago in the fast, hot inflation of spacetime that has been misnamed, in a juvenile metaphor, the "Big Bang" (as if our origins were some kind of video nasty or aerial bombardment ordered by the Joint Chiefs of Staff). It was not big (it was smaller than a quark), was not a bang (no one heard it), and its most salient job was not to be a firecracker, but rather to balance the forces of expansion and gravity with miraculous precision. How well balanced? The metaphor often invoked is that it's as if you threw a pencil in the air in a perfect vacuum so that it landed on its tip and remained there for the next 13 billion years. Whew. The balance of the forces is one part in ten to the 59th power. Is that enough to celebrate?

There are many further near-miracles in cosmic evolution that have been unearthed in the recent past, enough to inspire awe in any skeptic who can read. Cosmogenesis is becoming our Genesis story, one that roots us in time and cultural space, one that orients a global culture grown weary of past dogma. This narrative, it is true, shows creative destruction and nonsense; it shows real chaos and wandering. But it also reveals increasing organization, sensitivity, and further complexity growing out of the chaos. It reveals the way we are typical

LEFT: Metaphors of nature and cosmos—the emergence of an implicit system of reference.

BELOW: Charles Jencks, the Universe Cascade, Scotland, 2001, showing cosmic evolution over 13.7 billion years as a series of jumps in organization, each platform using rocks and other signs as a primitive media of expression.

cosmogenic beings, sensitive through our many senses to a self-organizing earth, recently understood through the metaphor of Gaia, in some ways as well balanced as the universe as a whole.

My view is that this story will become more and more widely shared and appreciated, it might sublate the world religions and philosophies until it is more or less accepted as *the* global orientation. If this were to happen it would become a proper subject of iconography, and that is what I have tried to explore in a Scottish landscape called the Garden of Cosmic Speculation. The speculation is that the basic elements of the universe and earth—the quarks, atoms, DNA, Gaia, black holes, galaxies, etc.—and the basic laws and themes, will become the new icons, the reference points for an art and architecture that is not yet fully born. The relevance for the iconic building is obvious, for these icons would provide further grounding to those natural and cosmic metaphors already emergent. They would extend, deepen, and make them more conscious.

The arts would interpret, celebrate, and heighten these discoveries, show their subjective side and our orientation to them both negatively and positively. The brute fact that five mass extinctions have occurred in the history of the Earth is one of these recent discoveries, and the way the fourth one led to the possibility of our emergence has a particular relevance for us just as does our understanding of the way we are at the beginning of the sixth. For good and bad reasons, the cosmogenic view is as inescapable as our embeddedness in the process. Hence, it is an unsentimental reason for those designing, or commissioning, iconic buildings—in all their expense and outrageous expression—to take note: if you're going to ask for a landmark that knocks the socks off your audience, why not ask for something more?

Notes

INTRODUCTION: THE BILBAO EFFECT

1. Carol Vogel, "Contemporary Art Strong for a Second Night," *The New York Times*, 13 Nov. 2003, p.A27.
2. Tom Dyckhoff, *The Times*, 2 Sept. 2003, p.19.
3. Peter Davey, "Outrage," *Architectural Review*, Oct. 2003, p.24.
4. Robert Booth, "Speed Merchants," *Building Design*, 31 Oct. 2003, and Part Two, "Fortune Cookie," 7 Nov. 2003, p.10.

JUDGING THE ICON

1. Vitruvius, *The Ten Books of Architecture*, translated by Morris Hicky Morgan, (Dover Publications, New York, 1960, from a 1914 edition), Book II, p.35.
2. Nikolaus Pevsner, "The Anti-Pioneers," Third Programme, 3 Dec. 1966; republished in the *Listener* and reprinted in Nikolaus Pevsner, *Pevsner on Art and Architecture: The Radio Talks*, edited by Stephen Games, (Methuen, London, 2003), pp.293–307; quote p.303.
3. For this and further discussion of mega-build and the AT&T see Charles Jencks, *Post-Modernism, The New Classicism in Art and Architecture*, (Academy Editions, Rizzoli, London and New York, 1987), "Wrestling with Mega-build," pp.118–234.
4. See Alex Frangos and Leslie Chang "Architects World-Wide Go East," the *Asian Wall Street Journal*, 18 Dec. 2003, p.A10.
5. These are the official figures, £7.33 billion, but my guess is that the total expenditure is double that since the local participants often had to put up half the money to get the Lottery Grants, and there was much hidden spending. See for instance, Jeremy Melvin and Amanda Baillieu, "The Luck Runs Out," *RIBA Journal*, Aug. 2004, pp.14–16.
6. Quoted in Mark Irving, "Being Miuccis," *Financial Times*, 21 June 2003, p.25. See also *Wired*, June 2003, edited by Rem Koolhaas.
7. *Ibid.*, p.26.
8. For the solar symbolism, see Charles Jencks, *Le Corbusier and the Continual Revolution in Architecture*, (Monacelli Press, London and New York, 2000), pp.287–92.
9. Nikolaus Pevsner, "The Anti-Pioneers," Third Programme, 3 Dec. 1966, *op. cit.*, p.303. The two main attacks were James Stirling's "Le Corbusier's Chapel and the Crisis of Rationalism," in *Architectural Review*, March 1956, pp.155–61, and Nikolaus Pevsner's *An Outline of European Architecture*, (Penguin Books, London, 1963), p.429. There were other attacks by critics, such as G.C. Argan, that typified the attitude of a whole generation of architects brought up on the tenets of rationalism.
10. See my *Le Corbusier and the Continual Revolution in Architecture*, *op. cit.*, pp.262–75 and references. One can find alchemical references in his autobiographical work, the *Poème de l'Angle Droit*, a group of lithographs and poems loosely connected around such themes. The precise meanings of this work are elusive and allusive, the images vary from Le Corbusier's personal signs—the sword above the cloud—to cosmic and carnal suggestions. The artist/architect developed the hybrid work over the years 1947 to 1953, and it thus becomes an important prelude to his inventions at Ronchamp. The series of oppositions one finds in the building can be seen here: the buttock and breast forms, the upturned horn, and the alchemical juxtapositions of water and sky, feminine

and masculine. Most importantly, the poem as a whole is conceived as an icon, or more particularly what Corbu called an iconostasis. This, in traditional Russian Orthodox terms, is that screen which separates the sanctuary of a church from the main body and on which icons are placed. These small paintings depict Christ, the Virgin, Apostles and Saints, and the priest perfumes the icons, the worshippers and the altar. Le Corbusier's *Iconostasis*, the prelude to the poem, is a set of right-angled blocks stacked into a cross with multiple arms. In effect, he was trying to design and elicit a new quasi-spiritual sign system, something based on alchemical, human, and cosmic meanings. It wasn't until his work on the state capital of Chandigarh in India (see pages 47–50) that this sign system was fully developed, but— and this is the importance for the general history of the iconic building—the *Poème de l'angle droit* is the secret text and imagery that leads directly to Le Corbusier's breakthrough building, Ronchamp. No poem, no iconstasis, no worship of cosmic signs, no iconic building. Like Gehry's "fish," a prop is expanded to the entire building enterprise.

11. Le Corbusier, *Oeuvre Complète Volume V, 1946–52*, (Girsberger, Zurich, 1955) p.72.

12. Le Corbusier, *The Chapel at Ronchamp*, (London, 1957), p.7.

ICONIC MEDIA WARS

1. Sarah Baxter, "Ego Wars Jolt New York's New Tower," *Sunday Times*, 21 Dec. 2003, p.25.

2. Christopher Grimes, "'Spirited' Collaboration for New Freedom Tower," *Financial Times*, 21 Dec. 2003, p.6.

3. Quoted in Arthur Danto, "The Abuse of Beauty," *Daedalus*, Fall 2002, p.35.

4. Philippe de Montebello, "The Iconic Power of an Artifact," *The New York Times*, 25 Sept. 2001. Quoted from *Monuments and Memory, Made and Unmade*, edited by Robert S. Nelson and Margaret Olin, (University of Chicago Press, London, 2003), p.319. This book also had the evocative fragment of the former WTC as a cover.

5. This and the quote above are from Daniel Libeskind, "Stone and Spirit" in Max Protech, *A New World Trade Center, Design Proposals from Leading Architects Worldwide*, (Regan Books, New York, 2002), p.85.

6. This democratic process and the World Trade Center saga are described by Alex Garvin in "Effect: Delivering Change," *RSA Journal*, Jan. 2004, pp.40–45. In correspondence he has mentioned that BBB were paid $3 million by the Port Authority for their work, the figure that I also remember being published. Garvin writes: "Their [BBB] contract involved engineering, market analysis, transportation studies, and a great deal more than the four plans they produced that we showed in July 2002. . . . Steven Peterson and Barbara Littenberg cost a small fraction of what the Port Authority spent on BBB." Obviously the unprecedented nature of September 11th, and the emotions involved, led to an unusual mixture of altruism on the part of some architects and hard bargaining on the part of others.

7. See Julie V. Iovine, "Appraisals of Ground Zero Designs," *The New York Times*, 9 Jan. 2003, p.B3.

8. For this estimate see Julie V. Iovine, "Ground Zero Spotlight: Architects Ambivalent," *The New York Times*, 1 Jan. 2003, p.20.

9. *Ibid*. The quotes in this and the previous paragraph are also from this article.

10. See, for instance, Hugh Pearman, "The Battle for Ground Zero," *Sunday Times*, 22 Dec. 2002.

11. Herbert Muschamp, "Nine Varied Designs Rediscover and Celebrate the Vertical Life," *The New York Times*, 19 Dec. 2002, p.A27.

12. Quoted in Jonathan Glancey "The Divided City," *The Guardian*, 17 Feb. 2003, p.14.

13. See, for instance. "Libeskind Vows Integrity," *Building Design*, 4 Apr. 2003. This was after he won the competition but such defence started in January as the attacks mounted.

14. For some of this political froth see Julie V. Iovine, "Finalists for Ground Zero Design Pull Out the Stops," *The New York Times*, 26 Feb. 2003.

15. See, for instance, Edward Wyatt, "Panel Supports 2 Tall Towers at Disaster Site," *The New York Times*, 26 Feb. 2003, p.B1; "Practical Issues for Ground Zero," *The New York Times*, 28 Feb. 2003, p.1.

16. For these double readings see Hal Foster, "In New York," *London Review of Books*, 20 March 2003, pp.16–17.

17. Paul Goldberger mentioned this to me in conversation on 18 Feb. 2004. Philip Noble, who, like Goldberger, is writing a book on the events at Ground Zero, also supplied information on which this and other sections are based. I am grateful to both of them for sharing their information and clarifying sources.

18. Edward Wyatt, "Practical Issues for Ground Zero," *The New York Times*, 28 Feb. 2003, pp.1, B2.

19. Daniel Libeskind, *Breaking Ground, Adventures in Life and Architecture*, (John Murray, London), 2004, p.180.

20. Quoted in "International News, Gulliver in Space," *RIBA Journal*, Dec. 2003.

21. Quoted in Damian Arnold, "Six Month Contract Lets Libeskind Start at WTC," *Building Design*, 7 March 2003, p.2.

22. "Interview: WTC Design Finalist Daniel Libeskind," www.dw-world.de, 5 Feb. 2003.

23. Edward Wyatt, "Shadows etc. . . ," *The New York Times*, 1 May 2003, pp. B1, B3.

24. For instance, Richard Meier shifts the grid of his museum in Frankfurt 3.5 degrees and that of the Getty Museum in Los Angeles 22.5 degrees for conceptual reasons concerned with the site. The shifts are only perceptual in plan and details, and they have to be explained with respect to a model, or helicopter view, before they can be fully appreciated. Conceptual or diagrammatic indexing is canonic with Eisenman and one of his great strengths.

25. Paul Goldberger, "Urban Warriors," profile of the Libeskinds, *New Yorker*, 15 Sept. 2003, pp.72–81; quote p.80.

26. Herbert Muschamp, "PATH Station Becomes A Procession of Flight," *The New York Times*, 23 Jan. 2004, p.B7.

27. Paul Goldberger, "Slings and Arrows," *The New Yorker*, 9 Feb. 2004, p.86.

28. *Ibid*, p.87.

29. See Alex Garvin, *op. cit.*, p.41.

30. Robin Pogrebin, "The Incredible Shrinking Daniel Lineskind," *The New York Times*, 20 Jun. 2004, Arts and Leisure, pp.1, 32.

31. Nicholas Wapshott, "Mistrust and Muddle Aggravate Twin Towers' Desecration," *The Times*, 28 Jun. 2004, p.14. The misquote was at the summation of Wapshott's article: "'We are living in a market economy,' he said with resignation. 'True art—you have to work with business.'" How did he know these words, misquoted from *The New York Times*, were said "with resignation"? And by what right did he not attribute the source?

32. I should declare a political and personal interest here to clarify my position. While I am a friend of Daniel and Nina Libeskind, and have worked with them, and a friend of many of the architects involved in the Ground Zero competition, my views are architecturally, not politically or personally,

driven. For instance, consider the possible differences over patriotic symbolism. In mid-January 2003, I organized a British pressure group, "Architects Against War," and it was supported by many of those I am writing about in this book, while some of my good friends refused to sign the petition. For the text see my website www.charlesjencks.com. This was published in the *Independent*, 20 Jan. 2003, p.13. The architectural group was a significant professional lobby, including presidents of the RIBA and members of the House of Lords. The hope was that it might trigger other professional bodies to come out against war. Their combined pressure could have forced Blair to back down, and if he did, then it would become quite hard for Bush to take a skeptical American public along for the ride. In the event, the other professions did not follow architects, but there were large anti-war demonstrations around the world, one of which was the biggest public demonstration in British history. Between one and two million people marched to Hyde Park. As one can see by the discrepancy in these figures, the measurement that day *did* depend on political views.

I can understand why some critics accuse Libeskind of wrapping himself in the flag, at the wrong time, and of some vulgar imagery but, on the whole, I think that his mixture of clear and enigmatic signs was much the most cogent of all the teams—*in spite of* its unfortunate timing. As the ironic comments in my text make clear I am not uncritical of the vulgarity and deplore the possible use the Republican Party may make of the symbolism, but my architectural views are not radically influenced, one way or the other, by war or politics. As for personal friendships they

extend to Foster, Eisenman, Meier, Greg Lynn, and several other members of the competing teams.

33. See Paul Goldberger, the *New Yorker*, 15 Sept. 2003, p.74.

34. Marina Warner, *Signs and Wonders: Essays on Literature and Culture*, (Chatto & Windus, London, 2003).

ICONIC DILEMMAS

1. *Building Design*, 20 Feb. 2004, p.2.

2. 3 May 2002. For a discussion see Rem Koolhaas and AMOMA, "E-Conography," in *Content*, (Taschen Books, London, Paris, 2003), pp.376–89.

3. Rem Koolhaas, "Delirious No More," *Wired*, June 2003, pp.166–9.

4. *Ibid.*, p.483.

5. Rem was staying with me in Cape Cod, August 2000, when he received a call to star, I seem to remember, as the Jackal.

6. Alex Frangos and Leslie Chang, "Architects World-Wide Go East," the *Asian Wall Street Journal*, 18 Dec. 2003, p.A10.

7. Rem Koolhaas, "Kill the Skyscraper," *Content, op. cit.*, pp.470–77.

8. See, for instance, Charles Jencks, *The New Paradigm in Architecture*, (Yale University Press, London and New Haven), pp.29–34, 252–3.

9. See Rem Koolhaas, *Content, op. cit.*, pp.483–501; quote p.486.

10. Ian Baruma, a mutual friend of Koolhaas and me, in the *Guardian*, 2002; see also Deyan Sudjic, "Beijing on the Brink," *Prospect*, Nov. 2003, pp.38–41.

11. Quoted in Kieran Long "The Greatest Show on Earth," *Guardian*, 12 Jan. 2004, pp.12–3.

12. Dewar's quotes here are from "Holyrood, a New Scottish Parliament," Visitor's Centre video made by Murray Grigor, 2003.

13. For this assessment, see, for instance Kirsty Scott, "When a Journalist is the

Story," *Guardian*, 8 Dec. 2003, Media, p.3. "Few issues have sickened Scots as much as the scandal of their new parliament building." This opinion is also repeated by Magnus Linklater, Ian Bell, and others who support the building.

14. Tim Luckhurst, "Wary Queen of Scots," *The Times*, 1 Dec. 2003, p.7.

15. Quoted in Grigor, *op. cit.*

16. See Robert Booth, "Holyrood Drama: History in the Making," *Building Design*, 27 June 2003, p.4.

17. Aaron Betsky, *Landscrapers, Building with the Land*, (Thames and Hudson, London, 2002).

18. The Fraser Report will have the details, as does his website, but the general points can be found in Deyan Sudjic "A National Treasure," *Observer*, 10 Aug. 2003, Review, p.10; and such sensationalizing news flashes as "Miralles Whim 'Added £53m to Cost of Chamber'," article by Neil Rafferty, *Sunday Times*, 21 Dec. 2003, p.9. See also a general report in *Building Design*, 27 Jun. 2003 and Kirsty Scott, "Dewar Legacy Leaves Scotland to Pick up the Bill," *Guardian*, 13 Apr. 2004, p.11. Robert Black's report, delivered on June 29th, 2004, faulted "the lack of clear leadership from the project managers . . . [and]. . . Paul Grice . . . [who said] he disagreed with some of the facts of the report." See Shirley English, "£431m Holyrood is 'High Class, but Too High Cost'," *The Times*, 30 June 2004, News, p.6; the architects were also criticized for "design slippage," not producing documents in good time.

19. The costs of the consultants were not high by the conventions of a crafted building. In June 2003, when the overall cost was estimated at £402 million, the consultants' fees were put at £60 million or 15 percent, not outrageous for a bespoke building. See "RMJM Hits Back at 'Ignorant' MSPs,"

Building Design, 27 Jun. 2003, pp.1,4.

20. Dan Cruickshank, in conversation and fax to me, 26 Mar. 2004. Among other things, he wrote: "Needless to say, growing costs caused massive problems and cut-backs. For example, in 1848 Parliament voted to reduce money available for completing the Palace from £100,000 to £50,000 and the Whig Government appointed a Royal Commission to complete the building."

21. For "lutes" and quotes from Renzo Piano and the "half-peeled onion," see Richard Fairman, "Putting Nowhere on the Concertgoer's Map," *Financial Times*, 3 Jan. 2003, p.11. For some of the other metaphors see Catherine Slessor, "Urban Orchestration," *Architectural Review*, May 2003, pp.64–8.

22. Fairman, *op. cit.*

23. Deyan Sudjic, "Landmarks of Hope and Glory," *Observer*, 26 Oct. 2003, Arts, p.6.

THE CHALLENGERS

1. Deyan Sudjic, "An Olympian who could Run and Run," *Observer*, 29 Feb. 2004, Review, p.6.

2. *Ibid.*, p.6.

3. Deyan Sudjic "Landmarks of Hope and Glory," *op. cit.*

4. See Maria Luisa Palumbo, *New Wombs: Electronic Bodies and Architectural Disorder*, (Birkhäuser, Boston MA, 2000), pp.78–83 where the blinking eye is seen as exemplifying the post-organic part of the new paradigm; also my *The New Paradigm in Architecture*, *op. cit.*, pp. 230–34, where some of the same views are expressed.

5. Deyan Sudjic "Landmarks of Hope and Glory," *op. cit.*

6. For these quotes and the argument, a long one, see Charles Jencks, "History as Myth," *Meaning in Architecture*, (Barrie and Jenkins, London, 1969), p.251.

7. See quote below and next footnote.

8. Charles Gates "Scorn as Alsop's Liverpool Choice Defies Public Vote," *Building Design*, 13 Dec. 2002, p.4.

9. Deyan Sudjic, "Can Liverpool be the Bilbao of the North?", *Observer*, 15 Dec. 2002.

10. These quotes and subsequent ones are from "Zaha Hadid 1996–2001," *El Croquis Monograph*, 103, 2001, pp166–7; 198.

TWO WINNERS

1. Martin Filler, "Victory at Bunker Hill," *New York Review of Books*, 23 Oct. 2003, pp.55–60.

2. Herbert Muschamp, "A Moon for the Hollywood Dream," *The New York Times*, 23 Oct. 2003, pp.E1, E5.

3. Leon Whiteson, "High Note, Gehry's Crown for Bunker Hill is a Fitting Tribute for Disney," *Los Angeles Times*, 15 Sept. 1991, K1, pp.14,15.

4. Muschamp, "A Moon for the Hollywood Dream," *op. cit.*

5. Jonathan Glancey, "Space Odyssey," *Guardian*, 8 Dec. 2003, pp.12–13.

6. Deyan Sudjic, "In a Glass of its Own," *Observer*, 28 Sept. 2003, Review, p.11.

SURPRISING CONCLUSIONS

1. Deyan Sudjic, "Landmarks of Hope and Glory," *op. cit.*

2. Charles Jencks, *The New Paradigm in Architecture*, *op. cit.* Here the enigmatic signifier is discussed and the emergent tradition of iconic building is seen as one of six important trends.

3. Barry Bergdoll has recounted some of this history in "Enlightened Problems," *Royal Academy Forum*, reprinted in *Architectural Review*, Oct. 2001, p.91–2; see also *The Blue Guide of Paris and Environs*, (Ernest Benn, London, 1977), pp.87–8.

4. Letter in *Le Temps*, 14 Feb. 1887, quoted from Norma Evenson, *Paris: A Century of*

Change, 1878–1978, (Yale University Press, New Haven and London), 1979. p.130.

5. From Eiffel's response to the *Le* Temps attack, quoted in Norma Evenson, *op. cit.*, p.133.

6. Unpublished article of 1912 by de Chirico, quoted in H.H. Arnason, *A History of Modern Art*, (Thames and Hudson, London, 1969, revised and reprinted 1985), p.294.

7. Quoted in Ruhrberg, Schneckenburger, Fricke and Honnef, edited by Ingo Walther, *Art of the 20th Century*, (Taschen, London and New York, 2000), p.134.

8. See "Judging the Icon", pages 56–63 and note 10 for a further discussion of Ronchamp.

9. See Hugh Aldersey-Williams, *Zoomorphic, New Animal Architecture,* (Laurence King Publishing, London, 2003), with an exhibition of that title at London's Victoria & Albert Museum, 2003; Günther Feuerstein, *Biomorphic Architecture, Human and Animal Forms in Architecture*, (Menges, Stuttgart and London, 2002).

Index

First published in the United States of America in 2005 by
Rizzoli International Publications, Inc.
300 Park Avenue South
New York, NY 10010
www.rizzoliusa.com

ISBN 0-8478-2756-9
Library of Congress Catalog Control Number 2005922828

First edition 2005

2005 2006 2007 2008 / 9 8 7 6 5 4 3 2 1

Printed and bound in China by Kwong Fat Offset Printing Co. Ltd.

Acknowledgments

The inspiration for this book developed from work I have done over the years on
metaphor in architecture and the enigmatic signifier. Some of this analysis appeared in
The New Paradigm in Architecture (2002) and previous editions of *The Language of Post-
Modern Architecture* (1977–). To explain how metaphors are partly coded in architectural
form I worked on drawings with others, and here some of them are reproduced. But
my greatest debt of gratitude goes to Madelon Vriesendorp, with whom I have further
explored such visual codes in all their variety and overtones.

Notwithstanding his reluctant sense of the plastic, my literary agent and old friend
Ike Williams has given me the usual benefit of his sharp eye for things architectural.
John Nicoll encouraged the development of this book from the beginning. Along with
his team at Frances Lincoln, Michael Brunström who edited it and Carolyn Clarke who
laid it out, he has steered the very complex mixture of thought, image and word to a
satisfying conclusion—at least very gratifying to me. My assistants, Bunny Firth and
Maureen Brown, helped with this layout and with corrections to the teext and images.
Many architects have helped supply images, and to them I am of course beholden, as
usual—in particular to Frank Gehry, Norman Foster, Rem Koolhaas, Will Alsop,
Daniel Libeskind, Zaha Hadid, Colin Fournier, Emilio Ambasz, and their offices. They
have all graciously supplied slides, CDs and drawings. The rest of the images are my
own photos, except those on the following pages:

Alsop Limited 144, 146, 147r, 148–9, 151, 151b (Richard Johnson), 152–3, 154, 155,
152–3 (Richard Johnson); **Emilio Ambasz and Associates** 206; **AMO** 105; **BBC
Scotland** 131; **Santiago Calatrava** 90; **David Childs, SOM** 65b; **City of Arts and
Sciences, Valencia** 166–7; **Carolyn Djanogly** 185a; **Steve Double** 156; **Eisenman
Architects** 162–3, 166–7, 168; **Foster and Partners** 13 (Nigel Young) 51, 184 (Nigel
Young), 187, 190–91; **Colin Fournier** 194, 195; **Gehry Partners** 9, 173, 174; **Zaha
Hadid Architects** 157, 158, 159 (Helene Binet), 160, 161a, 161b (Helene Binet);
Herzog & de Meuron title page, 47, 113; **Instituto de Tourismo de Espana
(Bravo)** 11; **OMA** 108–9, 111; **OMA/LMN Architects (Pragnesh Parikh)** 100,
102, 103; *Prospect*, **Architecture and Design in Scotland** 116, 121; **Max Protech**
73; **RMJM Architects** 114r, 122, 127; **Scottish Parliament** half-title, 118a; **Dennis
Sharp** 137; **Studio Libeskind** 65a, 95, 97, 99; **Tate Modern** 200 (Photo © Tate,
London 2005, painting © DACS 2005; **www.dbox.com** 169